HOUSING SHOCK
The Irish Housing Crisis and How to Solve It

Rory Hearne

Foreword by Leilani Farha

P

First published in Great Britain in 2020 by

Policy Press
University of Bristol
1-9 Old Park Hill
Bristol
BS2 8BB
UK
t: +44 (0)117 954 5940
pp-info@bristol.ac.uk
www.policypress.co.uk

British Library Cataloguing in Publication Data
A catalogue record for this book is available from the British Library

ISBN 978-1-4473-5389-8 hardback
ISBN 978-1-4473-5390-4 paperback
ISBN 978-1-4473-5392-8 ePdf
ISBN 978-1-4473-5393-5 ePub

The rights of Rory Hearne to be identified as author of this work has been asserted by him in
accordance with the Copyright, Designs and Patents Act 1988.

Cover design by Andrew Corbett
Front cover image: iStock
Printed and bound in Great Britain by CMP, Poole
Policy Press uses environmentally responsible print partners

This book is dedicated to those suffering from the housing and homelessness crisis, to those who work and volunteer to support people affected, and implement solutions, and to those who protest, campaign, educate and raise their voice for a right to housing for all.

The book would not have been possible without the support of Sinéad. It is for Leo, Aisling, Keelan and Erin – my dreams that became beautiful realities and make every day worth living.

This book is for the children of today and of the future, that they may have safe, secure, high-quality, environmentally sustainable homes that nurture their development, allow them to grow with dignity, and provide a socially just society and protects our common home – our planet.

Home, sweet home for all

Aisling, age 5

Contents

List of tables, boxes, figures and images

Tables

Boxes

Figures

Images

Acknowledgements

Thank you to those who have supported me on this journey to make this book happen, particularly Mary Murphy, Cian O'Callaghan, Padraic Kenna, PJ Drudy, James Wickham, Andrew MacLaran, Joe Larragy, Leilani Farha, John Bissett, Fergus Finlay and the extended Hearne family. Thank you to Mike, Sinéad, John, and Anne Marie for your comments. Thanks to Mel, Orla, Lorcan, Rita, Hugh, Niamh, Wayne, Rebecca, Collette, Ann and Aisling H, for your informative discussions and commitment to solving this crisis. Thanks to Tony and Tortoise Shack for our Reboot Republic Podcast in which we have endlessly discussed and highlighted housing problems and solutions.

Thank you to the Departments of Applied Social Studies, Sociology and Geography, and the Social Sciences Institute at Maynooth University.

Finally, thank you to everyone at Policy Press for publishing the book, especially Sarah Bird for believing in the idea and in me, and to Caroline, Emily, Leonie, Melissa and the team.

Foreword

Leilani Farha,
United Nations Special Rapporteur
on the Right to Housing

There are an estimated 1.8 billion people globally living in homelessness and grossly inadequate housing. These individuals and families typically endure stark conditions including a lack of access to basic services such as sanitation, running water, and electricity; no security of tenure; and housing that is simply unaffordable. Conditions such as these are not the result of some fault or misfortune of the people who suffer them, but rather are created and maintained by governments through their actions and inactions.

I am deeply concerned by the persistent failure of governments to recognise housing as a social good and a fundamental human right. Governments have yet to fully recognise the connections between the over-commodification of housing, which they promote in many ways, and the rising rates of homelessness and inadequate housing. Contrary to international human rights obligations, investment in housing has increasingly disconnected housing from its core social purpose of providing people with a place to live with security and dignity.

Particularly troublesome are those laws and policies that have allowed unprecedented amounts of global capital to be invested in housing as security for financial instruments that are traded on global markets, and as a means of accumulating wealth. This expanding role and new dominance of unregulated financial markets and corporations in the housing sector is now generally referred to as the 'financialisation of housing' and it is having devastating consequences.

In Ireland, homelessness has increased exponentially in recent years, with the number of homeless adults rising by nearly 95.9 per cent between 2015 and 2018, while levels of child homelessness grew by 227.7 per cent over the same period. The central causes of homelessness are issues related to the private rental sector. The lack of tenant protections – such as the ease with which a landlord can evict in order to sell the tenant's home or to move family members in, and, equally, the lack of long-term leases, means that tenants are extremely vulnerable to exploitation, housing insecurity and homelessness from the actions of investor landlords. Homelessness is one of the most egregious and damaging violations of the right to adequate housing.

The impact of homelessness on children in particular is known to be devastating on their development, both physically and mentally.

With financialisation, private-equity firms need to invest their money somewhere. So, like vultures flying over territories, they look for what they call 'undervalued properties' – homes where people are paying average or below-market-value rents. They purchase these people's rented homes and upgrade them – either cosmetically or by undertaking more substantial alterations – the cost of which is passed onto tenants, who can rarely afford the resultant rent increases. The result is that tenants are being pushed out of their homes – they either self-evict or fall into arrears and have an eviction process launched against them. Institutional investors – private equity firms, and pension funds, for example – don't view dwellings as housing, per se; rather, they view them as a tool, or square metres, from which they can extract profits and wealth, and leverage more capital. The financialisation of housing is, therefore, a vicious and violent cycle: the income stream from these buildings provides the securitisation for the investor to then buy more and more properties, and evict, or force out, more tenants. It's endless.

The financialisation of residential real estate undermines the enjoyment of the right to non-discrimination and the right to housing. Because the business model associated with financialisation demands short-term profits, there is heightened pressure placed on purchasing affordable housing – often where the most vulnerable communities are located – and then securing the highest possible return on investment through the persistent extraction of profits through monthly rents. The result of this is the constant escalation of housing costs for tenants. Turning housing into an investment leads to decision-making that is investor-driven, rather than tenant-centred. When the focus is on maximising profits, housing inevitably becomes less affordable, less available, less secure and less habitable.

Ireland has obligations under various international human rights instruments, in particular the International Covenant on Economic, Social and Cultural Rights, to which it has been a party since 1989, and more specifically Article 11.1 which states that 'The States Parties to the present Covenant recognize the right of everyone to an adequate standard of living for himself and his family, including adequate food, clothing and housing, and to the continuous improvement of living conditions.'

According to international human rights law, the Irish government is required to take progressive measures, to the maximum of available resources, to ensure access to adequate housing for all without discrimination. To address the issue of financialisation and its impact on the enjoyment of the right to housing, governments must develop policies and laws that include a full range of taxation, regulatory and planning measures in order to re-establish housing as a human right, promote an inclusive housing system, prevent speculation and limit the extraction of profits at the expense of tenants. This will require a transformation of the relationship between governments and the financial sector.

Countries must recognise the impact of the financialisation of housing on the enjoyment of the right to adequate housing, particularly for minority and vulnerable groups, and take concerted steps towards returning housing to its core function as a social good.

The question is, how can big capital be challenged? The answer may lie in a kind of currency. The currency is human rights: a strong currency based in moral and legal obligations. I have joined forces with the Office of the High Commissioner for Human Rights and United Cities and Local Governments. Together we are growing a global movement – 'the Shift' – knowing that around the world many are taking to the streets, courtrooms, legislatures, classrooms and boardrooms to demand change. The Shift is a platform to showcase and harness that energy and to support commitments and initiatives to secure housing as a human right. The Shift provides the alternative narrative: we are many and for us, housing is home.

The housing crisis is a global phenomenon. In this book, Rory Hearne provides a really important and insightful contribution to the global debate on financialisation, inequality and the right to housing. Every human rights organisation, government, state housing official, housing policy rights and law academic, housing activist, homeless charity and citizen should read this book, for its analysis of the potential dystopia on the road ahead, but also of the possibility of a positive affordable and sustainable future if we take the right actions.

What is particularly impressive is that alongside this brilliant critique of the neoliberal policies that are causing this crisis, Hearne also provides strategies for how tenants, those living with homelessness, non-governmental organisations, communities, trade unions and activists can get involved in creating change. He also offers cities and governments ideas for how they might get involved in solving the housing crisis.

The global housing crisis and the climate crisis are the two most challenging issues facing humanity today. Hearne provides insight and ideas as to how we can address both challenges at once. In proposing a new vision for public 'affordable, sustainable homes and communities' based on securing the right to housing for all, he shows that we can achieve affordable and secure housing while also meeting climate change targets and ensuring a sustainable planet that will provide, as he says, our individual home and wellbeing and ensure the sustainable wellbeing of our collective home.

There can be no more excuses. As Hearne says in the final chapter, the issue is not the lack of solutions, it is the absence of political determination to implement them. I agree with him. Let's act.

Preface: housing, home, and COVID-19

Our homes and housing systems have been the frontline defence in preventing the spread of COVID-19. Across the world governments told people to 'stay home'. But the COVID-19 pandemic 'has laid bare the pre-existing and vast structural inequalities in housing systems all over the world' (Farha, 2020). 1.8 billion people worldwide live with homelessness and grossly inadequate housing. Overcrowding and substandard housing makes prevention, self-isolation, and recovery more difficult. The importance of housing as a social determinant of health has never been more visible.

In Ireland, thousands live in unsuitable accommodation, institutionalised in homeless emergency accommodation, direct provision, or as 'hidden homeless'. The faultlines of policy that accepted homelessness as 'normal' has been starkly revealed.

The COVID-19 recession will push more householders into housing and financial distress with many unable to pay their rent or mortgage. If they had been living in public affordable homes, there would be fewer arrears and less stress as they would at least have the support and protection of an affordable home.

COVID-19 shows the failings of the dominant neoliberal policy paradigm which treats housing as an investment asset rather than its vital role as a home that can ensure the health and dignity of those living in it. These policies commodified housing by handing it over to the private market.

But signs of hope are evident in countries such as Ireland that discarded the neoliberal policy book and enacted unprecedented measures in response to COVID-19, such as freezing rents and banning evictions. It was previously insisted upon that these protections were unworkable or unconstitutional. Empty Airbnb properties have been used to house the homeless. These actions show that there is no actual reason that homelessness and the wider housing crisis cannot be solved.

Unfortunately, the global and Irish housing crises will worsen unless this radical shift in housing policy becomes a permanent change in direction. There is a tsunami of financial distress and evictions ahead if the pandemic housing measures are not extended for at least three years, and support for tenants and homeowners including rent and mortgage write-downs are provided.

In response to the last economic shock, the burden of adjustment was paid for by ordinary people through austerity cuts to public investment such as social house building. Ireland went from building 5,300 social housing units a year in 2009 to just 400 units in 2017. This time we must avoid the devastation of fiscal austerity, and instead bail out society and stimulate the economy through borrowing for investment. State responses should not just be about economic 'recovery' but about rebuilding and transforming our economies and society in a new way.

A new social contract is required to recreate our economies and societies as socially and environmentally just and sustainable in the (post) COVID-19 world – and a new green deal for housing must be central to this. The neoliberal policy imaginary was an ideological cage that foreclosed alternative ways of thinking about, and delivering, housing and homes – with housing restricted to its value as a privatised asset.

We need to reclaim, reimagine, and rebuild a vision for public housing for all, through inclusive quality design and expanding its availability and attractiveness to all income levels and household types. Housing, the 'wobbly' pillar of the welfare state, must be brought in to become a core competency of a reinvigorated empowering welfare state.

The private housing market will be in major difficulty and a new wave of predatory real estate and vulture funds could emerge. The folly of allowing the private market to dictate our housing system is apparent, but it will become even more disastrous if the state does not step in now.

Social and affordable house-building budgets should be hugely expanded to build public affordable homes and retrofit existing homes. This would provide a major employment and economic boost and deliver climate targets. Borrowing to build public housing is an investment – not a cost – and better value for money than housing benefits for private landlords. Planning and housing design will need to change to incorporate new living requirements such as sufficient indoor and outdoor space in homes, green spaces, and community spaces.

The spirit of solidarity witnessed in response to COVID-19 could be harnessed to involve local people and communities in rebuilding homes and communities together, such as through the cooperative housing model.

States must take radical action to ensure the right to housing – a fundamental right – is delivered for all. In Ireland a referendum is required to insert the right to adequate, affordable, secure housing into the Constitution in order to set a vision and aim for our housing system and policy and to oblige the State to realise and uphold such a right through all laws, policies and practices.

The failure to address housing and inequality has made our societies even more vulnerable to pandemics and economic crises. A housing system that ensures everyone has an affordable secure home is beneficial for all – rich and poor – as it better protects the whole of society and economy.

If we do not start to immediately reshape our housing system towards a rights and sustainability approach then the housing dystopia scenario I detail on page 16 of this book will become a reality. But COVID-19 shows that it could be worsened further with pandemics ripping through poorer overcrowded housing areas.

Housing is fundamental to our wellbeing, and home is the front line now and into the future. Ensuring affordable, high quality, sustainable homes for all is a political and societal choice, and in this new COVID-19 reality it has never been more clear that it also an urgent necessity. This book shows that we can, and we must, do it.

1

Introduction:
a new housing crisis

'To the people of Ireland. To the renters worried about
eviction or the next rent hike from their landlord, to
the couchsurfers, the overcrowded, the aspirant home
owners, the distressed mortgage holder, to the homeless
in emergency accommodation and on our streets, to the
commuter, the student, the disabled, the Traveller, and those
in direct provision [housing for asylum seekers]. Today, we
declare to you – we cannot be silent. We can no longer
be silent to your suffering and the suffering of our fellow
citizens. Today we have stood up and declared – that we,
the people of Ireland, do not accept homelessness and
the wider housing crisis as normal. We do not accept our
fellow brothers and sisters being left to die on our streets
for lack of homes. And because our Taoiseach [Prime
Minister] and our government have shown themselves
unwilling to take this crisis seriously, we are out here on
the streets – we, the citizens of this Republic – we will do
what this government is unwilling to do and so we declare
the housing crisis a national emergency.' (Excerpt from a
speech given by the author at the MyNameIs homelessness
protest concert outside Dáil Éireann, the lower house of
the Irish parliament, December 2017)

Our housing system in Ireland, and housing systems across the
world, are experiencing a structural 'shock'. We are in the midst of
an unprecedented housing and homelessness crisis. This is visible in
the dramatic increase in housing inequalities and exclusion, from
the rise in homelessness, mortgage arrears and foreclosures, to the
collapse in home-ownership rates and, in particular, the emergence
of 'Generation Rent' and 'Generation Stuck at Home'. This new
Generation Rent is being locked out of traditional routes to affordable
secure housing such as home ownership, social housing and secure
low-rent housing. They are being pushed into private rental markets
with unaffordable high rents and insecurity of tenure, or forced into

hidden homelessness, couchsurfing, sleeping in cars, or pushed back to live with their parents.

Ireland has had the largest fall in home ownership rates among European Union (EU) countries in the past three decades. Home ownership in Ireland fell from a high point of 81% in 1991 to 67% in 2016, while the proportion of young households owning their home dropped from 65% in 2004 to 33% in 2016. This is nothing less than a structural shock to the Irish housing system. It is a rupture in the Irish social contract whereby generations of people were guaranteed affordable home ownership or long-term, secure, social rental homes.

This book shows that the current housing situation and crisis is not a temporary blip, but a deep and profound structural crisis that is in danger of becoming a permanent crisis, a crisis without end for many people locked out of affordable, secure, high-quality and environmentally sustainable housing. Our national and global housing systems are in crisis and this is a key juncture.

We need to realise that this is a new era for housing. It is unfortunately a new, much darker dawn for those requiring affordable and secure homes. The fundamental driver of our current housing crisis is the marketisation of housing as it is opened up to the private market and private investors like never before and increasingly treated as an investment commodity, rather than a home meeting a fundamental social need. Through financialisation, housing has been turned into a global financial commodity. Recent years have seen an increasing involvement of institutional global private equity and wealth funds investing in housing, converting it from a home to an unaffordable, wealth-accumulating asset for investors, and this is only the beginning.

The housing crisis is hitting cities and urban centres the hardest, and it is most severe in the countries such as Ireland, the United Kingdom and the United States, countries that have followed the private speculative market approach to housing, reducing social housing, particularly through austerity budget cuts, opening up their housing systems to global finance and private equity investors rather than ensuring their housing system provides a right to a home for all. But even countries such as Germany, Sweden and the Netherlands, which had stable housing systems with strong social housing sectors prior to the 2008 financial crisis, are now facing rising unaffordability and shortages in housing. Ordinary people are increasingly unable to access affordable and long-term secure homes as the financialisation of housing is turning homes into investment commodities for the super-rich and global investment funds.

Millions of people are becoming homeless from climate-related extreme weather events, and being forced to migrate to other countries, where they will need homes. Millions more will be displaced in the developed and developing world in the coming decades, and will be in severe housing need. It is the most vulnerable, minority communities, those with disabilities, those in poverty and the elderly who will be disproportionately affected and have the fewest resources to recover from climate-related disasters.

The United Nations (UN) Intergovernmental Panel on Climate Change has made it clear that global emissions must be cut in half in just 11 years (by 2030) and we must get to net-zero carbon emissions by 2050. Speaking at the World Economic Forum in Davos in January 2019, climate activist Greta Thunberg said: "We cannot solve an emergency without treating it like an emergency." We must "act as if the house is on fire, because it is" (World Economic Forum, 2019).

The housing crisis and climate crisis are also inextricably linked. Ensuring existing homes are zero-carbon and energy-efficient, and that new homes produce zero emissions, both during construction and over their lifetime, is critical to achieving climate targets.

The construction of housing and the built environment is a major contributor to carbon dioxide production. In Ireland, 10% of the country's greenhouse gases are emitted from the residential sector – from our homes – in various forms. The location of new homes is also important in addressing climate change and creating sustainable communities into the future, with high-density design and proximity to transport and employment. There must be a fair energy-transition process that brings all citizens and all neighbourhoods along or else it will fall through and lead to rising citizen discontent. A Green New Deal based on a massive, publicly funded, deep retrofit of existing housing and the building of affordable sustainable public housing has the potential to radically reduce our carbon emissions and achieve a fair transition at the same time.

A crisis that affects us all

When the housing crisis is discussed by the media or when most people are asked who is affected by the housing crisis, it is often homelessness that is first mentioned. Homelessness is the most extreme end of the housing crisis, but people feel that that affects 'others' unlike themselves. Most people generally do not think about or associate the housing crisis with themselves or their family. However, this book shows a new reality of an ever-expanding housing crisis that affects you, no matter who you are or where you live. Everyone is touched by the crisis. It is increasingly likely that you, your children, your family, your community, city or country is going to be affected by it in some way in the coming years.

The housing crisis has extended across the globe and reaches across most sectors and groups in society, whether you are middle- or working-class, professional or trade, migrant or local resident. If you have children, you will be affected when they want to move to a city to go to university and cannot find affordable accommodation, or when they grow up and get a job and want to move away from home but find they cannot because there are no affordable homes to rent or buy. They could be still living at home in their 20s, 30s or even 40s, straddled with huge student debt, or forced to move back home with children of their own as they can't afford to pay escalating rents, or save for a deposit to buy a home as house prices stretch out of reach of the average earner.

Just over a decade on from the global financial crisis in 2008, in which the housing and property boom and bust played a central role, another global housing bubble has developed. House prices in many of the major cities have increased by over 50% in just six years, while wages and incomes have been stagnant or increased at fractions of these rates.

In 2018 alone, four of the top 35 global cities saw double-digit growth in house prices, including Barcelona, Shanghai, Madrid and Ireland's capital city, Dublin. Dublin had the second-highest growth in house prices of the 35 cities, with an 11% increase in 2018.

The housing crisis affects more people, and in more ways, than ever before. It is playing a major role in three of the greatest challenges facing our societies – rising inequality, climate change and the lack of environmentally sustainable and socially inclusive economies and cities. It is deepening political and social divisions, citizen exclusion and disconnection from globalisation, governments and communities. It also affects the economy and businesses in terms of the location of jobs and workers' wage demands. It is having a detrimental impact on people and societies' wellbeing and mental health, particularly on levels of anxiousness and stress, through a lack of long-term security, fear of eviction, or anxiety over paying rent or the mortgage, or being forced to choose between paying rent, having enough food in the house, or paying medical bills or school costs. Those unable to afford to rent or buy are stuck living at home with their parents, leading to overcrowding and intergenerational family stress.

The crisis affects when those in the Generation Rent cohort are able to move out of home and become independent adults, have relationships, start a family and have children. This results in delayed adulthood and delayed family formation, with huge societal and personal mental health implications.

Yet for each person born on this planet, a secure, adequate home is a fundamental human need and requirement to live in safety and dignity, to develop and grow. A home is a universal human requirement. We can see this from the devastating impact on children, families and individuals for whom this basic need is unmet, such as homeless people living on the streets or in emergency accommodation. A home should provide a place of safety, a secure base in which to raise children, and to rest and sleep; it is vital for our physical, social and emotional health, and for participating in society, being part of a community, and gaining employment and an education. Without a secure, healthy, home all of this is extremely difficult, if not impossible, to achieve. Human development is stalled, denied and impossible without a home. In recognition of this fundamental role of housing for people, Article 25 of the Universal Declaration of Human Rights, signed in 1948, states that: 'Everyone has the right to a standard of living adequate for the health and well-being of himself and his family, including food, clothing, *housing* and medical care and necessary social services ...' (United Nations, 1948: emphasis added). The right to adequate housing is included in Article 11 of the UN International Covenant on Economic, Social and Cultural Rights, ratified by 71 countries including Ireland and the UK. Article 2 (1) of the Covenant outlines that, by ratifying the Covenant, these countries have committed to 'take steps ... to the maximum of its available resources ... to achieving progressively the full realization' of the right to housing 'by all appropriate means' (UN, 1991). The specific definition of what this right to adequate housing involved was defined in 1991 by the UN as 'the right to live somewhere in security, peace and dignity' and requires 'adequate privacy, adequate space, adequate security, adequate lighting and ventilation, adequate basic infrastructure and adequate location with regard to work and basic facilities – all at a reasonable cost', and governments, states and city authorities are obliged to 'ensure security of tenure and that access is free of discrimination, and progressively work to eliminate homelessness' (UN, 1991: 7). This definition provides a clear vision for what ensuring the right to housing for all actually means, what states are responsible for, and what each person should have access to, at a minimum, in order to live a life with true human dignity and the opportunity to fulfil their potential.

This book calls, therefore, for a deepened and renewed understanding of the role housing plays in our lives, in our personal development, in society, our communities, environment and economies. Current housing systems and their resultant multiple crises are having a major impact on individual and societal wellbeing as they have a detrimental effect on inequality. Precarious housing affects people's mental health and ontological insecurity. We therefore need to rethink the role housing that plays in our individual lives, our societies, the environment and economy, explaining what a home means to people who are its primary users – those living in it, rather than investors and those seeking asset accumulation. We need to consider how housing is designed for energy efficiency and with what materials it is built, and how we live in our homes, their energy efficiency and their impact on meeting climate change targets. To do this, the book draws on social policy, political economy, human rights and social justice frameworks, concepts and theories in order to develop a richer understanding of housing's fundamental role in economic and social development and personal and societal wellbeing.

A new crisis unfolds in Ireland

The housing crisis that has unfolded in Ireland since 2013, especially a dramatic increase in family homelessness (initially concentrated in Dublin but then extending across the country) has become, as set out in the opening quote of this chapter, a 'national emergency' and social catastrophe.

Official numbers of homeless people (which just includes those in unsuitable emergency accommodation such as hostels, guesthouses, hotels and temporary 'Family Hubs') have reached record levels, with figures for July 2019 standing at 10,172, including 4,110 individuals and 1,686 families with 3,675 children. This is a 344% increase in the number of homeless families in just five years, and a 425% increase in the number of homeless children. In July 2014, there were 1,963 individuals, 344 families and 865 children who were homeless. These figures do not include rough sleepers on the streets, people living in cars or tents, those in unsuitable or overcrowded accommodation, couchsurfers, or those living in direct provision or domestic violence shelters. Leading homelessness campaigner Peter McVerry (McVerry, 2015: 7) has described the unparalleled nature of the crisis in the following terms:

We have a homeless crisis that is unprecedented in my 40 years working in homelessness. For the first time since the Famine, families are being told they have to live on the streets because there is no housing for them. Nothing is being done to stem the flow of homelessness. In the private rented sector people are being evicted because they can't afford their rents.

The crisis has extended to affect hundreds of thousands of people across the country, from low- and middle-income families to individuals, professionals, workers, students and elderly and disabled people. They are suffering from a range of impacts from unaffordable rents, unaffordable house prices, the fear and threat of eviction, overcrowding, substandard housing, long commutes between home and work, dislocation, anxiety and isolation. The substantial level of stress in relation to housing affordability in Ireland is shown by that fact that a third of the population in 2016 'worried about and/or struggled' to be able to pay their rent or mortgage every month (Focus Ireland, 2017: 2), and one in every nine people (12%) were worried they would lose their home. This increased to almost one in five (17%) of those aged 25–34, indicating the higher proportion of young people affected by the housing crisis, while 6% of the population (around 220,000 people) were worried about becoming homeless.

With house price rises and rent increases in double-digit figures from 2013 onwards, and a major housing shortage resulting in huge queues (including people queueing overnight) to rent and buy homes, it appears like a repeat of the property bubble and subsequent economic downturn following the growth of the so-called Celtic Tiger boom of 2000–08. The headline 'Housing crisis grips Ireland a decade after property bubble burst', which appeared in the *New York Times* in August 2019, shows how the latest Irish housing crisis has captured international attention. It also raises the point that a decade on from the last housing crash, it appears we are again in the midst of another housing bubble, with an impending crash just around the corner.

The new Irish housing crisis is exacerbating Ireland's already deeply entrenched inequalities, and producing new housing inequalities, on a scale unseen in contemporary Ireland.

The changing geography of housing in our cities in particular reveals the growing social and spatial inequalities within the housing system. These inequalities are visible and stark for anyone who takes a short walk around Dublin city centre or other regional cities such as Cork or Galway. You can walk in a matter of minutes between homeless people lying in shop doorways on the capital's main streets, past internet cafés where homeless people are charged ten euros a night to sleep on the floor or under desks, past bed-and-breakfast accommodation and hotels where homeless families and children stay in 'emergency accommodation', past houses with huge overcrowding. One-hundred-and-fifty people were living in just three houses in Mountjoy Square where a fire occurred in February 2017. In one five-bedroomed house up to 70 people were living, predominantly migrants, in 'dangerous, unhealthy and cramped conditions' (*Irish Times*, 2017a) with up to 17 individuals in one room, and about 36 people housed in the basement.

At night on the main streets of Dublin and other cities and towns across the country hundreds of homeless people queue to get food in nightly soup kitchens. In August 2019, a record 550 people lined up on College Green outside Trinity College at a charity soup kitchen. A quarter of those queuing had jobs but could not afford food and other basics after paying most of their income on rent. People queue for viewings for private rental housing across the city, while families outbid each other to buy homes in higher-income suburbs of Dublin. Six 'trophy' houses on one road in Dublin 4 postal district were sold for between €3 and €4 million each last year.

In Dublin's inner city, you can walk past the old social housing apartment complexes, where homes are affected by mould and damp, past other estates half boarded up, past derelict state-owned properties, past land and buildings owned by the National Asset Management Agency (NAMA) or private companies, past sites where hundreds of student apartments have been built by global vulture funds in a matter of months and those where global investor landlords such as Kennedy Wilson are building apartments to be rented at €3,000 a month, and past yet more sites with tens of thousands of square metres of commercial office space being built rapidly by international investors through real estate investment trusts (REITs). Houses and apartments across the country are being built or bought up by the new investor landlords, large private equity funds, companies and REITs. Who can afford to rent or buy these homes? The 'build to rent' model is turning what should be affordable homes for young families and workers into 'safety deposit boxes' – wealth-accumulating investment assets for the Irish and global wealthy.

In 2018, approximately 1,200 families became newly homeless in Dublin alone (Focus Ireland, 2018), while an additional 3,000 Irish people became millionaires (and one became a billionaire), in large part due to the housing crisis (on the back of rising asset and property values). Housing and property have provided a key source of wealth for Ireland's richest. A quarter of Ireland's wealthiest 100 people amassed their wealth through construction, property and building.

While most of the newly homeless families were evicted from the private rental sector, huge profits are being made from converting rental homes into short-term tourist rental lets. There were more entire homes (2,856 properties) available to let out on the Airbnb platform (an online marketplace for offering lodging, primarily homestays or tourist accommodation) for more than 90 days than there were properties available to rent as homes in Dublin (1,500) in July 2019 (*The Journal*, 2019).

Overcrowding is also becoming a much bigger issue, with the 2016 Census recording the first increase in the number of people per household in half a century in Ireland. There was a 28% increase in overcrowding between 2011 and 2016. In 2016, there were 95,013 permanent households with more persons than rooms, accommodating close to 10% of the population (CSO, 2017). In terms of groups most affected by this, non-EU nationals were found by the Irish Human Rights and Equality Commission to be at greater risk of overcrowding (Grotti et al, 2018).

Over 65,000 households (almost one in ten of all home owners with a mortgage) are still in mortgage arrears on their primary home and many are being sold off to vulture funds, while the debt of developers who owed billions has been written off by NAMA and the banks (Hearne, 2017). Those in arrears are in a state of constant anxiety and insecurity about their housing situation.

The housing crisis also threatens the economy. High rents and house prices and the shortage of accommodation affect companies and businesses in terms of their ability to recruit suitable staff, as workers are unable to afford or find suitable housing. Companies are questioning whether to locate in Ireland because of the housing crisis, which in turn is affecting Ireland's economic competitiveness.

Therefore, the housing crisis does not just affect a narrow range of groups, but affects everyone, through its impacts on social and economic inequality (generational, income, social class, ethnic and racial, and gender), on climate change and transition targets, on social exclusion and cohesion, on economic instability and competitiveness, and on politics.

Box 1.1 shows a selection of headlines from newspapers in Ireland in recent years, and provides an interesting snapshot of the housing crisis and who is affected.

Box 1.1: A selection of newspaper headlines from 2015 to 2019 dealing with the housing crisis (from the _Irish Times_, _Irish Examiner_, _Irish Independent_, _The Journal_)

- 'Life with mortgage arrears in Ireland: I had "seizures from stress"'

- '"The private rented sector is broken": survey says 96% of people found it difficult to find rental home'

- 'Average monthly rents across the country rose to a new record level during the second quarter of the year'

- 'Irish workers crippled by "crazy" rent prices forced to queue for soup kitchen'

- 'Gentrification: are Dubliners being squeezed out?'

- 'Dublin now in top 5 most expensive places to rent in Europe, research finds'

- '"Letting agencies said that a landlord will never choose me in the rental lottery because I have kids"'

- 'Housing crisis impacts families fleeing domestic abuse'

- 'The average cost of renting a property in Dublin is now over €2,000'

- '"There are two choices: stay in Dublin and pay the price or leave Dublin and pay the price"'

- '"I'm 27. I'm living at home. Going through the same hall door since I was in a school uniform"'

- 'The neverending race to secure affordable accommodation continues its painful existence in Dublin'

- 'Homeless Meath dad sleeping in shed as he recovers from brain injury'

- 'Mother and children forced to sleep at Garda station. Margaret Cash was unable to find emergency homeless accommodation'

- 'A mother whose partner drowned last year is sleeping in her car with her five children because she is unable to source emergency accommodation from Cork City Council'

- 'Irish colleges hiking prices of college accommodation as students face housing crisis'

- 'Students who have not yet received their Leaving Cert results already have to worry about finding accommodation'

The roots of this crisis: financialisation

In order to find a way out of this crisis, we must first understand how we got to this point of social catastrophe. The causes and roots of the crisis are contested. The dominant free market view argues that it results from an undersupply of housing from the private sector due to too much state intervention and overregulation leading to a lack of incentive to build, insufficient credit from overly restrictive lending rules, overly interventionist and conservative planning controls, rent regulation, and inadequate 'help to buy' subsidies. However, the critical analytical lens adopted in this book points to the evidence of multiple and successive failures, and inherent inequalities, of the private market provision of housing. This book reveals the negative sociospatial impacts of the speculative, developer- and finance-led housing provision model that has been introduced via neoliberalism, financialisation and marketisation. This new housing crisis has very long roots and results from policies and processes developing over the past 40 years, culminating in the 2008 global financial crash and further evolving and intensifying over the past decade. At its core, the crisis results from the way in which housing, and land, as real estate has been converted into a tradeable commodity and investment asset that has become central to the accumulation regime in the current period of financial capitalism.

Drawing on political economy, social and spatial justice, human rights and equality theoretical frameworks and values, this book shows that the contemporary housing problem and its multiple crises, while it is an extremely complex issue, it is not a 'natural' disaster or an accident of policy. It results from the specific neoliberal housing and economic policies pursued by government and the interlocking effects of growing social inequality and financialisation.

In the Keynesian period from the 1940s to the 1970s, housing, residential investment and real estate was generally a local or national market in most cities and countries. There was strong state involvement, either through state provision of social (council/public) housing, state-led urban development, and planning. But neoliberal housing, planning and economic policies implemented from the 1980s onwards involved a radical change involving the withdrawal of the state, government and local authorities from building and financing social and affordable housing, and the shift to entrepreneurial 'pro-private development' planning. This, combined with deregulation of capital flows across borders, the globalisation of finance, and new forms of financial products, led to the financialisation and commodification of all aspects of housing and residential development. Now housing provision is primarily provided through private developers, builders and housing markets, and, increasingly its provision depends on the investment decisions of financial markets, the super-wealthy and global investment funds. Private investment can now control the entire lifecycle of residential development – from land ownership and development, to finance and lending, management and renting, and ownership. All parts of the process of providing a home have been opened up to, and influenced, bought and controlled by, global flows of finance.

Total investment in real estate globally rose by 18% in 2018 to hit a new record of US$1.8 trillion. New ('dry powder') investment targeted at real estate globally rose from $130 billion in 2012 to $300 billion in 2018, while in Europe it jumped from €20 billion in 2012 to €70 billion. The investment flowing into invididual cities is staggering. In 2018, €55 billion was invested in New York alone, €40 billion into Los Angeles, and €30 billion into London, while €3 billion flowed into Dublin, putting it in the top 20 cities in terms of cross-border investments, ahead of Chicago, Melbourne and Copenhagen (Knight Frank, 2019).

Investors do not see housing in the same way that most of us do – as a home that provides people with a basic fundamental need. Investors see it as way to achieve the highest return (in the quickest possible way) from their investment. They make their decisions on what to do with their residential property and land – whether to evict, raise rent, sell, purchase, develop or leave land idle – based on profit maximisation assessments, with little or no consideration of the function of housing as home or land as a resource for homes. They treat housing purely as a profit-making asset, irrespective of the human cost. A speech by Steve Schwarzman, the chief executive of one of the world's biggest private equity firms, Blackstone, in New York in 2010, showed this clearly, when he said that the company was going to shift to Europe to buy up its distressed assets (including housing), at a time when governments and people had been sufficiently beaten up by the recession and willing to sell at any price:

> 'As we look at the current situation in Europe, we're basically waiting to see how beaten up people's psyches get, and where they're willing to sell assets…. You want to wait until there's really blood in the streets.'

Moreover, Ireland is playing a key role in the financialisation of housing across Europe and globally, thus facilitating growing inequality. Ireland has become a 'hub for the financing and management of tax-efficient cross-border investment in rental property assets' (Donaghy, 2013), enabling the conversion of homes into financialised assets.

The pace of expansion of the financialisation of housing, such as the investor 'build to rent' phenomenon, is frightening. What is clear is that the issue is not the lack of land, buildings or finance, but what the land and buildings in our cities and towns is being used for, and who invests in building what. There is a rapid process of gentrification under way whereby areas that once had affordable housing – many longstanding working-class neighbourhoods – are being turned into highly sought-after areas with high rent and houses prices, as investors and high-income owners buy up the housing. The result is that many historic communities are becoming increasingly unaffordable for local children to buy or rent in the area. Dublin is being hollowed out by short-term let 'touristification' and high-end rental gentrification.

Table 1.1 sets out headlines from various Irish and international news outlets from 2014 to 2019 and provides an interesting snapshot of these growing trends in housing such as Generation Rent, the financialisation of housing, new investor landlords, global funds, and the impact on citizens, affordable housing, poverty and politics.

Table 1.1: Headlines telling the story of a growing global housing crisis

Headline	Subheadline (where applicable), news outlet
'How the financial crash made our cities unaffordable'	'Since 2008, property markets in the world's major cities have "synchronised" and left nations and citizens behind', *Financial Times*, 15 March 2018
'A lack of affordable housing feeds Hong Kong's discontent'	aljazeera.com, 11 August 2019
'America's housing affordability crisis spreads to the heartland'	www.bloomberg.com, 30 July 2019
'"Generation rent" could become "Generation homeless" when they retire, warns report'	'More than 600,000 millennials may not be able to afford their rent by retirement age', *Huffington Post*, 17 July 2019
'If the tuition doesn't get you, the cost of student housing will'	'National developers are behind the proliferation of luxury apartments near college campuses, and they're driving low-income students farther away', www.bloomberg.com, 13 July 2019

(continued)

13

Table 1.1: Headlines telling the story of a growing global housing crisis (continued)

Headline	Subheadline (where applicable), news outlet
'America's battle over housing is just getting started'	'The surest way to bring down costs is to build more. Lots of people won't like that', www.bloomberg.com, 14 June 2019
'Working but homeless: a tale from England's housing crisis'	*Financial Times*, 18 December 2018
'Climate change exacerbates the affordable housing shortage'	'Disabled people and minority communities are disproportionately affected and have the fewest resources to recover from disasters', *Scientific American*, 7 August 2019
'A successful climate plan must also tackle the housing crisis'	'The Democratic nominee should be able to answer the question: what will your climate plan do for the housing crisis?', *Guardian*, 1 October 2019
'Almost 13,000 Dublin homes will be affected by climate change – EPA'	'Increased storms and higher sea levels will give rise to extreme coastal flooding', *Irish Times*, 6 November 2019
'Vacancies unfilled as rents push midwives out of city'	'Waiting lists for gynaecology care will rise in the National Maternity Hospital in the coming months', *Irish Herald*, 5 September 2019
'First-time buyers will miss out as cash-rich investment fund to swoop on new homes'	*Irish Independent*, 2 April 2019
'"Cuckoo funds" elbow young buyers out of housing market'	*Irish Independent*, 4 April 2019
'Our new overlords: private equity'	*Irish Independent*, 17 August 2014
'Foreign investor firms responsible for around a fifth of Dublin house purchases'	'The sales are mostly to large, mostly foreign private equity companies and real estate investment trusts (REITs)', *The Journal.ie*, 22 September 2016
'Housing crisis grips Ireland a decade after property bubble burst'	'Dublin has become one of the world's most expensive places to rent, ahead of Tokyo, Sydney and Singapore', *New York Times*, 8 August 2019
'German bank sees "generation rent" fuelling Ires, Glenveagh shares'	'Ireland has "a number of years of growth ahead of it", Berenberg analysts tell clients', *Irish Times*, 2019
'"What used to be low-rent areas will stay high now": how Airbnb is "worsening crisis" in some Dublin areas'	'While certainly not the cause of the housing crisis, campaigners say legislation is needed to prevent it exacerbating the problem further', *The Journal.ie*, 3 March 2018

Book outline

Following this introductory chapter, Chapter 2 provides an overview of Generation Rent and the new housing inequalities. Chapter 3 provides an overview of the homelessness crisis, its causes and impacts on families and children in particular. Chapter 4 outlines a new approach to understanding and measuring homelessness and the level of housing exclusion in Ireland. Chapter 5 explains my housing journey and community experiences of regeneration, austerity and human rights, and suggests a role for academics in social change around housing. Chapter 6 explains the origins of the current crisis and macro-level changes in Irish housing policy, from strong state support for social and affordable housing to neoliberalism and financialisation. Chapter 7 details the way in which the financialisation of housing has unfolded in Ireland through NAMA and REITs, while Chapter 8 explains the impact of financialisation on housing and inequality. Chapter 9 details the impact of Irish government housing policy, including austerity and marketisation, on social housing and the wider housing crisis. Chapter 10 introduces the new housing protest movements in Ireland, their actions and how they have evolved, as well as their impact on solidarity, politics and policy, and provides lessons from this social action for housing activism and policy change. Chapter 11 presents a human rights approach to housing, while the final chapter outlines a new vision for housing policy and solutions based on a Green New Deal for housing: affordable sustainable homes and communities for all.

Two potential housing futures

This book is about addressing the housing problems, needs, rights, desires and dreams of families, children, workers and communities, today and of future generations. The world is becoming ever more insecure, with precarious work, automation, inequality and climate change, and governments that promote the interests of real estate investors over tenants and home owners.

The housing crisis now affects us all, whether it is through our own personal housing issues, those of family members or our children in the future, its contribution to worsening climate change or its potential to meet climate targets and ensure a socially just transition, its impact on the economy and jobs, the costs of dealing with the crisis, and its impact on reducing societal cohesion and worsening inequality. The housing crisis now affects everyone.

I finish this opening chapter by setting out two potential housing futures. As I see it, present and future generations face two broad possible futures. The first is the housing dystopia, and represents the likely housing systems if we continue down the path of marketisation and financialisation outlined in this book. If we continue with these current policies, the housing crises will become even more extreme and, in Ireland's case, this could look like the housing dystopia described in Scenario 1. Unfortunately, current housing systems and policies are driving us over the cliff towards the first scenario. However, we also face the possibility, if we change direction, implement the right policies and deliver them rapidly, of achieving affordable, secure and environmentally sustainable housing futures for all, set out in Scenario 2. It is also clear that our housing futures are intimately linked with the climate and planetary future, inequality and the achievement of a socially just transition. Scenario 2 is the future towards which I believe we must move our policies. This book is about avoiding the first scenario and achieving the second. I set out strategies and policies required to get us there. We can do it. We can achieve Scenario 2, if we choose to. But if we want to do it, we must act now.

Scenario 1: housing dystopia

It is Ireland in the year 2040. The number of homeless people has reached its highest yet, at 90,000 people, including 10,000 families and 30,000 children living in emergency accommodation. Twenty families and their children froze to death on the streets of Dublin last winter as temperatures plummeted to lowest ever-recorded temperatures due to severe climate change. Housing affordability and precarity has reached unprecedented levels. Suicide rates have doubled, with rent and mortgage arrears contributing to huge personal and family stress. Houses and sites lie empty and derelict because people cannot afford to buy them and investors hoard them as land prices continue to rise. Generation Rent has become a permanent feature – a new 'housing precariat' – living in expensive, insecure, high-rise 'co-living' apartment blocks with major issues of stress, family breakdown, and decline of community and social cohesion. The wave of financialisation with 'cuckoo' investor funds buying up and building land and homes reached a high point in 2022 but crashed as part of the global financial crisis that year. As a result, co-living 'build-to-rent' blocks have been sold on by their investors and have become dilapidated, yet are still being rented out at huge rents because of ongoing housing shortages. They have become the tenements of the 21st century. A number of the most run-down blocks have been bought by the state and turned into family hub 'emergency' accommodation. Many of the 10,000 homeless families have been living for more than ten years in such emergency accommodation. Hotels and many of the inner-city apartment blocks (former homes but now used for short-term holiday lets) are full with tourists who enjoy the beautiful sites of our country but have to wind their way around the families living in tents along the streets of our cities. The state is spending €10 billion a year subsidising private property owners (including many vulture funds and global real estate investor landlords) to house low-income households, providing a key source of revenue for private investment funds. The city centres and inner suburbs have become intensely divided by the creation of quarters comprising luxury apartments built by high-tech companies where high-income workers and wealthy people live with beautiful parks, sustainable-energy homes, and neighbourhoods with solar panels and wind turbines providing zero-energy costs, high-end cafés and gyms. These developments have gentrified the city and pushed out its working- and middle-class communities. The city's homes have been hollowed out of their former communities and in their place are street after street of short-term Airbnb lets for tourists and luxury student accommodation (see Image 1.1). Working families live in overcrowded unsustainable homes, as they are unable to afford the cost of retrofitting and investing in renewable energy generation, and thus pay the highest carbon taxes; others commute huge distances to work from housing estates on the city outskirts or regional towns, rarely seeing their families or community. The smaller cities and towns around the country, considered unprofitable by investors as locations for building new housing, have declined further, and without suitable affordable accommodation have failed to attract new businesses.

Across Europe and the US, this dystopian housing scenario is repeated, with the numbers of homeless people growing exponentially and thousands dying each year on streets and in tent cities due to horrendously hot summers and freezing winters. Many climate migrants, displaced from flooded homes and destroyed countries, are part of the growing homeless population. The largest global cities are so socially divided that local municipalities have employed private security companies to keep homeless people off the main streets and force them into outskirt areas.

There is a very real possibility that this will be our housing reality in 2040. It is a dystopian nightmare that will unleash untold human costs on those affected and on wider society. Based on the current housing policy paradigm continuing, I would argue that not only is it highly possible, but highly likely. You may shrug and think that this is just fantasy horror, and that no modern democratic government and their citizens would allow such a state of affairs to develop. Nevertheless, just

Image 1.1: Hotels and homelessness in Dublin

pause for a moment and think about how homelessness numbers and unaffordable rents have already increased dramatically in the past five years and how they have become normalised, accepted and tolerated in such a short space of time. Without citizen action that brings about radical policy and political change, this may be our future.

Scenario 2: a future of affordable homes, flourishing communities and a sustainable planet

It is Ireland 2040. It is the 15th anniversary of the ending of homelessness and 20 years since the successful referendum that enshrined the right to housing in the constitution and the enactment of legislation that made the Irish state responsible for ensuring everyone has access to an affordable, quality, secure and environmentally sustainable home. Over the past 20 years, the state has used this overarching framework of a legal and policy right to housing to guide policy and implement a number of key measures to solve the 2013–20 housing crisis. These included raised taxes on real estate investor funds that cooled off their speculative investment. As a result, 'build-to-rent', co-living plans were redeveloped to provide larger, affordable homes for purchase and rent. Policy measures also included setting rent affordability mechanisms, leading to rent reductions, regulation to give tenants security of tenure, a ban on commercial short-term let platforms, the development of an EU public home-share platform, and the introduction of high taxes on vacant sites, and vacant and derelict buildings. Compulsory Purchase Orders were used by national and city government to buy up large amounts of derelict and hoarded land, with the help of public land banks, to build 300,000 new, public, affordable and environmentally sustainable community homes across the country. They are vibrant flourishing communities of long-term affordable rental, cooperative ownership and social housing, with mixes of incomes and family type, including sheltered, step-down homes suitable for elderly people and people with disabilities, with inbuilt, environmentally sustainable design features, accessible clean parks, playgrounds, community halls, digital hubs, urban farms, crèches, libraries and healthcare all integrated into the development. A range of people from nurses to teachers, cleaners, construction workers, IT workers, professionals, retail workers, artists, architects, musicians, volunteers and charity workers all live in the affordable sustainable communities. There are tens of thousands of construction workers, tradespeople, architects, planners and engineers employed in high-quality, secure jobs in the new national agency responsible for delivering and managing the developments, the National Affordable Sustainable Homes and Community Building Cooperative, which was set up in 2020. Tens of thousands more people are employed to maintain the developments to the highest standard. These workers are trained in specialist zero-carbon building skills as part of the Green New Deal 2020. The residents of these homes and communities are an integral part of a cooperative that manages each estate and block of apartments, as equal partners with local authorities, housing associations and smaller cooperatives. These organisations operate via a digital cooperative platform providing citizen planning and control over design, operations and data. Generation Rent has become a term that means having affordable, secure, high-quality and environmentally sustainable housing. It is a generation of people who are able to pursue the employment of their choosing, which fulfils their potential and interests, as they have the security of a permanent, affordable home. Levels of mental and physical health, equality and social inclusion have all improved. Our individual and collective wellbeing as a country is much better. Ireland is now a leading country in the delivery of affordable and environmentally sustainable homes, with people coming from across the world to visit how it shifted focus from an unprecedented crisis to implementing innovative globally leading solutions. Similar housing programmes have been rolled out across the world as part of a global 2025 agreement of ending homelessness and delivering affordable sustainable housing for all, meeting the right to housing and agreed climate change targets enshrined in the Green New Deal of 2020.

2

Generation Rent

It is the younger generations and lower-income households that are most affected by the housing and homelessness crisis. Huge aspects of their lives have become precarious and insecure, as a result of insecure, low-paid and often part-time jobs, and insecure and unaffordable housing.

Generation Rent is the new housing precariat, living with precarious housing, precarious work contracts and an inability to access mortgage credit, alongside unaffordable house prices and rent. There are workers paying over half of their wages on rent. A person with an average salary, renting the average home, now has to allocate 86.3% of their earnings on rent (UN, 2019).

Generation Rent results from growing housing unaffordability and increasingly precarious and low-wage employment, a trend that began in the 1990s and 2000s during the last housing boom and continued into the post-2008 global financial crisis and subsequent austerity period. They are being outbid by global investors, wealthy individuals and so-called 'cuckoo' funds (after the cuckoo bird, which pushes other birds' eggs out of their nests and moves in), turning homes into wealth-accumulating commodities, with the only option for Generation Renters being to rent co-living micro-homes.

Increasingly, these micro-apartments – essentially expensive 'shoebox' homes, sharing with dozens of other people, known as build-to-rent 'co-living' – are the only way for Generation Renters to afford to live in the biggest cities. In the US, up to half of renters in key cities face high housing cost burdens (unaffordable housing), spending more than 30% of their household income on rent (PriceWaterhouseCooper, 2019).

Many Generation Renters are also forced to live at home with their parents for much longer, perhaps unable to move out. Generation Rent could equally be described as Generation Stuck at Home, or Generation Home Birds. In Ireland, 82% of men and 75% of women aged 16 to 29 are still living at home with their parents, in contrast to Denmark where just 40% of men and 32% of women under 29 live with their parents (Eurostat, 2019).

Generation Rent also comprises construction workers (tradespeople, including plumbers, blocklayers, and electricians), who have become some of the most precarious workers in the economy. The practice of 'bogus self-employment' and 'subcontracting' has meant that many construction workers are without proper pay and conditions, leading to exploitation as well as issues of substandard quality of construction. This is preventing people from entering construction as a career, thereby contributing to the skills shortage in the sector.

Increasingly, Generation Renters also include people in their 30s and 40s and their children, and older people in their 50s, 60s and into retirement who are stuck living in the private rental sector.

For Generation Rent, home-ownership rates have fallen dramatically. In the UK, the proportion of people owning their own home fell from a high point of 73% in 2007 to 63% in 2016. Among low- to middle-income younger households (under-35s), the collapse has been even more dramatic, from a 58% home-ownership rate in 1997 to just 25% in 2013 (Institute for Fiscal Studies, 2018). In the US, home-ownership rates fell from 69% in 2004 to 63.7% in 2015, the lowest level since 1966 (Institute for Fiscal Studies, 2018).

Generation Renters also lack the safety net of social housing that existed in previous generations, as governments have withdrawn from building social housing in recent decades. The proportion of households in social housing dropped from 30% in the UK in 1980 to 17% in 2016 (Institute for Fiscal Studies, 2018). In Ireland, the proportion of households in social housing fell from a high point of 18% of households in 1961 to just 9% in 2016 (CSO, 2016).

This has meant that Generation Renters are being forced to get housing from the expensive and insecure private rental market. The trends in the shift among Generation Renters to the private rental sector in the UK and Ireland have been remarkably similar in recent decades and reflect the similar dominance of neoliberal policy and ideology that has radically reduced social housing provision in these two countries. The proportion of households in the private rental sector increased in the UK from 10% in 1995 to 20% in 2016. In the US, it grew from 31% in 2005 to 37% in 2016. In Ireland, the proportion of households in the private rental sector increased from 10% in 2006 to 19% in 2011, while the proportion of younger households in private rental in Ireland has increased from 16% in 1994 to 55% in 2016 (CSO, 2016).

This has major social, economic and political significance. In housing systems such as those found in Ireland, the UK and parts of the US, the private rental sectors, unlike in many European countries, are weakly regulated. They are insecure and unaffordable for tenants who have faced huge rent hikes in recent years. The increase in the number of households in the private rental sector, therefore, has considerable societal, policy, political and economic implications, as much larger numbers of households, for much longer periods of time, are living with housing stress and anxiety, poorer standards of housing conditions, and forced dislocation, all characteristics of the neoliberal Anglo-Saxon private rental sector. Those living in such private rental housing have little ability to plan for their future, plan families, or set roots in the community. This is having devastating impacts on families and children, affecting their ability to form friendships and attend local schools, and causing family and neighbourhood dislocation and disruption. In both Ireland and England, evictions from the private rental sector are the leading cause of new homelessness. You cannot make a long-term secure home in the private rental sector in these countries.

The implications are even more significant for the future, as, given the lack of affordable housing, many Generation Renters could be in rental accommodation for their entire life. The number of privately rented households headed by someone aged over 64 will more than treble over the next 30 years (Institute for Fiscal Studies, 2018).

Home ownership, for many people, has become a key way of surviving financially in retirement; it is their pension, their ability to pay for nursing home care, and perhaps a home or asset to pass on to the next generation. When Generation Renters retire in the future and are still living in the private rental sector, how they will they be able to afford to continue to pay the rent as their income drops to a pension? Shall we see huge increases in elderly poverty and homelessness?

In addition, Ireland is a country where a large cohort of Generation Renters were forced to emigrate in the austerity period from 2008 to 2013. The members of this 'lost generation' are now unable to return to their home country because of high house prices and rents, and there are still thousands of young people leaving Ireland because of the lack of affordable housing. This results in the country losing the human potential, talent and capital it has invested in, and leaves families spread across many continents.

The end of the home-ownership dream

There was a major oversupply of new housing in the period 2002–08, when, for example in just one year (2007), 78,000 housing units were built in Ireland. In contrast, only 8,000 new dwellings were completed in 2015. By 2018, a total of 18,072 new dwellings were being completed on an annual basis, but this is still well below the estimated figure of 35,000 per annum needed to meet demand (Central Bank of Ireland, 2019c). As a result, and due to an increase in population (including both domestic and immigration flows), employment and economic growth from 2013 onwards, house prices began to increase again. Figure 2.1 shows that over the period 2013 to 2019 house prices increased by 96% in Dublin and by 83% for the country as a whole. Dublin experienced the largest growth in property prices among 32 developed countries and cities between 2013 and 2018.

Many people, particularly those in their 20s and 30s, now struggle to buy a home of their own as house prices have spiralled beyond the reach of those on low and average incomes. The median price paid for a house in Dublin was €370,000 in February 2019. This was 9.3 times average annual earnings (€39,753) (ESRI, 2019). The Central Bank of Ireland defines affordable housing as 3.5 times gross income. For two people on the average wage, this is about €270,000, well below the median house price in Dublin (Central Bank of Ireland, 2019c).

Rent on the rise

Dublin and the Greater Dublin area comprise a large proportion (48%) of private rental tenancies in Ireland. In 2018, rents for newly rented properties increased by 11% in Dublin, and regionally, in Galway by 14%, in Cork by 10% and in Limerick by 8%. By July 2019, average monthly rents across the country has risen to €1,391 per month, in Dublin to €2,023 a month – a new record level – in Cork to €1,366 a month, and in Limerick to €1,225 a month. The increase marked the 13th consecutive quarter of record rents. Dublin has become one of the world's ten most expensive places to rent, ahead of cities such as Tokyo, Sydney, Barcelona and Paris, and with over double the average rent of Manchester and Toronto (ECA International, 2019).

Data from the state body, the Residential Tenancies Board (RTB, 2018), show that average Dublin rents, on existing rental properties, increased from €961 in the first quarter (Q1) of 2012 to €1,662 in Q1 2019, a 73% increase in that seven-year period. Average national rents increased from €744.72 in Q1 2012 to €1169 in Q1 2019, a 57% increase in seven years. In contrast, the Consumer Price Index, which measures inflation in the economy (the overall change in the prices of goods and services), registered almost little or no increase in costs in the period 2013–18. The rate of rental inflation is shown in Figure 2.2, with a dramatic increase in the rent visible from 2011 to 2018, reaching higher than the previous rental peak of 2008.

There was also the issue of the major shortage of rental properties. In Dublin, there were just 1,541 properties available to rent in

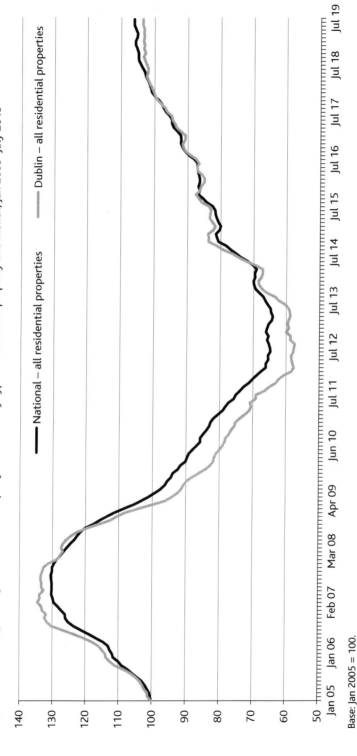

Figure 2.1: Percentage change in residential Property Price Index by type of residential property and month, Jan 2005–July 2019

Base: Jan 2005 = 100.

Source: CSO (2019b)

Figure 2.2: Average monthly rent (€) by location and year for a two-bedroom property

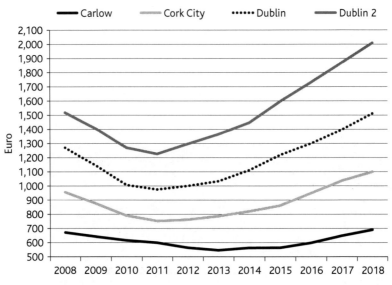

Source: CSO (2018b)

August 2019, well below the average of 4,700 for the preceding decade. The RTB (2019: 3) explains the extent and causes of the rental crisis as follows:

> Affordability issues in the housing market are resulting in an increasing number of people moving into the rental sector, exerting upward pressure on rents. As house prices continue to rise these affordability issues are likely to become more pronounced leading to further spill-over effects in the rental market. Despite the increase in housing completions in 2018, the level of supply remains significantly below the level of structural demand. A significant increase in the number of properties available for both sale and rent will be required to temper the rapid growth in rent prices.

Soaring rents have put immense financial strain on workers, students and their families, who are often paying for poor-quality accommodation with little or no security of tenure.

It now costs far more to rent than to pay a mortgage. Average mortgage costs in Dublin city centre are approximately €1,500 per month compared with an average rent of €2,064 (Daft, 2019).

Housing benefit: Housing Assistance Payment

Rising rents have also resulted in a growing gap between the rent limits set for state housing subsidies (housing benefit) to low-income tenants in the private rental sector (such as the Rent Allowance and the new social housing support, the Housing Assistance Payment) and the actual market rent. The rents for most of the homes in the private rental market are higher than the state rent limits payable to people on state housing benefits. This, along with the high level of competition in the private rental market, has meant that low-income households – and particularly vulnerable groups such as young people, people leaving care, migrants, Travellers, those with disabilities and mental health difficulties, and lone parents – are increasingly subject to discrimination and exclusion from the private rental market, and consequently forced into homelessness. It has also meant that a majority of those in receipt of state benefits in the private rental sector are also making 'top-up' payments to landlords to cover the gap between the state housing benefit and market rents. This is likely to be pushing already low-income tenants further into poverty. As explained by the charity St Vincent De Paul (SVP and Threshold, 2019: 2):

> The national average rent rose 18% between Q2 2016, when the Housing Assistance Payment (HAP) limits were set, and Q4 2018. As a result, those eligible for housing income supports are increasingly priced out of the market. Households 'top-up' their rent beyond 30% of income threshold, meaning that already limited financial resources for food, clothing and utilities are reduced to unsustainable levels. This causes untold stress and worry for households. This shortfall in HAP payments can impoverish some households, meaning they are forced to seek assistance from charitable organisations, such as SVP. Worryingly, 48% of respondents in receipt of HAP who were surveyed by Threshold, pay a 'top-up' directly to the landlord. These amounts range from €20 to €575 a month. The average 'top-up' payable was €177. This is in addition to the differential rent paid directly to the local authority which averages €223 a month. Working households, whether part-time or full-time, as well as those in receipt of social welfare were paying 'top-ups' across the range.

There are major issues in the private rental sector relating to the lack of enforcement of regulation and penalties for landlords. The law allows landlords to evict tenants if they state that they are moving a family member in, or are selling or renovating the property, or if the tenant is unable to pay increased rents. Such evictions have been the single largest factor causing the rise in homelessness. Even those who can afford their rents find that they have little security in a rising market. Leases can be for as little as six months.

Less than a third of tenancies in the private rental sector in Ireland are for a longer duration than 12 months. This means that over two thirds of private rental tenants are living on a year-to-year lease and therefore living with huge insecurity.

The extent of problems in the private rental sector is shown by the fact that over 3,700 tenants contacted the Residential Tenancies Board in relation to issues of dispute with their landlord in 2018. There were 503 complaints from tenants about the unlawful termination of tenancy (illegal evictions) by landlords in 2018, an increase on the 320 complaints in 2015. There were 1,396 complaints in 2018 about the validity of the notice of termination issued by the landlord. In 40% of cases, the reasons for termination included the landlord's intention to sell or substantially refurbish or renovate the dwelling, or requiring the dwelling for the landlord's own or family use (RTB, 2019). Tenants are often unaware of their rights. The Irish private rental sector is therefore an insecure form of housing tenancy.

The housing charity Threshold (2018: 4) explains that:

> The rental market in Ireland, though improving, is still insecure, unaffordable and of poor quality. Tenancies can still be ended for no reason. Moreover, rents grew 6.9% nationally in 2018. Tenants cannot create a home or even desire a home in the private rental sector when they can be so easily evicted. When rents are beyond levels of affordability. When the quality of their home puts their health at risk … not enough has been done to make the rental sector an attractive, viable and secure place to call home.

Threshold surveyed tenants and found that 71% rent because they cannot afford to buy.

Table 2.1 provides an insight into the difficult housing situations of tenants in the private rental sector through a summary of case studies provided by RTB and Threshold.

Table 2.1: Case studies of housing situations in private rental sector

Case study 1: €3,900 awarded to a tenant in overpaid rent because the landlord threatened to sell the property if the tenant did not pay an illegal rent increase	A tenant had been paying €1,200 in rent in 2016 and a year later, an agent acting on the landlord's behalf informed the tenant that if they were to pay an increase in rent of €1,500 the landlord would allow the tenancy to continue. However, if the tenant did not agree to this, the landlord would proceed to sell the property. The tenant felt they had no choice and paid €1,500 a month for the next 13 months. After being made aware of their rights, the tenant turned to the RTB. It was found that the landlord had served an invalid Notice of Rent Review, and the tenant was awarded the amount that had been overpaid over the 13 months.
Case study 2: €20,000 awarded to a tenant where a landlord was found to have penalised the tenant and abused the termination process	In this case, the landlord had sought to invalidly increase the rent and the tenant did not accept this. The landlord subsequently served notice of termination on the grounds that their brother would be moving in. The tenant moved out, but could not find suitable accommodation, resulting in them moving into a log cabin in a friend's back garden, which was no longer suitable or big enough to allow their child to stay with them. Subsequently, the tenant saw the rental property advertised online, with a rent increase of €500 more than they were paying and took a case to the RTB. It was found that both the Notice of Rent Review and Notice of Termination were invalid, and that, as a result, both the tenant and their children suffered severe disruption to their lives.
Case study 3: family with one child evicted into shared accommodation	A couple with one child living in Galway city were paying €775 per month in rent for their home. The landlord wanted to increase that by €500 to €1,275 a month. Galway is in a designated rent pressure zone, so this increase of over 60 per cent contravenes the law in this regard. Assisted by Threshold, the tenant successfully challenged the rent review. However, while the landlord did not increase the rent, the tenants were served notice of termination of the lease. They are now living in a room in a shared house, as they have been unable to find any alternative affordable accommodation.
Case study 4: family successfully challenges illegal eviction	A family based in north County Dublin had been living in a property for eight years. The rent was low and the landlord said that it was not sustainable to keep it at that rate into the future. However, the rent could only be raised by a maximum of 4 per cent, meaning that it couldn't be brought in line with the price of similar properties in the area, so that landlord issued the tenants with an invalid notice to leave the property, on the basis that renovations would be carried out and the property then given to the landlord's son. The notice failed to comply with the Residential Tenancies Act 2016, and the tenants remain in situ. The landlord must now issue a new 224-day notice to comply with the legislation before attempting to remove the tenants from the property.

(continued)

Table 2.1: Case studies of housing situations in private rental sector (continued)

Case study 5: **lone parent at risk of homelessness**	A lone parent of two children was told that her landlord was selling the Cork city property she lived in. Threshold represented the tenant at an RTB hearing, and won because the landlord had issued an invalid notice of termination. However, the tenant has now received a new, valid, notice of termination, on the grounds again that the landlord is selling the property. The tenant is now on the social housing waiting list, but is finding it difficult to find accommodation, raising the risk that she may become homeless.
Case study 6: **HAP tenant in substandard accommodation in private rental**	Vera lives in a two-bedroom terraced house with one child. There is no heat, damp throughout the house and no hot water in the kitchen. The kitchen consists of an alleyway leading to a backyard with no place to sit. The rent is €660 per month with the tenant paying a 'top-up' every month. After an inspection by the Council, the landlord installed a heater in the kitchen but then put up the rent as a result. A council representative told the tenant: "Be thankful that the landlord put in the heater.'

A structural shift in Ireland's housing system: decline in home-ownership rates and rise in private rental sector

Prior to the 2008 financial crash, the rate of home ownership in Ireland stood at 76%. This was down from a high of 81% in 1991. The home-ownership level has declined even further, from 69.7% in 2011 to 67.6%, a rate last seen in 1971. The rate in rural areas is 82% and in urban areas 59.2% (Hearne, 2017). Table 2.2 shows that the extent of collapse in the home ownership rate in Ireland is one of the largest in the EU since the crash.

Given the lack of social housing, the decline in home ownership has meant a dramatic increase in the proportion of households in the private rental sector, doubling from 9.9% in 2006 (145,317) to 18.5% in 2011 (305,377). Including unregistered tenancies, around 750,000 people in Ireland now live in the private rented sector. That is almost one in five of all households (Hearne, 2017). It is double the number of households that lived in the sector over a decade ago. In the cities and towns it is even higher. In Dublin, it is estimated that one in four households is living in the private rental sector. These households are living in a situation of persistent and pervasive housing anxiety and housing stress – worrying whether the landlord will increase the rent further or issue a notice to quit and whether they have to join the thousands more looking for another home, uprooting their children, losing their local connections and supports.

Table 2.2: Percentage of population in ownership tenure status in various EU countries, 2007 and 2014

	2007	2014	Change
Ireland	78.1	68.6	−9.5
United Kingdom	73.3	64.4	−8.9
Iceland	86.4	78.2	−8.2
Estonia	86.8	81.5	−5.1
Latvia	86.0	80.9	−5.1
Slovenia	81.3	76.7	−4.6
Euro Area	71.4	66.9	−4.5
Denmark	67.1	63.3	−3.8
Bulgaria	87.6	84.3	−3.3
Luxembourg	74.5	72.5	−2.0
Austria	59.2	57.2	−2.0
Spain	80.6	78.8	−1.8
Greece	75.6	74.0	−1.6
Cyprus	74.1	72.9	−1.2
Belgium	72.9	72.0	−0.9
Finland	73.6	73.2	−0.4

Source: Eurostat (2018)

This underlines the significance of the increase in the number households living in the private rental sector. The Irish private rental sector does not have the tenant protections, or the affordable, high-quality rental properties that are the norm in many other European countries. The private rental sector in Ireland does not provide a secure, affordable home. The expansion of the private rental sector in Ireland in its current form, therefore, means an increase in the number of people suffering from housing distress. It also houses a greater proportion of low-income households, as those on higher incomes and from wealthier backgrounds are more likely to have the financial means to purchase housing; rising rents and insecurity therefore affect such low-income households even more, contributing to poverty and inequality.

This represents a dramatic structural shift within the Irish housing system. In Ireland in recent decades, a core objective of government housing and economic policies has been to increase home-ownership rates. The expansion of the private rental sector shows the extent to which these policies have failed.

Figure 2.3 shows the changing nature of housing tenure of young Irish households. Since 1991, there has been a collapse in the proportion of younger age groups owning their own home. Just 30%

Figure 2.3: Tenure of young Irish households (25- to 35-year-olds)

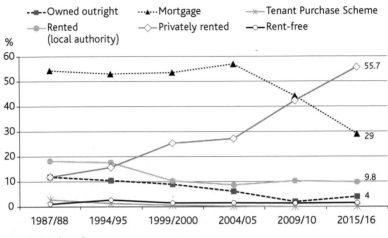

Source: CSO (2016)

of 25- to 34-year-olds owned their home in 2016. The level of home ownership among this age group was almost double that level (at 68%) in 1991. In 1991, the majority of people aged 26 owned their own home, but in 2016, the age threshold had risen to 35. In 2016, over half of 25- to 34-year-olds were in private rented accommodation, three times the level of renters (at 15%) in 1991. The proportion of those in the 35–44 age group renting from a private landlord increased from 5% in 1991 to 24% in 2016 (CSO, 2016).

The CSO data (2016) shows the distribution of renting and ownership within the population according to householder age. It shows a large bulge of renters among the 20 to mid-30s age group, a bulge of owners with a mortgage in the mid-30s to late 50s age group, and a very large bulge of owners without a mortgage in the 60-plus age group. It also illustrates that between 20% and 30% of those in their 40s are renting. Figure 2.4 shows the increase in the number of householders who rent by different ages between 1991 and 2016, with a particular rise in households in their 20s, 30s and 40s.

The biggest decline in home ownership levels has been among the younger generations, but in particular among low socioeconomic classes. Data from Eurostat (2017) shows that there has been a proportionally equal fall in home-ownership rates between 2007 and 2014 for those above 60% of the median income (falling from 82.9% to 72.7% – proportionally a 12.3% decline) and for those below 60% of median income (from 55.1% to 47.6% – proportionally a 13.6% decline). However, the fall for those below 60% of median income is

Figure 2.4: Number of householders who rent by age in 1991 and 2016

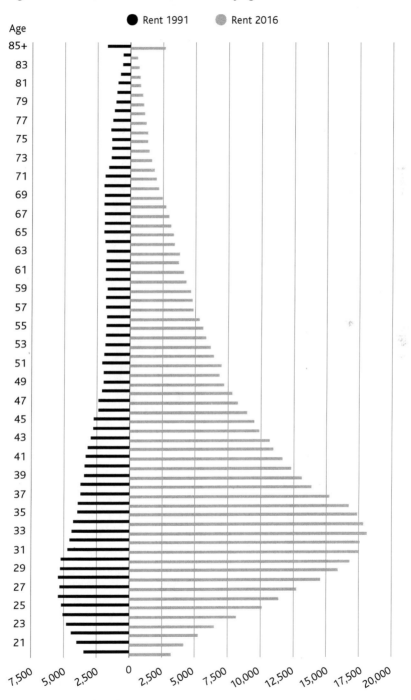

Source: CSO Ireland (2016)

more significant as it brings home-ownership rates in that category below 50%. The households below 60% of median income are going to face much more difficulties in paying rents in the private rental sector than those on higher incomes.

Generation Rent extends its reach

The Department of Housing, Planning and Local Government acknowledges that young people and those on low incomes are unlikely to be able to afford to buy a home in their communities:

> The incomes of many households are such that aspiration to home ownership in the communities in which they came from and work is unlikely to be realisable: this is despite the fact that in the recent past households in similar relative economic positions may well have bought houses in those communities. (Department of Housing, Planning and Local Government, 2016b: 26)

Our understanding and classification of Generation Rent needs to be expanded to include the growing middle-aged and *older* renting demographic. Generation Rent does not just apply to those in their 20s and 30s, but now extends to the middle-aged and older generations as shown in the increase in the number of people renting in their 40s and 50s. The proportion of 45- to 54-year-olds living in private rental accommodation increased from 3% in 1991 to 11.6% in 2016. Given that most renters in their 40s are unlikely to get a mortgage due to the length of the repayment period, the 24% who are renting in the private rental sector are unlikely to ever become owners (Hearne, 2017).

With regard to post-retirement age households, the number of people over the age of 65 is expected to reach 1.4 million by 2040, or almost a quarter of the population, up from 13% of the current population. There is therefore going to be a dramatic increase in the coming years in the number of elderly people in the private rental sector. Currently only 2% of those aged 65 and older are renting from a private landlord, but this will increase to between 15% and 25% in the coming decades, as those currently renting in their 40s and 50s are unlikely to be able to buy and will remain renting for life. Pensioners becoming homeless from the private rental sector is already a reality, and an estimated 150,000 age-friendly accommodations will be needed by 2031 (Hearne, 2017). But how will elderly people access this 'rightsizing' accommodation from the private rental sector?

There are not huge profits to be made in 'rightsizing', so the private market will not address this social need. Housing policy makers need to address the issue of who will house the older Generation Rent.

This raises critical policy issues pertaining to the capacity of the current younger population and increasing proportions of the middle-aged population to become owner-occupiers in the future. It has significant implications for wealth inequality and the welfare state in terms of pension and poverty among elderly people in the future. It suggests that urgent reform of the current housing system and rental sector is required to provide an affordable secure home for these new Generation Rent households excluded from home ownership and social housing.

Increasing housing cost overburden rates

Young people on low incomes are most severely affected by the issue of housing affordability than young people on higher incomes. In 2014, 53% of young people aged between 25 and 29 years from a lower-income background (below 60% of median income) were affected by a housing cost overburden rate, but only 5% of young people above 60% of the median income were affected (Hearne, 2017).

In terms of household type, there is a similar pattern to poverty and deprivation trends. The housing cost overburden rate among single-parent households has doubled since 2007. In 2015, three times the proportion of single-parent households were affected by the housing cost overburden rate as were households without children. Given that most single-parent households are headed by women, this reflects the strongly gendered impact of the crisis (Hearne, 2017).

Housing cost overburden is primarily an issue of the private rented sector. In 2015, just under a fifth (18%) of tenants renting at market price were affected by a housing cost overburden rate. This is over six times the rate of those with a mortgage or loan (at 2.7%) and five times the rate of those in subsidised accommodation (3.7%) (CSO, 2016). As Table 2.3 shows, the consistent poverty rate of those in the private rental market is almost five times that of owner-occupants

Table 2.3: Consistent poverty rate (%) by tenure status and year

	2009	2010	2011	2012	2013	2014	2015	2017	2018
Owner-occupied	2.5	3.4	3.8	5.4	5.6	5.1	4.6	3.5	2.5
Rented at market rate	8.3	10.6	6.8	9.9	10.0	10.5	11.3	10.6	11.2

Source: CSO (2019a)

and has increased consistently in recent years, despite the economic recovery and the decline in poverty among owner-occupiers. Similarly, the deprivation rate for private renters is 25%, which means one in four households in the private rental sector is affected by deprivation, compared with just one in ten home owners.

Generation Stuck at Home

Generation Rent includes those forced to live at home with their parents as they cannot afford to move out into the rental sector, or because they have been evicted from the private rental sector or have been unable to meet mortgage payments and have had their former home repossessed, cannot access social housing, or are trying to save for a deposit to buy a home. This is Generation Stuck at Home and Figure 2.5 demonstrates that Ireland has one of the higher proportions of this generation (young people, aged 16-29) living with their parents in the EU, with over 80% of young men and 75% of young women living at home, in contrast to countries like Denmark where just 40% of young men and 32% of young women live with their parents.

This data shows that problems relating to access to affordable housing that first emerged during the boom years of the mid-2000s have escalated in recent years and are having a marked impact on the lives of young people in Ireland. This is having profound personal impacts, such as reduced levels of household formation. Generation Rent and Stuck at Home are more likely to rent accommodation and they are getting married and forming family units at a later age. For growing cohorts of younger generations, and particularly low-income households, Ireland is becoming a post-home-ownership society.

Generation Rent is also seen as a major investment opportunity for global finance property speculators and investment funds building expensive 'co-living' and 'build-to-rent' micro-apartments.

It is important to understand that Generation Rent is not just a temporary phenomenon. It is a long-term trend with major implications for the future. The Economic and Social Research Institute (ESRI, 2019) estimates that a third of renters in the private rental sector have 'high' housing costs, and this has been the case over the period 2004–18, not just during the current crisis.

The expansion of mortgage credit in the period 2001–07 masked the growing unaffordability crisis (which also then contributed to the mortgage arrears crisis). The Central Bank of Ireland's macroprudential mortgage lending rules implemented in the wake of the financial crisis that limit loan-to-value and loan-to-income ratios, combined

Figure 2.5: Share of young people (aged 16–29) across Europe living with their parents, 2017

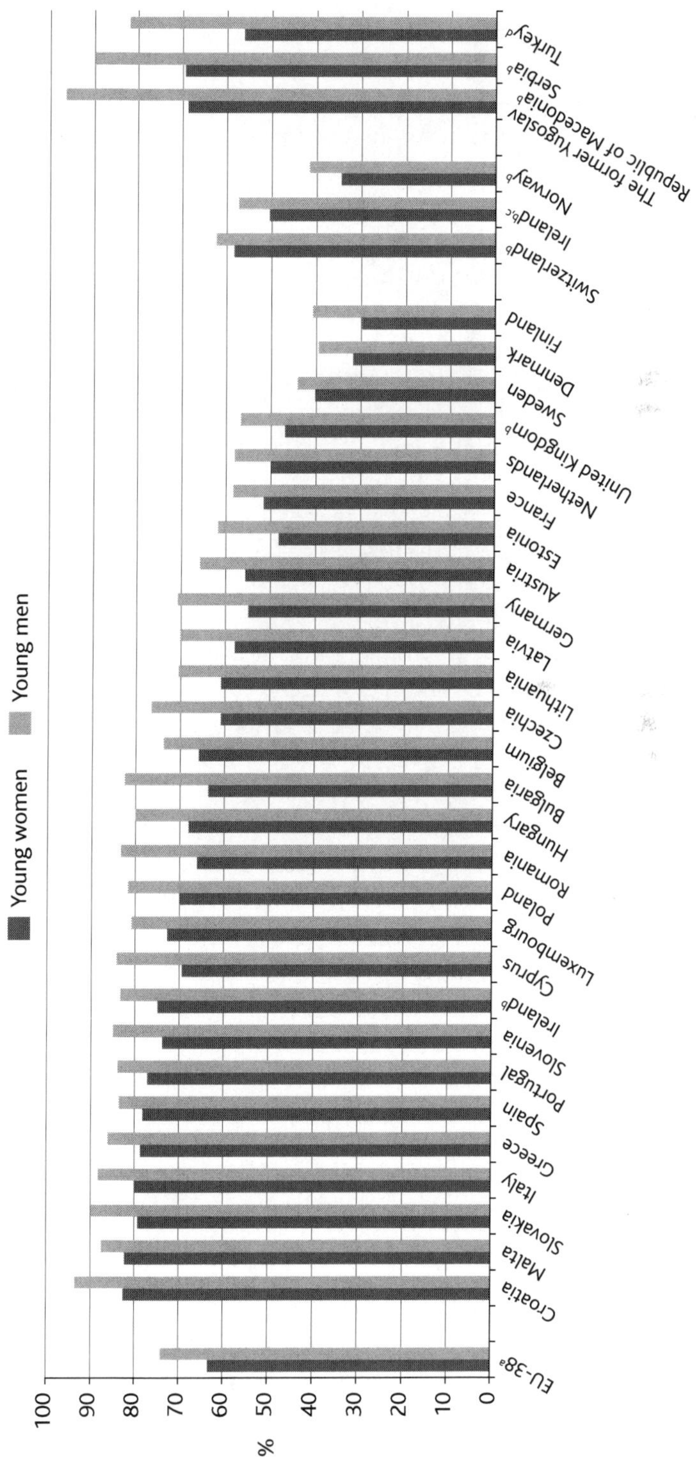

■ Young women ■ Young men

Notes: [a] Estimates; [b] 2016; [c] Provisional; [d] 2015.
Source: Eurostat (online data code: ilc_lvps08)

with a decline in incomes and the rise of precarious, 'gig' economy work among younger generations, has meant a dramatic reduction in the ability of younger households to access mortgages to enable them to purchase a home. Furthermore, the increase in the proportion of income spent on rent means less money available to save for a deposit, and this combined with increased deposit requirements also affects the ability to borrow and buy a home.

An increasing proportion of Generation Rent households will be renting permanently in the private rental sector – and in Ireland this currently means being in unaffordable and insecure housing. This is a dramatic cultural and societal shift. The so-called 'dream' of home ownership will become more and more unattainable for a large proportion of Generation Rent. It has become a home-ownership illusion. Instead Generation Rent will be stuck in the nightmare of the insecure and unaffordable private rental sector.

Therefore the decline in home-ownership rates and the associated increase in private renting present a major challenge for the Irish housing system and for government policy. This includes rising residential insecurity, generational and social class inequalities, and ultimately, the failure to provide affordable and secure housing for increasing numbers of existing and new households.

Student housing crisis

Students are another group of Generation Renters who are affected by the rental crisis. In previous decades, many students moving away from home to attend college or university obtained accommodation in the private rental sector. However, with the shortage in the rental sector, unaffordable rents and increased competition for accommodation, students who cannot afford the high rents are being squeezed out. Students are suffering at the hands of rogue landlords taking advantage of the accommodation crisis. Students' unions report that they are overrun with casework on accommodation. They face issues such as a lack of student accommodation, and the accommodation that is available is either too expensive for the average student to afford or is in very poor condition. There are countless horror stories of students and their families in a panic at the start of term trying to get accommodation in the midst of a wider housing crisis characterised by huge demand, massive deposits, unaffordable rents and poor standards. The housing crisis even affects students' education and mental health, particularly among those from lower socioeconomic backgrounds. Some students are not able to take up their studies because they cannot access or afford accommodation in the cities or towns of their chosen college or university.

As the Union of Students in Ireland explains: 'This is no longer an urban issue. We are seeing rental price hikes from Carlow to Sligo and everywhere in-between. Students need protection, and every student deserves an affordable place to call home and to study' (USI, 2019: 3).

The student housing crisis has been worsening each year and is likely to continue to worsen. Yet this might seem surprising, given that in Dublin city centre new student accommodation blocks are one of the main new forms of residential accommodation being built. Six thousand purpose-built student accommodation units have been built, mainly by private real estate investor developers, in the past three years, with another 14,000 planned by 2024. The problem is that they are expensive and out of reach of most students. In Dublin, only 20% of the new units are rented to students from Ireland. With student numbers due to increase by 27% by 2030, with a large increase in the numbers of international students attending Irish universities, these units they are being used as a 'cash cow' for Irish third-level (higher and further) educational institutions (international students pay much higher fees and are seen as key strategy of overcoming government underfunding of third-level education). The new student units being built will be insufficient, and continue to set ever higher market rents, and therefore will not address the domestic demand for student accommodation. Most Irish students will be stuck seeking accommodation in the crisis-ridden private rental sector or forced into long commutes. This is also affecting postgraduate and PhD research students who are also providing essential tutoring and other work at the third level. Postgraduate students have been reported to be sleeping in their cars during work placements. PhD students have explained that they struggle to find accommodation in Dublin as the PhD stipend is insufficient and does not cover living costs. This pushes students into poverty and some even cut back on food to save on costs. Others decide that they simply cannot afford to keep studying, and feel 'forced out' as they can no longer consider a future in Ireland.

Downsides of the home-ownership 'dream': the mortgage arrears crisis

The problem facing Generation Rent is that, in the absence of public rental and affordable housing for all, the only path to a secure home is home ownership, which requires taking on a huge level of debt, because of the high cost of housing in the private market.

Most renters view purchasing a home as the only way to achieve long-term security – their own 'forever' home. Because of the insecurity in the private rental sector, many households feel pressured and forced into home ownership. They see no alternative but to push for a mortgage, to enable them to purchase a secure, high-quality home. But this adds to the demand for houses, which increases prices, and in turn leads to further pressure on the Central Bank of Ireland to relax its lending rules, enabling banks to lend greater amounts. Quickly we return to the scenario of a credit-fuelled housing bubble, with the potential for a similarly disastrous outcome to that of the 2008 global financial crash that saw a mortgage arrears crisis.

That crisis, which still leaves a legacy a decade later, has caused huge stress and trauma to those in arrears, but also to tenants (Generation Renters) who face increasing rents or evictions when buy-to-let properties in mortgage arrears go into receivership or are repossessed. Indeed, there are many lessons to be learned for our housing systems and housing policy from this particular aspect of the housing crisis. Ireland now has one of the highest ratios of mortgage arrears (also referred to as 'non-performing loans', or NPLs), in the EU.

There was a dramatic increase from 2009 onwards in the proportion of households and buy-to-let landlords falling into arrears on their mortgage. With easy borrowing, many had purchased homes at inflated prices at the height of the housing boom. Due to unemployment, cuts to wages and hours of work, illness, new childcare costs or other challenges, families and individuals were unable to repay mortgages. As Figure 2.6 shows, the total private residential mortgage accounts for principal dwelling homes (PDHs) affected by arrears of over 90 days increased from 3.3% in 2009 to 7.2% in 2011, and reached a high point of 12.9% in 2013 (Central Bank of Ireland, 2019a). At the end of March 2019, 62,834 PDH accounts were in arrears, equating to 8.6% of all PDH mortgage accounts (almost one in ten mortgage accounts). Six per cent of PDH accounts (43,643) were in arrears of more than 90 days, double the rate of PDH mortgage arrears in 2009. Over the period 2009–18, almost one in six (15%, or 111,504) of all PDH mortgage accounts got into some level of difficulty and were restructured (for example, via arrears capitalisation, reduced payment or interest only).

It is also clear from Figure 2.6 that the proportion of those in long-term arrears (over 720 days) has grown substantially. In December 2018, there were 28,000 households in such long-term arrears.

The community development non-governmental organisation, Community Action Network (CAN), in partnership with the School

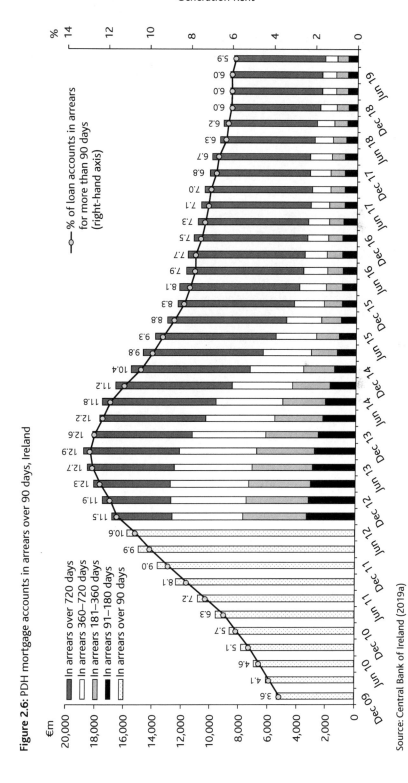

Figure 2.6: PDH mortgage accounts in arrears over 90 days, Ireland

Source: Central Bank of Ireland (2019a)

of Law at the National University of Ireland Galway, undertook a series of surveys, interviews and public meetings with those in mortgage arrears (CAN, 2018). They found that thousands of people continue to face multiple challenges and obstacles as they interact with banks and private equity funds, as well as government programmes and a legal system that are meant to protect their rights, but which, for the most part, are failing them.

Furthermore, the rate of PDH repossessions in 2017 was double the level in 2012 (increasing from 602 in 2012 to 1,417). The rate of repossessions increased from 2014 onwards, reaching a high point of 1,694 repossessions in 2016 (Central Bank of Ireland, 2019a). As Table 2.4 shows, a total of 8,000 homes were repossessed over the seven-year period from 2012 to Q1 2019.

The European Central Bank is putting pressure on the Irish 'pillar' banks to dispose of these NPLs to other entities such as vulture funds. 'Non-bank entities' such as global investment companies and vulture funds are buying up distressed mortgages in increasing numbers. Their intention is to maximise asset value return and there is concern about the level of pressure they will put on already distressed home owners in arrears.

In contrast to the trend of declining PDH mortgage arrears, arrears on residential mortgage accounts for buy-to-let properties remains very high, with almost one in five (19,671, or 18%) in arrears in 2019 (Central Bank of Ireland, 2019a). At least 14,000 of these homes in long-term arrears are at serious risk of repossession. Tenants in buy-to-let properties in arrears are in a vulnerable position, at the mercy of rent receivers and with little legal right to protection from eviction or rent increases.

Table 2.4: Repossessions of PDH homes in Ireland, 2012–19

Year	Repossession by lender
2012	602
2013	766
2014	1,311
2015	1,195
2016	1,694
2017	1,417
2018	895
2019 Q1	127
Total	8,007

Source: Central Bank of Ireland, *Residential Mortgage Arrears & Repossessions Statistics* (various years)

The mortgage arrears crisis stemming from the 2000s is still clearly far from resolved. The human cost of stress and anxiety is also ignored and downplayed by government and policy makers. Households in arrears are in a difficult situation, facing potential homelessness if they lose their home. This legacy crisis has also left a cultural mark in Ireland, with a wariness on the part of younger generations (and their parents) of the heavily indebted home-ownership model and the asset-based welfare approach of buy-to-let property as a pension or investment for the future. The mortgage arrears crisis revealed the other, less trumpeted, side of the home-ownership 'dream' – the nightmare of the unpaid mortgage and arrears. The etymology of the word 'mortgage' lies in the Old French for 'death pledge', an apt description of the situation many Irish households in mortgage arrears feel they are in. Fear, worry and stress over unpaid mortgages has dominated many people's lives over the past decade in Ireland and led to a sense of despair and hopelessness among many householders. Some in arrears have died by suicide. It highlights that the current heavily indebted home-ownership model is not a viable, sensible or desired option for increasing groups of people.

Research by the Irish Housing Agency (Housing Agency, 2018) shows that a staggering 25% of all mortgaged home owners in Ireland experience 'some difficulty' in affording their mortgage, while half of mortgaged home owners in Dublin experience 'some difficulty' in paying their mortgage. This also raises major questions about the viability of the asset-based welfare approach of housing as an investment for future pension and nursing home care.

Home ownership, therefore, is not an 'ideal' form of housing tenure, as it can lead to household over-indebtedness and unaffordability, as the housing crash and mortgage arrears crisis in Ireland have shown. The current dominant way of achieving home ownership is through a financialised, heavily indebted, mortgaged-based system. This is in stark contrast to the socialised form of affordable home ownership that Ireland provided its citizens up to the 1990s. The underlying problem today is one of a lack of supply of affordable housing. Increased access to credit without an affordable supply will lead to increased house prices and a credit–house price bubble like 2008.

3

Homelessness: the most extreme inequality

There is no inequality greater than homelessness and persistent housing insecurity. The United Nations (UN, 2017: 5) describes homelessness as:

> ... an egregious violation of human rights, threatening the health and life of the most marginalized.... Homelessness is the unacceptable result of States failing to implement the right to adequate housing. It requires urgent and immediate human rights responses by the international community and by all States.

Imagine the entire population of Irish towns such as Wicklow, Tramore or Ballina being uprooted overnight, along with their children, forced into homelessness. A national outrage and emergency action by government would surely swiftly follow. Yet homeless figures from November 2019 show that a population equivalent to one of these towns – 10,514 people, including 1,733 families and 3,826 children – are homeless and living in emergency hostels, hotels or Family Hubs, a type of emergency accommodation described in more detail later in the chapter. The number of homeless children has risen by a shocking 440% since 2014 (Department of Housing, Planning and Local Government, 2019b).

Homelessness is a deeply traumatic event, especially for children, leaving emotional scars that may last a lifetime. At least 12,000 children have experienced the trauma of homelessness at some point in past five years in Ireland. Children are affected emotionally and developmentally from spending many months, and in even years, in emergency accommodation. They have been damaged, emotionally and developmentally, in a form of structural violence resulting from the housing crisis and government policy failure. The psychological stress and poor living conditions associated with homelessness has significant negative health effects, especially in mental health (Hearne and Murphy, 2017).

Homelessness has increased exponentially since 2013, when Ireland entered a period of economic recovery. The number of homeless families and children in emergency accommodation increased by a staggering 344% between 2014 and 2019 (Department of Housing, Planning and Local Government, 2019b).

Figure 3.1 shows the scale in the increase of family homelessness from 2014 to 2019. This is a new phenomenon for Ireland. In 2013, in the Dublin region, between ten and 20 families per month presented as newly homeless. By 2014, this increased to an average of 32 families per month and by 2015 to 62 new families per month. By 2018, on average, between 80 and 120 families presented as homeless every month in Dublin (Focus Ireland, 2019).

This rise results from the challenges faced by vulnerable families and individuals on low incomes from unprecedented levels of rents, lack of tenant protections, low pay or unemployment, austerity cuts to social welfare supports, and a lack of social housing.

It is the more vulnerable sections of society that experience the highest levels of homelessness. Those affected in particular include people on low incomes, disadvantaged women and children in lone-parent families, migrants, Travellers, people with disabilities, young people leaving care, and single men. A profile of homeless families in September 2016 showed that these families were mainly young, with 67% under the age of 36. A majority (60%) were born in Ireland and 40% were migrants, of which 20% were from the European Union (EU) and 20% non-EU (Hearne and Murphy, 2017).

The extent to which families headed by lone parents, and in particular by lone mothers, have been affected by homelessness is shocking. Nationally, 60% of homeless families are headed by lone mothers, yet female-headed, lone-parent families represent 20% or one in five of all families with children in Ireland. In Dublin similarly, the majority of homeless families were headed by lone parents (65%), of which 86% were women. Couples with children comprised 30% of all homeless families (Hearne and Murphy, 2017).

Figure 3.2 shows the changing profile of homelessness in the growth in the numbers of children becoming homeless. In 2011, 17% of the homeless population comprised children (aged 0–19). In 2016, however, children made up 29% of homeless people.

Migrants, especially those from non-EU backgrounds, are at greater risk of homelessness, poor housing quality and discrimination within the housing system. They make up 13% of the normally resident Irish population, but account for around 25% of homeless people.

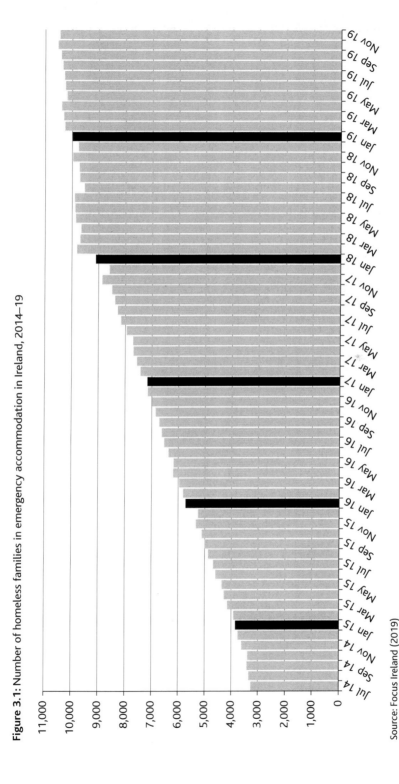

Figure 3.1: Number of homeless families in emergency accommodation in Ireland, 2014–19

Source: Focus Ireland (2019)

Figure 3.2: The changing profile of homeless in Ireland: the increase in child homelessness (children with their families in emergency accommodation), 2014–19

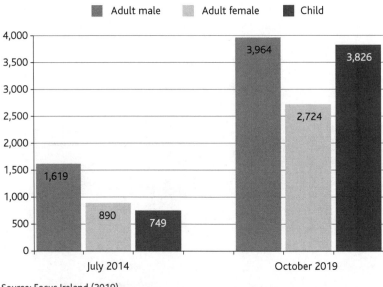

Source: Focus Ireland (2019)

Housing crisis is principal cause of homelessness

The main reason for family homelessness in Dublin over the period of 2017–18 has been issues in the private rental sector. A majority (60%) of new families presenting as homeless state the private rental sector as the primary reason for becoming homeless. The second reason stated is family circumstances (including family breakdown, overcrowding and so on) (Focus Ireland, 2019). These data reflect only the immediate cause of entering the homeless system; research by Focus Ireland (2018) has shown that many families who had their last stable home in the private rented sector 'double up' with other family members or friends, sometimes for several months, before presenting as officially homeless. According to the Focus Ireland research, around half of the families identified as homeless due to 'family breakdown' in the Dublin Regional Homeless Executive data (DRHE, 2018) were evicted from private rental tenancies, and for a portion of them family circumstances only describes the ultimate breakdown of their temporary doubling-up arrangement. Weak tenant protections, short leases and high eviction rates in the private rented sector, along with rising rents and associated unaffordability and the termination of leases by landlords (as landlords seek to sell their property or seek higher-paying tenants), are the main issues causing homelessness.

What is distinct about this period of homelessness is the range of individuals and families presenting as homeless. Some are employed and living in emergency accommodation, or are sleeping in their cars and going to work. Statistics and figures do not adequately capture the personal, real-life impact of the crisis on individuals, families and children. It is therefore very important to listen to the voices of those directly affected. Their stories show the devastating impacts of being homeless. We should remember when hearing these stories of homeless workers, families, carers and young people that they are not unique. There are tens of thousands of families and children facing homelessness or living in housing insecurity and exclusion in Ireland, as outlined in Chapter 4.

The Irish government (Department of Housing, Planning and Local Government, 2016b: 18) accepts that homelessness 'is a complex phenomenon' and outlines its causes as follows:

> ... usually the result of a number of inter-related issues, including mental health issues, addictions, relationship breakdown, family issues, domestic violence, financial loss, economic insecurity, rent arrears, tenancy issues, anti-social behaviour, crime, prisoner release and the vulnerability of migrants, among other factors. Consequently, a successful whole-of Government response is required in relation to such issues, if the current homelessness issue is to be tackled effectively.

However, these factors describe a range of within-person and family issues, and make little reference to the systemic and structural factors that result in people becoming homeless. Taking the view that people only 'fall into homelessness' due to personal behaviour, such as addiction and relationship breakdown, takes responsibility away from policy makers to have to change the structural causes of homelessness. Structural causes that have caused the huge rise in homelessness in Ireland in recent years are the housing crisis, weak tenant protections and lack of social housing, interlinked with economic issues of inequality, low wages, discrimination and poverty.

Furthermore, the decade-long shift in government housing policy away from providing secure, affordable council housing to relying on the private rental sector to provide subsidised social housing has been a key factor in creating the conditions for rising family homelessness in the last six years. Issues of insecurity, unaffordability and substandard accommodation prevalent within the Irish private rental sector have become even more influential on homelessness as a result of the reduction in the direct state provision of social housing and the increased reliance on the private rental sector to provide social housing.

As the Irish Human Rights and Equality Commission (IHREC, 2019: 3) explains:

> The Commission believes that the provision of social housing is central to the solution to the homelessness crisis. The Commission is disappointed by the Government's attempt to take the emphasis off the human face of the homelessness crisis, and instead to recast the crisis as the by-product of market dynamics, or the price our society pays for progress. The Commission believes that the rise in homelessness has been significantly exacerbated by Government policy choices in this regard. The decision to withdraw from building social housing and to instead provide rent supplement for private renters has made low income households extremely vulnerable to shocks in the housing market. The impact of homelessness on families and children is a particular concern.

Structural causes of homelessness

Another structural cause of homelessness is the social housing benefit system in Ireland. As pointed out in Chapter 2, the growing gap between rents being charged by landlords and housing benefit limits (for Rent Allowance and Housing Assistance Payment) has meant that thousands of families are facing homelessness as a result of the inadequacy of state housing support to cover rising rents. This can lead to evictions if tenants are unable to pay existing or new rents. Moreover, families and individuals on low incomes who have been evicted, as well as those seeking housing to escape from overcrowded situations or domestic violence or family breakdown, are often unable to obtain alternative private rental accommodation because of housing shortages and high rents. Even with the state-supported Housing Assistance Payment (HAP), which is the government's main form of social housing support, vulnerable families and individuals struggle to get private rental accommodation because they are outbid by higher-income tenants or suffer discrimination as a result of landlords choosing tenants deemed more suitable.

Under HAP, the local authority pays the rent direct to the landlord and the tenant pays the local authority a lower, differential, rent based on their income. There is also a specific Homeless HAP, available in Dublin, whereby in order to find accommodation for a homeless person, or a person at risk of homelessness, the local authority pays the private landlord rent that is up to 50% greater than the HAP limit (20% outside Dublin). But it is the responsibility of the tenant to source their accommodation in the private rental sector. This means they are competing with others to get accommodation from landlords and estate agents.

Carers and those with a disability face particular challenges in relation to housing, homelessness and housing exclusion. The experience of Tracy and her family, outlined in Box 3.1, shows the extra challenges and suffering faced in trying to find suitable and affordable accommodation in the midst of an unprecedented housing crisis. Tracy's situation also highlights another downside to HAP – the extreme difficultly for families with special needs to find suitable housing in the private rental sector.

Box 3.1: Housing experience of a family with a child with disabilities

Tracy and her two boys, Declan aged 9 and Brendan aged 13 (who is severely disabled), faced the threat of becoming homeless

Tracy's older son, Brendan, who has just turned 13, was born with congenital cytomegalovirus, which means he can't walk or talk, and has severe epilepsy, cerebral palsy and scoliosis. He is not expected to live longer than 18. Tracy has a Master's degree and worked as a therapist and with non-governmental organisations before she had to leave her career behind to become Brendan's full-time carer when he was three years old. She explains that currently they live in a private rented house in Kildare that has major problems.

"The house is so cold and so draughty, the boiler leaks kerosene, there is no light coming into the kitchen, the ceiling is not insulated. The environmental health officer said it is in violation of various standards. It is half under construction and there are rolls of fibre glass insulation in the attic which is open and the wind sweeps down through to the rest of the house and I am worried about it affecting Declan [her other son who is nine years old] and Brendan's lungs. There is mould growing on the ceiling in the bathroom. I have no lease and the landlord is unregistered". It is, she says, "unsafe unsuitable, unfit and its putting Brendan's health at risk, and mine as I try to care for him in a place that's not suitable and not modified and can't be modified for Brendan's needs".

There is a shower chair sitting unbalanced in a bathtub – no safety rails – and she is unable to use a hoist as the doorway is too narrow and the hoist legs cannot go under the tub. Tracy describes it as "dangerous, inhumane and risking Brendan's life as well as my health and safety as his carer as I am forced to carry Brendan in my arms across a wet floor, through doorways, from one room to the other".

She has been trying to find somewhere else in Kildare to rent, and that would take the Housing Assistance Payment. Tracy is eligible for the HAP scheme. However, she has found it impossible to find landlords that will take the family. Landlords, she feels, are discriminating against her: "The landlords were saying they don't think the house would suit my son's needs – I heard that a number of times."

Tracy is terrified of becoming homeless. She says: "Brendan can't go into emergency accommodation – a hotel or B&B. He needs to have his medical bed as it helps with pressure sores and his scoliosis – he needs his oxygen near his bed and this can't happen in a hotel or B&B."

Modification grants are only available for local authority housing or for a family that owns their own home. Renting someone else's home does not allow the family to avail of any home modification grants, which means the family cannot modify the home to safely and properly care for the disabled family member. As Tracy explains: "If a family with a disabled child is left to the private rental market, they are left at a tremendous risk of homelessness. They could be given notice to vacate after a 12-month lease and be back at the near impossible task of trying to find a suitable rental house again. If they are not made homeless, they are more than likely forced to settle renting an unsuitable, unsafe house."

A social house, she says, would be more appropriate as it can be modified to suit Brendan's complex healthcare needs. "We need a long-term house that we can make a home secure for our future and modify for Brendan's care." She wants a permanent home as she doesn't want to ever have to leave the home where Brendan will spend his last years with her and his brother.

"I want to stay there, in that home – in our home – where he was for his remaining time, which I hope and pray is a good number of years still to come. I don't want to ever have to leave behind the home where all those final memories will have been created."

She explains also that Declan needs to be settled: "Every day he mentions the word homeless.... That's not an exaggeration. He asks, 'When we become homeless what will happen? I don't want my friends to know.' Every day there is at least one sentence involving 'homeless'. This is not fair and not right so I'm trying to do everything I can to rectify it."

The crisis hits the vulnerable the hardest – women and children

There is an important gender inequality dimension to the Irish housing crisis – at its most acute, the majority of homeless families are headed by lone mothers. The lack of housing options means that victims of domestic violence (predominantly women and children) are even more vulnerable; alternative housing options are not available to them, and women have few alternatives but to stay in refuges for longer than otherwise would be the case if there was sufficient affordable and social housing available. This has the knock-on effect that thousands of women looking for emergency accommodation are turned away because refuges are constantly full (Safe Ireland, 2016).

Ireland's rate of female homelessness is double that of other EU states. In the Dublin region, for example, women comprise 47% of the total adult homeless population. This compares with a figure of between 20% and 33% homeless women across Europe (Mayock and Bretherton, 2017).

The high level of representation of lone parents within homeless families results from rising poverty among lone parents who suffered the harshest cuts during the austerity period and from the 'welfare to work' policies implemented between 2008 and 2015. The level of deprivation in lone-parent households was 42% in 2018, almost three times the general household rate of 15%. The consistent poverty level in female-headed, lone-parent households increased from 13% in 2010 to 26% in 2015, compared with the general increase in poverty in Ireland from 6.3% to 8.7% in the same period (Hearne and Murphy, 2018).

Travellers also experience high levels of discrimination in accessing housing in Ireland, and are almost ten times as likely to report discrimination as the White Irish population.

In 2017, I undertook research with homeless families in emergency accommodation (Family Hubs) in Dublin as part of a participative action research project (Hearne and Murphy, 2017). The homeless families were mainly headed by lone mothers, who also identified the particularly gendered experience of discrimination within homelessness and the housing crisis. The families suffered multiple aspects of stigmatisation, as they were discriminated by landlords within the private rental sector for being single mothers, HAP recipients and being homeless. When they contacted landlords advertising rental properties, the landlords asked if they were single, if they were in relationships, and their age. As one mother explained:

> 'I have been in the Family Hub for six months and I have had no replies to emails from landlords. I am still looking for accommodation through HAP. The agencies and landlords keep asking for work references and past landlord references. But we don't have that. They say they do not take children and they do not allow children in the house. When I tell them that I am a single mom – they say the viewing list is full, but there is a waiting list and they will put my name on that. But I never get back a reply. They are saying they are not taking me because I am a single mom because they think I can't pay.' (Hearne and Murphy, 2017: 22)

The homeless families explained that even with the higher rental subsidies provided in the Homeless HAP, they still found it extremely difficult to compete for the limited (and increasingly expensive) private rental accommodation available on the private market (Hearne and Murphy, 2018). They also described the impact of discrimination they experienced from landlords. Families felt depressed and rejected with consequent negative impacts on self-esteem. As one mother explained:

> 'The very few replies from my emails I do receive are asking for current work reference and landlord references. The trouble is I do not have a landlord reference as I ran into rent arrears in my last home. I do not have a current work reference either, as I am not working. I feel like I am at a loss trying to find a home for my kids and I simply do not have what they are looking for.'(Hearne and Murphy, 2018: 21)

In January 2016, housing assistance was introduced as a new category in legislation under the Equal Status Acts 2000–2018, to protect against discrimination in the provision of accommodation. The provision of private rented accommodation is considered a service under the Equal Status Acts 2000–2018, which prohibits discrimination, directly or indirectly, on a number of grounds including gender, family status, sexual orientation, race, membership of the Traveller community, disability and being in receipt of HAP. This means that it is illegal for landlords to discriminate against people in receipt of HAP, Rent Supplement or other social welfare payments in relation to the provision of accommodation. Nor can landlords, letting agencies or property advertisers discriminate in advertising on the grounds of housing assistance. Some examples of discrimination include using terms such as 'Rent Supplement not accepted' and 'professionals only' in property ads; refusing to allow a person to view a property or let to them because they are in receipt of Rent Supplement, HAP or other social welfare payments; and ending a tenancy or not renewing an agreement because tenants are in receipt of Rent Supplement. The Irish Human Rights and Equality Commission (IHREC, 2019) has stated that the introduction of the housing assistance ground is an important first step towards the recognition of a socioeconomic ground in equality legislation. Tenants suffering discrimination have taken successful cases to the Workplace Relations Commission (WRC) whereby their complaints have been upheld and landlords have been fined (the maximum fine is €15,000) for breaching the Equal Status Acts 2000–2018. One landlord was fined €12,000 for refusing to accept a tenant in receipt of HAP. However, there are challenges for tenants in bringing cases forward, such as the lack of awareness of pathways and processes to access justice, for example through the WRC. It can also be difficult in some circumstances to demonstrate that discrimination has occurred. But importantly, those suffering discrimination often do not have the capacity, energy or resources to pursue cases. The enforcement of Irish discrimination law relies heavily on the individual complaints-led model. This means that discrimination will simply go unchallenged unless an individual takes action.

As the IHREC (2019: 5) explains, 'For individuals who may be at risk of homelessness, and are focused on finding a place to live, it is unreasonable to expect that they can refocus their energies on pursuing a complaint.' Over two years after its introduction, the housing assistance ground remains one of the most common reasons for people to contact the IHREC Your Rights information service, and it is apparent that there is 'systemic discrimination' against people in receipt of housing social welfare payments.

Emergency accommodation: detrimental impacts on family and child wellbeing

The government's landmark housing plan *Rebuilding Ireland* (Department of Housing, Planning and Local Government, 2016b), launched in July 2016, acknowledged that emergency accommodation provided for homeless families is inappropriate 'other than a short period of time' and that 'it is widely acknowledged that any medium to long-term period living in a hotel seriously impacts on normal family life and is particularly detrimental to children' (Department of Housing, Planning and Local Government, 2016b: 35). The government committed 'to ensure that by mid-2017 hotels are only used in limited circumstances for emergency accommodation for families' (Department of Housing, Planning and Local Government, 2016b: 34) and outlined various initiatives to meet this housing need.

In May 2016, 622 homeless families in Dublin were accommodated in hotels and bed and breakfast (B&B) accommodation, and families with children who present as homeless and are still being provided with emergency, temporary accommodation in hotels and B&Bs. In February 2019, 740 families with 1,724 children were being accommodated in hotels in the Dublin region (DRHE, 2018). This represents a 20% increase in the number of families in hotels since the commitment to end the use of hotels in *Rebuilding Ireland* over three years ago.

Meanwhile, the amount of time families are spending in emergency accommodation has increased in recent years, with the consequence that parents and children are exposed to the detrimental impacts of living precariously for longer periods. Figure 3.3 shows the amount of time families spend in emergency accommodation before exiting homelessness over different months between 2017 and 2019. It

Figure 3.3: Duration in emergency accommodation for families in Dublin, 2017–19

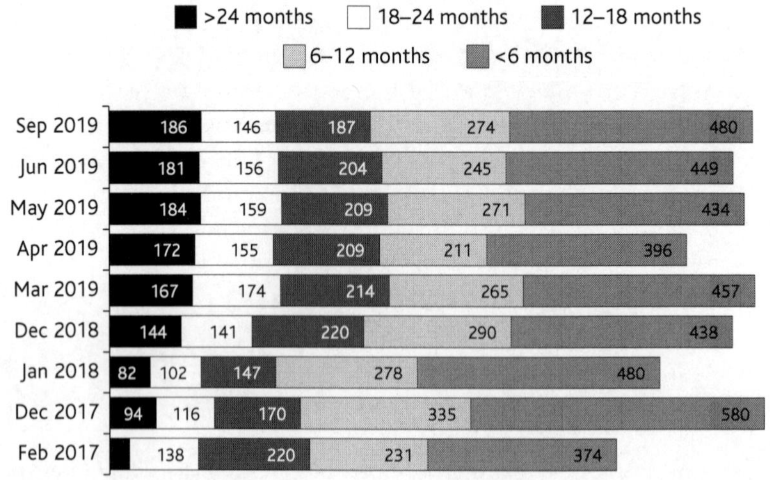

Source: Focus Ireland (2019)

reveals that the number of families spending more than two years in emergency accommodation doubled between February 2017 and May 2019. Furthermore, two thirds of the families (823 families) in emergency accommodation in May 2019 had been there for longer than six months.

Moreover, the practice of self-accommodation, whereby families find their own emergency accommodation in a hotel or B&B that is then paid for by their local authority, continues to operate in certain circumstances, despite an acknowledgement by the Department of Housing, Planning and Local Government (2018: 3) that 'self accommodation is something we need to ... reduce and bring to a close'. Self-accommodation is still necessary because of the lack of emergency accommodation, with families being told to contact hotels and B&Bs themselves to ask about availability. Increasingly, there are no hotel rooms available or hotels refuse to take the local authority payment. Self-accommodating families are sometimes forced to leave hotels at peak tourist times such as Christmas or Easter, or, in Dublin, when large events are held, and must try to source alternative emergency accommodation or make other arrangements such as sleeping in cars or couchsurfing. Between 2016 and 2018, there were periodic reports of families having to sleep rough or seek shelter in Garda (police) stations.

In a statement to Seanad Éireann (the upper house of the Irish parliament) on 30 January 2019, the Minister for Housing, Planning and Local Government (Minister for Housing) accepted that emergency accommodation has a detrimental impact on people's lives:

> 'The most distressing aspect of the challenge we face is the damage being done to people living in emergency accommodation. Damage is being done to society and individuals and families because they have to spend time in emergency accommodation. There are too many living in emergency accommodation. It is absolutely unacceptable that people still have to go to hotels for emergency accommodation.'

Research and regular media reports have also highlighted the damaging impact of homelessness on family life and functioning, on children's education, and on parents' and children's physical, social and emotional wellbeing.

A report from Temple Street Children's University Hospital (2019: 1) highlighted that 842 children who attended the hospital's Emergency

Department in 2018 were discharged with no fixed address. This was an increase of 29% on the 2017 figure. According to the report, although the children's presentations are varied and complex, the majority of them 'stem from the fact that these children are living in completely unsuitable, cramped and temporary accommodation'.

A report by the Faculties of Public Health Medicine and Paediatrics, Royal College of Physicians of Ireland (2019) provides evidence for the impact on children's health of living in inadequate housing, and describes the effects of instability caused by frequent moves or prolonged temporary housing on children's emotional, social and mental health. The report shows that homelessness and inadequate housing have the following effects:

• higher risk of preterm pregnancy and low birthweight;
• higher rates of asthma, respiratory illness and infectious diseases;
• poor nutrition and obesity;
• less access to developmental opportunities, play and recreation and social activities;
• poorer emotional and mental health and increased behavioural difficulties;
• less access to preventive healthcare and lower rate of childhood immunisation;
• poorer educational opportunities;
• difficulties in the relationship between parents and their children.

The report shows that the impact of negative experiences in childhood on a person's health and wellbeing is immense. This impact lasts well beyond childhood and can be seen in early and later adult life. Early childhood and early adolescence are particularly vulnerable times. Poor housing conditions contribute to these negative experiences, increasing the risk of severe physical and mental ill health and disability during childhood and early adulthood by up to 25%.

Children thrive in stable and nurturing relationships where they have a routine and know what to expect. Homeless children are more likely to have higher rates of developmental, emotional and behavioural problems than housed children, with as many as 38% of homeless children having disorders of clinical significance. Behavioural problems are often a reflection of the stresses that children and their parents are going through. A study of children aged 4–8 years living in family emergency accommodation found they were three times more likely to experience emotional disturbance than children of similar age from low-income households (Faculties of Public Health

Medicine and Paediatrics, Royal College of Physicians of Ireland, 2019).

The increase in homelessness in recent years has also seen a corresponding increase in expenditure on the provision of homelessness services. In 2017, €116 million was provided by the Department of Housing for homelessness services, an increase of 18% on the 2016 budget allocation. In 2018, €141 million was spent on homelessness services in Dublin. Of this, €118.3 million was spent on temporary emergency homeless accommodation (including short- and long-term hostels, hotels and Family Hub accommodation for homeless families), representing 83% of the entire budget. Private hotel operators were paid €49.3 million, and €13.8 million was spent on other private emergency accommodation, meaning hostels and Family Hubs operated by private companies. Approximately €50 million was paid to homelessness charities such as Focus Ireland, Peter McVerry Trust, DePaul, the Salvation Army and others operating hostels and Family Hubs in Dublin. Most of these non-governmental services provide essential support for homeless individuals and families, without which the crisis would be significantly worse. Of the entire budget, just €4.7 million (3.3%) was spent on homeless prevention and supports to keep people in their homes, including just €928,000 on contact and outreach services for the Housing First programme (Department of Housing, Planning and Local Government, 2019a).

In 2017, national broadcaster RTÉ aired a radio programme describing the reality of living in hotel emergency accommodation from a child's perspective (RTÉ Radio, 2018). Amanda, an 18-year-old living with her mother, spoke about how the experience had affected her. Amanda had been living in emergency accommodation (a hotel) for two years after her family became homeless. Her mother, who gave up work when her children were born, was unable to keep up the mortgage repayments when her marriage broke down and she was unable to find a job because her skills were considered out of date. Amanda explained how she has been bullied, struggled with her mental health, and forced to repeat fifth year in school as a result of being homeless: "I feel like I've been [robbed] of most of my life ... these are the years that I'm supposed to be focusing on getting a decent education, making friends, and going out and living my life."

She described the hotel where she had been living for two years as "rotten" and "mouldy": "it's degrading for everyone having to wake up and look at the dirt around you, the mould in between walls and behind curtains and everything else. It's horrible." Although she dreamed of becoming a councillor and teacher – inspired by her current situation to help others overcome their challenges – Amanda worries that being homeless would prevent her from going to college. She believed she would struggle to study for her Leaving Certificate while living in a hotel, particularly because of the impact on her mental health:

> 'It's a struggle every day, getting up and even just taking the blankets off yourself in the morning. It's horrible…. People need to know that it is deadly to live like this. You feel like you have no life left, living in here with no help, no sense of security. You just think, "What's the point?" You really do.'

The tragic experience of lone parent Danielle Carroll, who died by suicide in emergency accommodation, further demonstrates the devastating impact of the housing and homelessness crisis on children and families. Danielle was 27 when she died by suicide in the emergency accommodation she was sharing with her two sons. Danielle struggled with the pressure of securing a home for her family after she had to leave her rental property because the landlord put it up for sale. She was left devastated after being told just days before her death that the offer of a council house near her parents' home and her son's school had been withdrawn. Danielle had viewed the house on offer in Tallaght, south Dublin, and was overjoyed at the prospect of moving there with her family. But less than two weeks before she died, she was informed by South Dublin County Council that the property was being withdrawn. In a hand-delivered letter to the council she wrote the following:

> I am understandably devastated at this this news as I was ready to start a new chapter in my life. I haven't broken the news to my children yet and I don't want to break their hearts any more….
>
> I was so happy and finding a place I could call my own home, to be finally to be able to walk my kids to school, to walk over to my family when I felt I needed support. For it to be taken away from me yet again, although I appreciate the offer in Lucan it would disturb everything more than it already is and I would have to change my childs [sic] school where he is very settled and happy. With my mental health issues I would like to be local to my family…. I don't want to move somewhere that me and my kids would be

invisible for the rest of our lives. I would really appreciate
if you would take all of this into consideration.

This heart-breaking story shows the devastating human impacts of
homelessness, as well as highlighting the wider lack of social housing
and the centrality of social housing in providing a home for those on
low incomes and in vulnerable situations.

Danielle's death sparked a huge outcry and last year her family spoke
about it and read out Danielle's letter at the inaugural Danielle Carroll
Summer School, which brings together campaigning groups to discuss
housing and homelessness. Danielle's sister described the impact of the
death on their family:

> 'There are people dying yearly, weekly since our Danielle
> and what's being done? I feel it's getting worse. We are
> completely empty, trying to move on for our children and
> hers. It's a struggle ... but almost two years on Danielle's
> death has demolished us all. Her little boys miss their
> beautiful mammy. She was such a devoted mammy. Her
> sons were her life. None of us will ever be the same. We
> miss her and we hope she's at peace.'

Erica is a lone parent and homeless campaigner who spent almost two
years in emergency accommodation with her daughter. She spoke to
me about the shame and stigma of being homeless, particularly if you
speak out publicly about your circumstances, and about the impact
on children:

> 'Children coming to emergency accommodation are
> frightened ... they are going to school and pretend to be
> ok. Until my little girl had a breakdown at school we didn't
> let the school know we were homeless. Children don't
> want to let the school know – because they are afraid of
> the stigma that would be attached to them.'

Erica believes the stigma around homelessness is getting worse:

> 'I don't understand why members of the public are targeting
> homeless people and persecuting them for something that
> they have no control over. I find that really upsetting –
> people should feel safe and secure and be able to come
> out and say, "I am homeless and this is my story." They

shouldn't feel afraid of being attacked by media or members of the public – because it's not their fault – they are being persecuted for something they have no control over.'

She says that the impact on children is the hardest to watch:

'Children have no choice. As adults we make the decisions for our children and when you are homeless you genuinely don't have much choice – you have no power – and you lose that control. So imagine how it feels for a child – as an adult it irritates you and you get angry about it – but a child feels they can't express themselves because they don't have any control.'

Erica organised a protest against homelessness to coincide with the 100-year commemoration in 2016 of the Easter Rising (to establish an independent Irish Republic) and associated Proclamation. She explained that she felt she had to take to the streets and organise the protest in order to:

'... stare at power in the eye and hold it to account for the experiences of poverty that are facing my child daily. Her playground is a hotel corridor: I rarely get to provide her with a home cooked meal. As I tuck her in at night, I can't even afford her the dignity of leaving the room. This isn't the Republic that people died for and I feel duty bound to demand that my daughter be cherished equally in the eyes of this State. I am doing this to highlight that our children matter and that a home is the minimum we should be affording our children on this anniversary of an event associated with such strong themes of equality and what it truly means to live in a Republic.'

Family Hubs: institutionalising women and children

Given the failure of government to build new social housing, low levels of private sector supply and increasing levels of homelessness, government policy shifted rapidly in early 2017 to approve the creation of a new type of supported, temporary, emergency accommodation for rising numbers of homeless families. These new Family Hubs are purpose-built or specifically adapted premises to house homeless families and children. Hubs are being provided in a variety of refurbished buildings, including former religious institutions such as Magdalene Laundries (or asylums, usually run by Roman Catholic orders), convents, warehouses, retail units and hotels. Family Hubs have been promoted and presented by policy makers and government as a better alternative to hotels and B&Bs, and are therefore legitimated in the public discourse as a positive improvement for homeless families. Despite the absence of a research or evidence base to justify their development, Family Hubs expanded rapidly across Dublin and in other parts of the country through 2018 and 2019. By early 2019, there were 26 Family Hubs in operation across Ireland (22 in Dublin, and one each in Cork, Limerick, Kildare and Louth) providing accommodation for 600 families. There were 98 families in one hub, 50 in another, with numbers ranging from 12 to 40 families in others.

The public image of the Family Hub as a positive one has been actively reinforced through energetic public relations activities, including launches, press releases and promotional videos that seek to reassure that Family Hubs are a positive policy development. However, participative research that I undertook with my colleague, Mary Murphy, with homeless families in a Family Hub in Dublin found that these hubs are detrimental to family wellbeing (Hearne and Murphy, 2017).

The project involved meeting with the families weekly over a period of ten weeks, and undertaking trust-building exercises, facilitating discussions of their issues, providing educational materials and information on key housing policies and the right to housing, and initiating a process of 'co-construction' of families' experiences of homelessness and housing policy research.

We found that certain rules and conditions operating within the Family Hub meant practical restrictions on the ability to live a normal family life. For example, living behaviour was monitored with strict curfews, visitors were not allowed, overnight leave rules only allowed a maximum three days per month permitted absence. There were also restrictions on movement (a ban on being in others' rooms) and parental rules included a ban on holding and/or minding other people's children.

Mothers described the undermining of their role and capacity to parent as a key factor leading to feelings of depression and low self-esteem. In keeping with Mayock and Bretherton's (2017) finding of the infantilisation of female residents in homeless shelters, mothers in the Family Hub in our research reported feeling "demeaned", "spoken down to" and "like a child", as if they were still "in school" or "in prison". They described the consequences for their physical and mental health, including increased use of anti-depressants and other prescription medications:

> 'When I came here first I was much happier. Spending time here takes something away from you. I'm just fed up [visibly upset, crying – pointing to her head] ... now I don't want to talk to people anymore ... I just want to be on my own ... it's the system ... my child asks me when are we going to live in our own house and have our own toys – I say, "I don't know."... you have to keep the children inside ... you cannot bring your friends here ...what is it like that your children remind you to "sign out" when you leave this place in the morning – what kind of life is that? And with all the stress you have to stop yourself from yelling at the children. You have to be in the room with your children so when they go to sleep, you can't watch the TV, you have to go to sleep too. It's not right for a mother and two children – a boy and a girl – in one room here. All the time.'

This finding is in line with the international literature, which shows that emergency homeless accommodation fails to facilitate normal family living. As with Milburn and D'Ercole (1991), we found that monitoring and rigid rules meant living in circumstances that may undermine otherwise effective parenting practices and the capacity to parent autonomously, with related issues of stigma and discrimination and what parents report as humiliating and dehumanising experiences that affect parental stress and mental health. The tensions posed by implementing child protection guidelines in the context of communal living, for example, required a range of restrictions that limited the capacity to parent. This led to mothers questioning their worth as parents – the core element of maternal identity. Family Hubs can be seen, therefore, as a form of 'therapeutic incarceration', as they operate akin to a prison-like regime that destroys personal autonomy. Gerstal and colleagues (1996) used the term therapeutic incarceration to describe the move of voluntary homelessness agencies into service-intensive programmes with unintended consequences for the personal autonomy of homeless residents. Issues of reduced autonomy, hidden conditionality and surveillance are common in analysis of various types of institutional care settings and welfare policy (activation, prisons, elder care as well as homeless services).

The Ombudsman for Children's Office in Ireland undertook its own independent research into Family Hubs and found that children living in such emergency accommodation expressed feelings of sadness, confusion and anger. In its report, *No Place Like Home* (OCO, 2019: 3), it makes the following observations:

> Six months in a Family Hub is one quarter of a two year old's life. It is more than half of a school year for a teenager studying for their Junior or Leaving Certificate.... Children told us about what it is like to share a room with their parents and siblings, what it is like to go to school from a Family Hub, to study and do homework. They told us about what it is like to have to go to bed and turn off all the lights when their younger brother or sister is going to sleep. Space, privacy, noise, not being able to have visitors, feelings of shame and embarrassment, were all issues raised by the children who talked to us. This consultation confirmed something we already know: children are strong, children are resilient, but children are aware. Children see what is going on and they are affected. One child said the hub was 'like a children's jail', another said one of her biggest sources of unhappiness in the hub was noise caused by fighting. She explained that she and her mum tried to make it into a game, trying to guess what the 'screaming' might be about. 'The noise keeps me awake, I feel tired when I go to school. I feel like my eyes feel like they are about to go to sleep.' Another said, 'The rules are very strict. The worst is that you are not allowed to have friends in your room. They just expect you to sit on your own. And not being allowed to be anywhere without your mam, you're not even allowed to sit in the room for 10 minutes by yourself. I know it has safety issues but nothing terrible is going to happen ... if we break the rules we will get kicked out. It's like a prison ... it's just horrible.'

The Irish Human Rights and Equality Commission (2017: 2) expressed concern that 'the use of family hubs has normalised family homelessness, which may lead to families being institutionalised'. It also found that the rules and conditions applying to the use of communal spaces and visitors may affect the autonomy and mental health of parents, noting that 'developmental delays, emotional attachment issues, self-harm and accidental injuries have been reported with regard to children'.

As explained earlier in the chapter, there has been no policy rationale provided by government or policy makers to explain the development of Family Hubs. This is because they are a short-term crisis response used for practical and political reasons. But ultimately they result from housing policy failure to address the rising numbers of homeless families. The hubs provide an immediate solution to the urgent need for shelter for homeless families in crisis and to the requirement to meet statutory child protection obligations, but they also play an important role in legitimating the government response as adequate. Hubs are also being used as a political solution by government to claim it is fulfilling its promises to reduce the use of hotels and B&Bs to house homeless families. Family Hubs also appeal to underlying paternalistic assumptions that homeless families need therapeutic supports and the gendered assumption is that, even with increased housing supply, a minority of families would remain vulnerable to homelessness.

The term Family Hub has been deconstructed effectively by Mayock and Bretherton (2017), who highlight the intentional feminine imagery in the language of the Family Hub. It is evoked as a positive, warm, central place in a home – revolving around the care of the mother. The name itself, therefore, is a gendered construct that attempts not only to destigmatise such centres, but also to hide their reality, to try to undermine and downplay their actual or potentially harmful nature.

Family Hubs need to be understood as a new form of institutionalisation of poor mothers and their children, restricting their ability to live a normal life and producing developmental regression in children. Such institutionalisation follows a long Irish history of gendered forms of social violence inflicted on poor mothers and their children. Family Hubs have been introduced under the cloak of clever and manipulative language, but they are still a form of emergency homeless accommodation. Ireland is creating another generation of poor families, predominantly women and children, who are being forced into institutionalised settings. Family Hubs are another attempt to normalise and legitimise, and achieve societal acceptance of an unethical policy and social crisis of unprecedented levels of family, lone-parent and child homelessness. The solution to homelessness is not emergency accommodation; rather, it is the provision of permanent, affordable homes. The Irish government cannot claim at some future point that it did not know that these hubs are an abuse of human rights of these families and children, as I outlined in my speech to the MyNameIs protest in front of the Dáil Éireann in December 2017:

> 'Think of that child in a Family Hub or other emergency accommodation – who has to get up each morning and go to school – ashamed – unable to bring their friends back to

play, unable to tell their friends where they live – thinking that nobody cares about them – that their country doesn't care – that they aren't worthy of a home. We know that spending time in this emergency accommodation is having a devastating impact on the wellbeing of parents and children. We are robbing the childhood away from a generation of children. And when it comes to the tribunals and enquiries in decades to come as to how this happened, and how was it allowed to happen even when it was known the damage they cause to parents and children? The Taoiseach, Minister for Housing, Department of Housing, all know. Indeed I presented on our findings to the Oireachtas Committee on Housing and they were raised directly with the Taoiseach in the Dáil – you will not be able to say you didn't know.'

4

The normalisation of homelessness

The Irish government has argued that Irish homelessness levels are normal in comparison with other countries. The then Taoiseach, Leo Varadkar, publicly stated that "we are actually a country ... that has a low level of homelessness" (*Irish Independent*, 2017). The data being used to draw this conclusion were drawn from a report by the Organisation for Economic Co-operation and Development (2017) that stated explicitly that the figures set out could not be compared because they were compiled based on different definitions of homelessness. The Taoiseach also stated: "There always have been a certain number of people in emergency accommodation for one reason or another, particularly people who become homeless suddenly who were not on the housing list." Moreover, a former chair of the state Housing Agency wrote: 'Homelessness is a dreadful thing when it happens to someone, but it is a normal thing, it happens' (*The Journal*, 2017: 26).

It is, in fact, very difficult to compare homelessness in Ireland with other countries because it is measured quite differently in each country. Some countries measure the number of people without shelter, others only measure those in specialised emergency accommodation, and yet others have a much broader view and include people who are living with friends and families because they have no alternative. Ireland actually has a narrow definition of homelessness – the number of people staying overnight in emergency accommodation paid for by the Department of Housing, Planning and Local Government on any night in the reference week.

What is clear is that for Ireland, the scale of, and rate of increase in, homelessness is currently greater than anything in recent history.

Focus Ireland, a non-governmental organisation (NGO) providing services for people who are homeless, highlights that homeless organisations have never claimed that Ireland has a particularly higher rate of homelessness than other countries, but that 'homelessness is too high, that it could be much lower and – in recent years – that it is growing appallingly and unnecessarily'. Homelessness, Focus points out, must be tackled, 'not because it is higher than some international averages, but because it is wrong and avoidable' (Focus Ireland, 2018: 34).

Professor Eoin O'Sullivan from Trinity College Dublin compared Ireland's homelessness level with three similar countries: Denmark, Finland and Norway. These countries include a range of people who are living in overcrowded accommodation or who are at risk of homelessness (for example, prisoners whose sentences end within three months and have nowhere to live on release) in their homeless figures. O'Sullivan (2016) explains that Ireland does not even count these groups, let alone include them in its homeless figures. The deduction of these groups from the Finnish, Danish and Norwegian figures allows for a more genuine comparison, which shows Ireland moving from a position in 2008 when it had a lower level of homelessness than the comparator countries, to a position from 2015 onwards where the level is significantly higher.

This is the worst homelessness and housing crisis since the early part of the 20th century, when in 1911 nearly 26,000 families lived in terrible, overcrowded conditions in inner-city tenements (slums) (National Archives of Ireland, 2019). It is this change over time in scale of the crisis that should be the political and policy focus, along with the human impact of the crisis. We should not be trying to normalise thousands of children growing up in inappropriate emergency accommodation such as hotels or Family Hubs (described in more detail in Chapter 3). This level of homelessness should not be deemed acceptable, either ethically or as a society. The housing crisis is a moral and policy failure of a system that has the resources and wealth to solve it. Homelessness is preventable and can be radically reduced and even eliminated, as is the case in Finland.

It is important to challenge the normalisation of homelessness and the housing crisis because this narrative of normalisation places the blame and responsibility for the crisis on to the victims. Some senior state officials have claimed publicly that homelessness is often due to past behaviours. This exacerbates feelings of stigma and shame among homeless people and those threatened with homelessness. It pushes them into silence and deepens their social exclusion. It silences them from seeking help from services (something they are ashamed about) and it silences them from speaking in the media or campaigning about the issue (the desired outcome of certain government and state officials).

There is a homelessness crisis not because of some failing or past behaviour of those who are homeless, but because the policies of successive governments have focused on promoting a private market and speculative developer approach to housing provision. Governments have not built sufficient social housing for decades, nor put in place legislation to protect tenants in the private rental sector. The public comments from government about 'normal' levels of homelessness, in the face of the critique of NGOs, media, academics and opposition politicians highlighting the crisis, are an attempt by the authorities to downplay and minimise the homelessness and housing crisis and to portray rising public concern and anger as unnecessary. Such comments attempt to divert attention away from the actual causes of the crisis – away from market policies and government failure and on to those it is claimed are 'scamming' the system or are the cause of their own misfortune – the 'undeserving poor'. It is about the lack of political willingness to do what is necessary.

The government, however, has prioritised the interests of the banks, real estate investors, vulture funds, landlords and developers over the housing needs of children. Behind the rhetoric there is an indifference to the suffering caused by the housing crisis. The government has refused to prevent the flow into homelessness through measures such as improving tenant protections and leases, limiting landlords' ability to evict families into homelessness, and freezing unaffordable rents, thus failing to provide routes out of homelessness; rather, it has facilitated the lack of social and affordable housing supply.

Rather than asserting individuals' right to a secure home, and nurturing empathy and solidarity among the public that could enable major policy change (some of which could be unpopular), the government and state officials foment a bitterness, indifference and even anger among the wider public towards vulnerable homeless families and individuals.

New measures for monitoring homelessness and housing exclusion

The United Nation's (UN) Sustainable Development Goals (SDGs) are a collection of 17 global goals designed as a 'blueprint to achieve a better and more sustainable future for all' (UN, 2017: 14). They were set in 2015 by the United Nations General Assembly and intended to be achieved by the year 2030. The SDGs have become a key policy target for the Irish government and internationally. However, reaching at least three of the goals is simply not possible without decisive action to end homelessness. SDG1 requires eradicating poverty in all its forms, and SDG 3 requires ensuring healthy lives and promoting wellbeing for all at all ages. Housing is a key social determinant of health and homelessness and housing insecurity is associated with ill health and dramatically lower-than-average life expectancy. SDG11 requires making cities and human settlements inclusive, safe, resilient and sustainable, and includes ensuring access for all to adequate, safe and affordable housing. By definition, this includes preventing and addressing homelessness and addressing issues of housing affordability and insecurity of tenure.

However, in order to achieve the goal of eliminating homelessness and housing exclusion, and ensuring the right to housing for all, an adequate understanding and measurement of the true scale of homelessness and housing exclusion is required in the first instance. The measurement of homelessness and housing exclusion is an area that is hotly contested by policy makers and housing advocates. In order to implement policy objectives that aim to prevent homelessness and reduce its impact on vulnerable households requires information that reflects the reality of the process of homelessness and housing exclusion. Therefore, hidden homelessness should be made visible by policy makers and service providers. As Edgar (2007) explains, this means

> ... having an understanding and measurement of homelessness which includes the situation of people who live in insecure housing, are forced to move constantly between inadequate housing situations and those who are forced to live in housing which is unfit for habitation by commonly accepted norms....Where policies aim to ensure that fewer people should become homeless, information is needed to monitor accurately the total number of homeless households, the number living in temporary or insecure/inadequate housing and the number who are potentially homeless or are threatened with homelessness. (Edgar, 2007: 11–12)

However, Ireland's monthly homelessness statistics use a very narrow and contested definition of homelessness, and while they provide a useful monitoring mechanism, they are inadequate to capture the scale of housing need and exclusion.

As Focus Ireland (2018: 3) explains:

> Five years into the homeless crisis, we still know too little about who is becoming homeless and why. This absence of reliable information undermines our ability to plan services and change policies to prevent people becoming homeless.... Much of the required information is available administratively, but has so far been primarily used to make

short-term political points rather than collated and analysed
to inform long-term policy making.

While the monthly homeless figures provide a useful monitoring
mechanism, they are frequently inadequate in capturing the scale
of the crisis – and the constant focus in the media on the monthly
homeless figure, such as 10,275 people in September 2019
(Department of Housing, Planning and Local Government, 2019b)
means a reduction in the breadth of public debate and understanding
of the wider housing crisis.

The monthly homelessness figures are only the tip of the iceberg
in terms of hidden homelessness. They do not include rough
sleepers, people living in cars, tents or overcrowded accommodation,
couchsurfers, those in direct provision (a system for providing
accommodation for asylum seekers), Travellers in substandard sites,
or women in domestic violence refuges. Nor do the figures include
tenants with unaffordable rents or insecure leases, those living in fear of
eviction or rent hikes, or home owners in mortgage arrears. As shown
later in this chapter, the real scale of the housing and homelessness
crisis is around 260,000, or one in six households (half a million
people), fifty times greater than the official homelessness figures and
four times the number of those on social housing waiting lists.

There are very real social policy and ethical philosophical questions
to be asked about a policy approach that does not measure as homeless
those women who are staying in refuges, fleeing domestic violence.
What provision is planned to ensure these women and their children
have the ability to gain housing that can provide them safety and
prevent them from being forced to return to situations of domestic
violence? How does policy plan to meet their housing need if they
are not included in the statistics?

Ireland's homelessness crisis continues to worsen, but policy will only
be effective if it responds to an accurate level of housing need. We need
to understand properly the scale of the crisis and particular housing
vulnerabilities if we are to respond effectively. It could be argued
that because of Ireland's narrow definition of homelessness, policy
has failed to respond adequately to the crisis. It is blind to the wider
hidden homelessness crisis behind the ongoing rise in presentations
as people's housing situation becomes even more precarious. If there
were an acceptance among policy makers of a broader measure of
homelessness, policy could be more effective and holistic.

Previously unseen forms of homelessness and housing exclusion have
emerged in recent years and existing measurements are not capturing

the scale of people affected, particularly the most vulnerable, including lone parents and children, women in domestic violence refuges, migrants and Travellers.

Ireland's measurement of homelessness and housing exclusion (HHE) has not been updated to respond to new groups affected, resulting in prevention being largely absent in the Irish policy response. In a hard-hitting report, the European Commission (Daly, 2019) stated that Ireland needs better and more accurate HHE data, analysis and monitoring:

> There are serious gaps in the definition and counting of the extent of HHE in Ireland.… homelessness is conceived only as encompassing those in emergency accommodation and there is only an approximation of Housing Exclusion (and no explicit definition) through the numbers assessed as being in housing need and therefore on the housing waiting lists. Clear and inclusive definitions and full enumeration of each should be a priority for the future. The current reality in Ireland is that the statistics are unreliable and incomplete and this also hampers planning as well as efficiency and effectiveness in service provisions. (Daly, 2019: 15)

There is a requirement therefore to redefine and reconceptualise our understanding and approach of homelessness and housing exclusion in Ireland. The UN Special Rapporteur on the Right to Housing (Farha, 2017: 21) provides a useful three-dimensional approach anchored in human rights that undermines 'moral' explanations of homelessness as personal failures and instead recognises patterns of inequality that deny those who are homeless their rights. The first dimension addresses the absence of home in terms of both its physical structure and its social aspects. The second dimension considers homelessness as a form of systemic discrimination and social exclusion, whereby 'the homeless' become a social group subject to stigmatisation. The third dimension recognises homeless people as resilient in the struggle for survival and dignity and potential agents of change as rights holders. An inclusive human rights-based definition of housing should thus consider the security domain (security of tenure, exclusive occupation and affordability); the physical domain (sufficient quality of accommodation in terms of durability, amenities, protection from weather and so on) and quantity of accommodation (not severely overcrowded); and the social domain (ability to enjoy social relations, privacy and safety).

The European Typology of Homelessness and Housing Exclusion (ETHOS) framework, developed in 2005 by the European Federation of National Organisations Working with the Homeless (FEANTSA) is outlined in Table 4.1 and provides another very useful classification to define and measure homelessness and housing exclusion. The European Commission has agreed on the ETHOS definition for measuring homelessness and housing exclusion.

The ETHOS framework does not refer to individuals but to living situations and calls an adequate living situation 'a home'. Three domains are identified as constituting a home; living situations that are deficient in one or more of these domains are taken to represent homelessness and housing exclusion. These three domains of home are described as: 'having a decent dwelling (or space) adequate to meet the needs of the person and his/her family (physical domain); being able to maintain privacy and enjoy social relations (social domain); and having exclusive possession, security of occupation and legal title (legal domain)' (Edgar et al, 2004: 5).

According to this model, a population can be categorised into three groups at the time of enumeration: the homeless population; the population experiencing housing exclusion; and the adequately housed population (not experiencing homelessness or housing exclusion).

There are seven theoretical categories of homelessness and housing exclusion which are included in the ETHOS typology (Table 4.1), consisting of 13 categories containing 24 discrete living situations (FEANTSA, 2007). These categories are grouped under four headings: roofless, houseless, insecure, and inadequate accommodation.

This broader definition of homelessness and housing exclusion is backed up by the report (Faculties of Public Health Medicine and Paediatrics, Royal College of Physicians of Ireland, 2019: 3), which shows that the health and wellbeing of children is affected not just by homelessness but also by overcrowded or poor housing, and by frequent moves from one accommodation to another. Homelessness and inadequate housing, the report points out, 'may cause adverse childhood experiences with resultant mental health effects that may be lifelong'. There is an extensive literature on the health inequities and substantially lower life expectancy for those on the lowest incomes compared with those who have better access to education and resources. The authors of the report cited above point out that 'such differentials in health experience are likely compounded by the effects of homelessness and inadequate housing' (Faculties of Public Health Medicine and Paediatrics, Royal College of Physicians of Ireland, 2019: 3). Inadequate housing is one cause of adversity in childhood.

Table 4.1: ETHOS classification framework

Conceptual category	Operational category	Living situation	Generic definition
ROOFLESS	1 People living rough	1.1 Public space or external space	Living in the streets or public spaces, without a shelter that can be defined as living quarters
ROOFLESS	2 People in emergency accommodation	2.1 Night shelter	People with no usual place of residence who make use of overnight shelter, low threshold shelter
HOUSELESS	3 People in accommodation for the homeless	3.1 Homeless hostel	Where the period of stay is intended to be short term
HOUSELESS	3 People in accommodation for the homeless	3.2 Temporary accommodation	
HOUSELESS	3 People in accommodation for the homeless	3.3 Transitional supported accommodation	
HOUSELESS	4 People in women's shelter	4.1 Women's shelter accommodation	Women accommodated to experience of domestic violence and where the period of stay is intended to be short term
HOUSELESS	5 People in accommodation for immigrants	5.1 Temporary accommodation/reception centres	Immigrants in reception or short-term accommodation due to their immigrant status
HOUSELESS	5 People in accommodation for immigrants	5.2 Migrant workers' accommodation	
HOUSELESS	6 People due to be released from institutions	6.1 Penal institutions	• No housing available prior to release
HOUSELESS	6 People due to be released from institutions	6.2 Medical institutions (*)	• Stay longer than needed due to lack of housing
HOUSELESS	6 People due to be released from institutions	6.3 Children's institutions/homes	• No housing identified (e.g. by 18th birthday)

(continued)

Table 4.1: ETHOS classification framework (continued)

Conceptual category (continued)		Operational category	Living situation	Generic definition
INSECURE		7 People receiving longer-term support (due to homelessness)	7.1 Residential care for older homeless people	Long stay accommodation with care for formerly homeless people (normally more than one year)
			7.2 Supported accommodation for formerly homeless people	
		8 People living in insecure accommodation	8.1 Temporarily with family/friends	• Living in conventional housing but not the usual place of residence due to lack of housing
			8.2 No legal (sub)tenancy	• Occupation of dwelling with no legal tenancy/illegal occupation of a dwelling
			8.3 Illegal occupation of land	• Occupation of land with no legal rights
		9 People living under threat of eviction	9.1 Legal orders enforced (rented)	• Where orders for eviction are operative
			9.2 Repossession orders (owned)	• Where mortgagee has legal order to repossess
		10 People living under threat of violence	10.1 Police recorded incidents	Where police action is taken to ensure place of safety for victims of domestic violence
INADEQUATE		11 People living in temporary/non-conventional structures	11.1 Mobile homes	• Not intended as place of usual residence
			11.2 Non-conventional building	• Makeshift shelter, shack or shanty
			11.3 Temporary structure	• Semi-permanent structure, hut or cabin
		12 People living in unfit housing	12.1 Occupied dwellings unfit for habitation	Defined as unfit for habitation by national legislation or building regulations
		13 People living in extreme overcrowding	13.1 Highest national norm of overcrowding	Defined as exceeding national density standard for floor-space or useable room

Note: Short stay is defined as normally less than one year; long stay is defined as more than one year.

(*) Includes drug rehabilitation institutions, psychiatric hospitals etc.

Source: FEANTSA (2005)

The experience of poor housing has been shown to increase the risk of severe physical and mental ill health and disability during childhood and early adulthood by up to 25%. The authors highlight that:

> Instability caused by frequent housing moves puts additional stresses on families. Such instability can cause not only psychological distress but can disrupt access to primary care health services, reduce the ability to achieve balanced nutritional intake and reduce access to physical and social activities. For the older child, it can reduce their educational opportunities if they have to move school or relocate a distance from school. The longer that such instability lasts, the greater the impact. (Faculties of Public Health Medicine and Paediatrics, Royal College of Physicians of Ireland, 2019: 9)

Ireland's level of homelessness and housing exclusion

Michael Martin, the leader of the main opposition party in Ireland, Fianna Fáil, and the Taoiseach (the Irish Prime Minister) both accept that the housing crisis is a major social crisis and an emergency. The following is a transcript from a debate between the Taoiseach and Michael Martin in the Irish parliament on 3 October 2018, the same day that a national protest on housing organised by the Raise the Roof coalition took place:

> Michael Martin TD: The lack of housing and the level of homelessness are an appalling blight on our society and, without question, represent an emergency. It is an emergency that demands urgent, effective and targeted action. Too many families and children are homeless. Rents are far too high. Too many people are waiting far too long for council houses. Young working people cannot afford to buy houses. Students' third level experiences are compromised and diminished by the housing crisis and the high cost of accommodation.... We all know, from the people we meet at our clinics, the countless number on social housing lists who are living with their parents and other families and of the ensuing strain and stress for all concerned. It is an emergency that has lacked any effective intervention....

The Taoiseach: I know that the issue of housing is of huge concern to people across the country and that many will express that concern by attending the protest today. I know that many people are frustrated by the pace of delivery. I, too, am frustrated by it, as is everyone in government. It is an emergency. I am on record as having said that as far back as January or February of this year, if not long before that. Of course it is an emergency. If it was not an emergency, we would not be spending €60 million a year to put people up in emergency accommodation, we would not have brought in rent caps in urban areas and we would not have brought about fast-track planning. They were all emergency measures brought in because this is an emergency.... I have acknowledged before that the country faces a housing crisis. (Varadkar, 2018)

While the speeches show that both leaders and parties accept that there is a crisis and that it is an emergency, they stand over official housing statistics that significantly underestimate the real level of housing need and exclusion in Ireland. While homelessness is measured by the monthly statistics covering the number of individuals in state-funded emergency accommodation, the official level of wider housing need is estimated based on data provided from local authorities on their individual area social housing waiting lists. These waiting lists provide a measurement of who has applied for and subsequently qualified for social housing support.

There has been a dramatic growth in recent decades in the numbers of households that qualify for social housing support on the local authority waiting lists. Table 4.2 shows that in 1996 there were 28,000 households on waiting lists, in 2005, 42,000 households, and by 2016, 90,000 households. Official statistics show a reduction to 71,858 households on the waiting lists in 2018 (Housing Agency, 2018). But this can be explained in large part by the reclassification of tenants in receipt of state housing benefit in the private rental sector. Tenants receiving the Housing Assistance Payment (HAP) and those under the Rental Accommodation Scheme (RAS), whereby local

Table 4.2: Number of households on housing waiting lists, various years

1996	2005	2016	2018
28,000	42,000	91,600	71,858

Source: Hearne and Murphy (2018)

authorities draw up contracts with landlords to provide housing for an agreed term for people with a long-term housing need, are considered to have their housing needs met and are no longer counted on the waiting lists.

Dublin City has by far the greatest identified need for social housing support, with 16,514 households on the waiting list, representing over one fifth (23%) of all households that qualified for housing support. The four Dublin local authorities combined (Dublin City Council, Dún Laoghaire–Rathdown County Council, Fingal County Council and South Dublin County Council) have 31,196 households on their waiting lists. Together, the four Dublin authorities account for 43.4% of the national total. In the Mid-East (Kildare, Meath and Wicklow) and Louth region, 9,946 households identified as qualifying for social housing support. This region now accounts for 13.8% of the national figure.

Many have been on the waiting lists for an extended period of time. Over a quarter (19,185) of the 71,858 households qualified for social housing support were waiting for more than seven years on the lists (Housing Agency, 2018).

The housing waiting list is also broken down by housing type. The majority (54.2%) of those qualified for social housing support are unemployed. But in reflection of the high housing costs and issues of low pay, just under a quarter (17,000) of all those on the lists were in employment. Just under 60% of households qualifying for social housing support are in the private rented sector, with most in receipt of the rental income support, Rent Supplement. Single-person households are the predominant household grouping, accounting for just under half (33,556) of households, with lone parents with children numbering 22,000 (30%) and couples with or without children 15,000 (22%). The majority (74.6%) of those qualifying for social housing support are Irish citizens, and 25.4% are non-Irish nationals, mainly from countries in the European Union or European Economic Area. There are 4,037 households on the waiting lists that qualify as the result of a specific requirement stemming from a member(s) having a physical, sensory, mental or intellectual impairment, and a further 1,967 households with the specific requirement of a member(s) being aged 65 years or more (Housing Agency, 2018).

However, these estimates of housing need are restricted to the numbers of households that qualify for social housing. As explained earlier, these figures do not include tenants who are in the private rental sector in receipt of social housing supports like the HAP or those under the RAS, who are deemed to have their housing needs met and are taken off the waiting lists. Yet, these tenants are based in the private rental sector and do not have security of tenure, so should still be considered in housing need and kept on the waiting list. The largest decrease in the number of households on the waiting list in 2017 and 2018 has been due to a fall in those in receipt of Rent Supplement – a reduction in 10,181 households between 2017 and 2018 alone. This can be largely explained by the transfer of households from Rent Supplement (on the waiting list) to the HAP scheme (taken off the waiting list). There was an increase in HAP tenancies by 13,589 between 2017 and 2018 (Hearne and Murphy, 2018).

Moreover, the waiting lists do not include some homeless households, those in direct provision or and those in domestic violence refuges, who are all clearly in housing need. Furthermore, there are approximately 28,000 home owners in long-term arrears on their mortgage, and who are also clearly in major housing need, yet just 873 are recorded on housing waiting lists as qualifying for social housing due to an 'unsustainable mortgage'.

Another significant factor in explaining the failure of social housing waiting lists to reflect the real level of housing need is the maximum income threshold above which households are unable to apply for social housing. In Dublin, the maximum income threshold for a single person is €35,000 and the maximum threshold for a family of three adults and four children is €42,000. In counties like Carlow, Monaghan and Westmeath, the single-person threshold is €25,000 and for a three-adult and four-child family it is €30,000. Moreover, applicants for social housing must first be accepted by the local authority to get on to the waiting list and then maintain their place over time. There have been issues of local authorities deleting households from waiting lists due to a lack of correspondence with households.

Given the level of insecurity in the private rental sector and its role in causing homelessness and housing distress, the 67,000 HAP and RAS households that are in the private rental sector should be included on the housing waiting lists. If we combine these with the 28,000 households comprising those in long-term mortgage arrears and direct provision, those living in domestic violence refuges, Travellers and other homeless people, it brings the total housing need figure to 177,964 households. Furthermore, we know that the housing crisis and need for 'affordable' housing extends to many more households than these. It includes many renters in the private sector who are paying more than 30% of their income on rents (the internationally accepted definition of 'affordable' housing being no more than 30% of income). While it is difficult to estimate how many households this includes, the Economic and Social Research Institute (ESRI, 2019) estimates that a third of renters in the private rental sector have 'high' housing costs. This equates to 85,000 households in need of affordable housing currently in the private rental sector.

Adding this to our figures here gives a total of 261,564 households. This equates to 16%, or one in six of all households in Ireland (likely to be over half a million people) facing severe housing unaffordability and insecurity, and in need of social and affordable housing. This figure is almost four times that in the current social housing waiting lists. It shows that the real housing need in Ireland is over four times greater than that indicated by official social housing waiting list figures.

And this figure does not include aspirant home owners who cannot afford current house prices. Neither does it include students, adult children living at home with parents, couchsurfers, the 100,000 home owners with mortgages who are in a state of a 'restructured' mortgage, nor the tens of thousands living in substandard quality housing. In reality it is likely that almost a third of households in Ireland experience some form of housing insecurity, affordability issue or substandard housing. And this figure is likely to increase in the coming decades if we consider Generation Rent and Generation Stuck at Home, the generation coming after them, and the growing elderly population. This shows that the real scale of the crisis is currently hugely underestimated by government and policy makers. These figures demonstrate a significant increase in the numbers of people excluded from the housing market and a substantial growth in households affected by unaffordability, insecurity and substandard housing. The problem with this is that if policies are based on denial

Table 4.3: Number of households affected by homelessness, housing exclusion and insecurity in Ireland

Housing need	Number of households
Social housing waiting list	71,858
HAP	47,000
RAS	20,306
Homeless	2,000
Direct provision	5,400
Traveller in unsuitable conditions	1,600
Domestic violence refuges	1,400
PHD (Principal Dwelling House) arrears over 360 days	28,000
Total social housing need	177,564
Private rental unaffordable	85,000
Total 'real' affordable housing need	261,564

and an underestimation of the real scale of housing unaffordability and social housing need, they will clearly be ineffective in meeting the actual level of housing need.

This crisis, therefore, is not a temporary housing and homelessness crisis but a structural crisis of unaffordable housing that affects low- and middle-income individuals and families, workers, elderly people, people with disabilities, students and disadvantaged minority groups. Furthermore, the current housing statistics do not include any assessment of a major aspect of housing deprivation that is not given much consideration – that of substandard housing. Directly linked to this is the area of energy efficiency of homes, which affects poverty, health, and climate change targets.

Substandard housing

Within the public and policy debate on the housing crisis the issue of access to an affordable home is to the fore. What are considered much less, but are as important, are issues of standards, quality, design (space, light, access to nature) and, increasingly, energy efficiency. And this relates not just to houses and apartments, but also to the surrounding neighbourhood.

The Grenfell Tower disaster in the UK in 2017, where a fire broke out in block of flats in London causing 72 deaths, brought the issue of inadequate standards to the top of housing debates. In Ireland, there are huge problems with substandard apartments built during the boom years of the late 1990s and 2000s. Lack of proper fire safety standards coupled with poor design and poor materials mean that there are hundreds of thousands of apartments within the private sector, both owner-occupied and rented by tenants, that are of poor quality and requiring major refurbishment. The case of Priory Hall, a Dublin apartment complex deemed to be a fire hazard, is a prominent example and shows what happens when the building process is not regulated properly. There was also a fire that destroyed four floors of a hotel and apartments in Dublin's northern suburb of Ballymun in 2018. Substandard housing is widespread in the private rental sector in Ireland. More than 80% of private rental accommodation that was inspected last year failed to meet the minimum standards required by law. Of the 25,814 dwellings that were inspected, a total of 20,414 were substandard. Landlords whose properties fail to meet standards are issued with an improvement letter or prohibition notice, or served with legal action, depending on the level of non-compliance. A total of 7,104 dwellings were served with notices for improvements to be carried out last year but legal action was only initiated in 61 cases (Threshold, 2018).

The housing charity Threshold (2018: 7) has stated that complaints about substandard dwellings is one of the biggest issues it deals with:

> Many of our clients throughout the country are living in properties lacking in necessities such as heating or hot and cold running water, or are plagued with damp and mould.... Furthermore, when there are issues with properties that constitute a breach of standards this has a negative impact on tenants – damp, poor ventilation and lack of heating contribute to ill health; portable heaters, overloaded sockets, broken windows increase the safety risks.

This has major implications in relation to meeting climate change targets. The private rental sector has very poor energy-efficient housing and it is tenants who are affected most by having to pay high energy bills. To cut carbon emissions as quickly as possible means transforming home energy systems, stripping heating oil and natural gas out of very home in the space of a decade or two, and enabling far less energy-intensive modes of transportation. In order to meet the climate targets, a major refurbishment and retrofitting is required in the private rental sector. Who will pay for this? How will it be done without leading to further rent increases and evictions? These are questions that policy must address.

Furthermore, within the social housing sector there are a number of both older and relatively new local authority high-rise flat complexes and estates with substantial issues of substandard housing and poor design. The extent of the problem is shown by the fact that 20 different communities took a Collective Complaint to the Council of Europe in 2015. I was involved in researching and drafting the complaint, which demonstrated how the social housing stock was below acceptable living standards, with major problems of mould, dampness and sewerage ingress. Seventy per cent of the tenants surveyed across the 20 estates found their homes cold or difficult to heat; 75% of homes had mould; 37% had water coming into their building; and 75% complained about the standard of maintenance by the local authority. One in five said that a medical practitioner had advised them that their health was in danger as a result of the housing conditions. In the south Dublin estate of Balgaddy, 448 homes, built between 2004 and 2007, have serious structural problems have led to years of leaks, damp, mould and electrical problems. The local authority blamed tenants for causing most of the problems, until it was challenged by tenants in one estate, Dolphin House, using a human right to housing campaign (explained in more detail in Chapter 5). A tenant on one of the estates describes the housing conditions and their impacts:

> 'My bathroom is full of mould. I had to take my shower down because it was full of mould, it fell down. And I have a hole with a leak coming through the light in the bathroom that pours every time it rains. It is just full of damp.... You will see the wall is starting to crumble in the corner where the first leaks started. The plaster is coming off the wall. There is a huge hole. It plays on your mind, it affects your mental health an awful lot.... I took that house in good faith that it was going to be a house for life. And now it's not. It's crumbling down around me. I've lived in this for 13 years. It does take its toll on you.'

Other issues such as poor design, inadequate local services and community infrastructure worsens problems of poverty, isolation and anti-social behaviour, which can devastate communities.

There is a clear requirement to retrofit Ireland's social housing stock that would bring it up to standards that would radically reduce its carbon emissions, and also help with fuel poverty and the health and wellbeing of tenants.

Finally, issues of substandard housing affect Travellers, Ireland's indigenous minority ethnic population who have suffered extreme discrimination and denial of rights in Ireland, particularly in the area of housing. Traveller-specific accommodation is inadequate, unsafe, sometimes without running water and poorly maintained by local authorities, and there are considerable issues of overcrowding. Traveller organisations such as Pavee Point (2016: 19) have been highly critical of the way in which government and local authorities fail to acknowledge or respond to their housing crisis:

> The term 'sharing' of houses and halting bay sites is a euphemism for Travellers living in chronic overcrowding. The term 'basic' service bays refers to sites that are often flooded, rat infested and lack sufficient facilities. The term 'unauthorised site' refers to Travellers who are forced to live at the roadside due to lack of access to private rented accommodation, social housing and/or Traveller specific accommodation.

There are 585 Traveller families living by the side of the road and 1,115 in 'shared housing', accounting for 15% of the Traveller population. These Travellers are in effect homeless, but they are excluded from government statistics on homelessness. Furthermore, Travellers make up 9% of the homeless population but just 1% of the overall population. Ten people, including five children died tragically from a fire at a local authority-provided 'temporary' emergency halting site in Carrickmines, South Dublin, in 2015. This chapter shows, therefore, that the housing shock is just not a temporary housing and homelessness crisis but a structural crisis of unaffordable housing that affects low- and middle-income individuals and families, workers, elderly people, people with disabilities, students and disadvantaged minority groups. Furthermore, the current housing statistics are inadequate and do not include an assessment of 'hidden' homelessness and housing exclusion, or a major aspect of housing deprivation that is not given much consideration – that of substandard housing. Directly linked to this is the area of energy efficiency of homes, which affects poverty, health, and climate change targets.

5

Working for social justice: community, activism and academia

It is often argued that academics are supposed to do research and write books that present knowledge and analysis in an 'objective' and 'non-political' format, and remain in the safe and closed spaces of academia, leaving politics and policy making to the politicians, policy makers and media. However, a genuinely 'objective' analysis would highlight the incontrovertible evidence of huge harm being done to societies from the current neoliberal policy hegemony in housing. I make the case in this chapter that a mature, open democracy must have space for academics, researchers and policy analysts to play the important role of 'public intellectuals', undertaking participatory and critical research, and 'academic citizens' to provide a voice in the public sphere that challenges inequalities and presents alternatives, and thus proactively contribute to social change in areas such as housing. Indeed this is necessary to avoid the groupthink and uncritical policy that contributed to the 2008 global financial crisis and subsequent Great Recession.

This chapter begins with outlining aspects of my own housing journey and provides strategies for achieving a fairer and rights-based housing system. This book is not a typical policy or academic work. But then I am not a typical academic author or policy analyst. Driven by the desire to challenge injustice and inequality and bring about real social change and social justice, I have worked with, and for, disadvantaged communities and wider civil society for my entire adult life. I have been an activist and campaigner, a researcher, community worker, policy analyst, author, lecturer, media commentator, and, more recently a podcaster. Some of this work has taken the form of paid jobs, but much of it has been voluntary. I hope this book will inspire community workers, activists, academics, policy analysts and researchers who seek to achieve empowerment, participation and social justice in their work.

A personal housing journey

We all need a home. We all have a housing journey. We have memories of our childhood and of growing up in our home. And as adults, we face a challenge of finding our own home. Then if have you children, the need for a long-term, secure, home in a safe neighbourhood becomes paramount in your priorities.

For the first ten years of my life – the formative years – I lived in a house that my parents rented from a private landlord, in the small Irish town of Tramore. I loved our first home. I can remember the cosy sitting room, playing games in the garden, the arrival of the first digital alarm clock radio in the house (it was the 1980s after all), and a robot I received as a present one Christmas. I remember the grilled liver for dinner and the excitement when an elderly neighbour brought a bar of Cadburys chocolate for us (that meant a square or two each among five of us!) after our Saturday evening bath, playing 'hide and go seek' with my best friends who lived on the street, and having all my school friends over for my birthday. However, I also remember holding my mom's hand as we walked up the long drive to the landlord's giant house on the other side of the town. I remember my parents asking the landlord repeatedly to fix the leaks in the roof of the house. Then the landlord decided to sell the house and we had to move (in Ireland landlords have the right to vacant possession of their property no matter how long a tenant has been living there). We were offered the opportunity to buy the house, but my parents felt the work needed to improve it was beyond their budget. We had to move to another rented house. I felt I had been wrenched away from my closest friends and my home – to a strange house that I never felt was home. I lost my best friend. It even seemed that all our lives were much more stressful in our new rented house. When I was 12 years old, we bought our permanent, forever home and I remember my mother and father's proud smiling faces as they brought us to our new house. Nevertheless, the experience of (in my child's perspective) losing my first home had an impact. I saw and experienced housing inequality and dislocation. I did not understand it, but I felt it, and it stayed with me, as a source of understanding of social inequality and a motivation to act for social justice. Reflecting on it now, it taught me the importance of a long-term, secure home, especially for children, in forming bonds of friendship and gaining a sense of belonging and stability.

My experience (along with my mother's encouraging talks about the values of social justice) led to an empathy and compassion that I have, since then, always felt for excluded and homeless people and those suffering injustice and inequality. It also led to a desire to effect change towards equality. I do not want any child to experience poverty, inequality and housing related stress and dislocation.

After completing my Leaving Certificate, I moved to Dublin to study geography at Trinity College. Housing, planning, urban economics and social justice were key parts of my degree. Finding accommodation in Dublin was also a challenge and I lived in typical, student substandard housing and temporary sublets. Inspired from what I learned about public house-building programmes of affordable, mixed-income and well-planned homes, in Ireland and Europe, I made student housing a central issue during my presidency of Trinity College Students' Union in 2000, and as Campaigns Officer for the Union of Students in Ireland in 2004. I organised a 'sleep out' protest on Dublin's O'Connell Street, to protest at the student accommodation crisis in 2004, at the height of the Celtic Tiger economic boom.

Communities, regeneration and public–private partnerships

Having been involved in Global Justice Movement protests and World Social Forums, including attending global justice protests against the International Monetary Fund and World Bank summit in Prague in 2000 and the G8 summit in Genoa in 2001, I wanted to do more research on the rising inequality associated with the global neoliberal financial order. So I started a PhD in the Department of Geography at Trinity College in 2004, researching how, despite being the dominant economic and public policy approach under neoliberalism, privatisation through public–private partnerships (PPPs) was actually failing to deliver accessible and quality public services. One of my main case studies in Ireland involved researching the regeneration of disadvantaged social housing communities through PPPs.

Around this time, Dublin's local government authority, Dublin City Council, in partnership with private developers, was engaged in the speculative redevelopment of some of the city's most marginalised social housing estates through PPP regeneration. Twelve estates comprising just over 2,000 social housing units (10% of the city's entire social housing stock) were in the process of undergoing PPP regeneration. Decades of underfunding of local government had resulted in inadequate investment in maintenance and management of these estates, leaving tenants suffering from substandard housing conditions such as overcrowding, dampness and poor-quality neighbourhood infrastructure. The PPP plans being developed by the local authority and private developers placed little value on the existing communities. The plans involved the breakup of the communities by 'de-tenanting' the residents off the estates in order to redevelop them, mainly as gentrified private housing with a much-reduced amount of social housing. The local authority viewed the plans positively because the cost of redevelopment was being covered by the transfer of the public land to a private developer to undertake private residential and commercial development.

The estates were three- to four-storey flat (apartment) complexes, built between the 1950s and 1970s, to rehouse families from Dublin's notorious tenements. They were large, inner-city social housing estates in the Irish context and comprised substantial parcels of public land. For example, of the estates under regeneration, the Dolphin House estate contained 18 acres (7.28 hectares), O'Devaney Gardens 16 acres (6.47 hectares), St Michael's Estate 14 acres (5.7 hectares) and Fatima Mansions 11 acres (4.45 hectares).

These areas, particularly Fatima Mansions and Dolphin House (part of the Rialto community area), had a long history of voluntary community development activism. In the 1990s, the state provided funding to local voluntary groups in marginalised areas to enable them to employ community development workers. They worked to challenge both the causes and effects of poverty by empowering communities to self-organise and demand equality in treatment from the state. They highlighted social inequalities, proposed and implemented community-based solutions, interventions and services. They also played a key management and coordinating role in local childcare, health, youth service provision, and supporting communities to participate in state–community initiatives around estate management, policing and regeneration.

The communities were critical of the proposed PPP regeneration plans and made the case for genuine community consultation and decision making in the development of the masterplans for regeneration, for increased provision of social housing units, for community facilities, and for 'social regeneration' within the PPPs. A number of the community groups active on the PPP estates in Dublin came together to form a new city-wide tenants' network, Tenants First, in 2003, which aimed to be a 'strong collective voice for local tenants'.

As part of my research, I went out and visited the communities. I saw a housing injustice as the state sought to take this very valuable land (after a decade of hugely inflating land prices in Dublin city) away from the communities, thus breaking them up – it placed little value on these disadvantaged working-class areas. The local authority was also seeking to move away from its responsibility of managing and providing social housing. I got involved in Tenants First as a form of participatory action research to support the communities in their campaign for better housing and community conditions.

In 2006, I also wrote a series of articles for Vincent Browne's *Village* magazine, on disadvantaged areas such as Bray, Clondalkin and Coolock, among others, that, despite the economic boom and their designation for funding under the RAPID programme (an initiative focused on tackling social exclusion), continued to suffer from a lack of housing and services and from high unemployment. During this time, I went to meet the communities and saw that deep inequalities persisted in Ireland despite the Celtic Tiger boom.

Becoming a community worker as communities hit by austerity

As the funding awards I had obtained from the Irish Research Council and the Combat Poverty Agency came to an end in 2007, I needed money to pay the rent and finish my PhD. I took up a part-time position as a community worker and policy adviser with the Dolphin House Community Development Association, and started what was to become some of the most incredible and intense years of my life, working with and for this extremely disadvantaged, but proud and strong, community.

The knowledge I gained working with the communities in Dolphin House and the wider Rialto and Inchicore area over the next six years in social housing, community development, social change, social justice and rights was an education in the fullest and truest sense.

A key part of my role was to work with the community in making the case to Dublin City Council for a community-orientated regeneration plan and developing that plan in consultation with the community and its architects. I combined my previous political and community-organising experience with my academic research and writing skills to develop reports, policy proposals and analysis for on behalf of the community to the council, to the Department of Housing, Planning and Local Government (formerly Department of Environment, Community and Local Government), local and national politicians, community policing forums, Health Service Executive (HSE), and even the United Nations.

I went door to door in the community and got to know the residents, their hopes and worries, challenges, strengths, ideas and dreams. I was invited into their homes, drank a lot of tea and sat with them in meetings in temporary Portacabins (which formed the community centre where I worked). I walked the estate and chatted to the young people and elderly residents, and got involved in summer projects with the homework club and the kids. I led the implementation of a ground-breaking consultation on the proposed PPP plans that achieved the Irish Planning Institute Community Participation Award of Excellence.

Then in May 2008, the financial crash unfolded and private developers withdrew from all the Dublin PPP projects (except for Fatima Mansions, which was being completed at the time). We held protests outside city council meetings. But in December 2008, the council announced that the regeneration projects were 'no longer viable' under the PPP process, and that communities would have to wait for regeneration when there was an 'upturn' in the market and PPPs became viable again – a scenario unlikely to happen for years into the future (the market did return, a decade later, and the failed zombie PPPs were resurrected in areas such as O'Devaney Gardens). To make matters worse, in 2008 the Fianna Fáil–Green Party and Progressive Democrats coalition government commenced the first in a series of harsh austerity Budgets (continued by the Fine Gael–Labour government elected in 2011) that effectively eliminated state funding for building and regenerating social housing. The council abandoned the regeneration plans and focused on de-tenanting and demolition.

I remember the communities being devastated at the time. They were under siege from drug dealing and antisocial behaviour, along with rising unemployment resulting from the economic crash. The coalition of community groups representing the areas, Tenants First, called for 'solidarity' from the Irish public, as they described the collapse of the regeneration plans as "the death of our hopes and dreams" (Tenants First, 2008: 2). They felt abandoned by the state just as the recession hit and austerity cuts to social welfare and lone parents pushed them over the edge.

But these were their homes, and despite the deprivation and austerity the tenants retained a pride in, and strong connection to, their local community, and they spoke of their family and historical connections to these places and their identity as tight-knit, inner-city, 'working-class' neighbourhoods (Bissett, 2008; Hearne, 2011). They wanted to stay in their community and not to be 'de-tenanted' to areas they had no connections with or support in. However, they also needed proper healthy homes and proper facilities.

The regeneration had held out the promise of an end to some of their terrible living conditions such as the pervasive mould in their flats that caused asthma in their children, and the vile smells and sewerage that constantly flowed back up their baths and sinks causing skin and eye irritation and infections, and an end to the drug dealing and antisocial behaviour. Above all, it promised a new beginning. However, with the withdrawal of regeneration, any hope of a new beginning was wrenched away from them.

Working daily in Dolphin House at this time, I saw at first hand the devastation of austerity policies. I also saw how substandard and overcrowded housing affected every aspect of the lives of people living in poor housing. But I also saw how affordable public housing was essential to the residents for their daily survival. These are vulnerable, low-income communities, deeply affected by inequalities and social exclusion. I saw the importance of their neighbours and community as a daily resource to get through the stress and harsh grind of poverty. Ultimately, I saw how social housing – public rental homes – despite the stigma and misconceptions attached to it, provides secure homes and strong communities.

A tough decision

At this time, I was finishing writing up my PhD and I faced a decision about whether to follow the typical academic route and try to get a postdoctoral research position in a university, or whether to continue working in Dolphin House. I remember going to a Regeneration Board meeting in Dolphin House with the community, city council and Fergus Finlay, the chair of the board and chief executive of children's charity Barnardos. The meeting was utterly depressing as the council representative told the community that there was no prospect of regeneration in the short to medium term. The sense of hopelessness and despair among the community representatives was visible for everyone. As I walked out of the room, which was a converted flat, and into the centre of the block of flats, where the stairwells smelled of urine and the walls were filthy and cracking, the sense of utter devastation that was going to hit this already battered community struck me like a steam train. Fergus turned to me and said, "Barnardos can try get funding to make your post full time for at least a year. The community needs you to keep the regeneration going." I had become part of the community, an outsider welcomed in. So I decided that if ever there was a time to put my principles and beliefs of social justice and empowerment into practice, this was it. So I spent the next five years, along with the local community workers and residents, supported by Fergus and Barnardo's, working at Dolphin House with the community, trying to improve the living conditions, developing new plans, and trying to reinstil hope and nurture a belief that a better future was possible. We battled against, and worked with, the council's architects and housing department to get them to shift their approach. We organised protests as part of the Big Push campaign of community organisations against the austerity cuts. We produced policy proposals such as *Housing for Need not Greed*, the Tenants First Action Plan for Sustaining Homes and Communities (Tenants First, 2009).

However, conditions on the Dolphin House estate deteriorated in 2009 and 2010, particularly illegal drug dealing and antisocial behaviour, and maintenance issues of sewage inflows and dampness. Public meetings we organised to call for a safer community received bomb threats and residents were threatened by local drug gangs. It was a frightening time for residents and for us as community workers. Then in 2009, Community Action Network, a non-governmental organisation (NGO), approached us about developing a new approach.

The human rights-based approach: Rialto Rights InAction

With the support of the Dolphin House Community Development Association, the Rialto Youth Project, Fatima Groups United and the Rialto Network, we brought tenants and community workers together to form the Rialto Rights InAction Group (RRIAG), an innovative human rights campaign focused on the right to decent housing conditions and the right to community-based regeneration that would sustain the existing community and change the unequal power relationship between the council and tenants. We used community development organising principles to educate and train tenants in human rights and empowered them to demand that the council meet their rights to housing and participation in decision making on issues such as estate management and regeneration planning. We held four public human rights 'hearings' between 2010 and 2014 where tenants spoke and asserted the responsibility of national government to address their issues. These received widespread media attention.

We lobbied senior council officials and government ministers. It was a difficult campaign for the tenants as they were worried that the council would punish the tenants involved, and how it might stigmatise Dolphin House further. It was extremely brave of this vulnerable community to engage in such public critical action. Despite the challenges faced by their disadvantage, they were empowered through the human rights campaign to stand up to their landlord and the wider Irish state that had, for decades, denied responsibility and blamed tenants for the problems. Eventually, in 2012, the Minister for Environment, Community and Local Government and Dublin City Council accepted responsibility to address the problems and agreed to deliver and publicly fund the regeneration of the estate. Six years later, the first phase of the council-led regeneration of 110 units was completed (see Image 5.1).

Image 5.1: Dolphin House regeneration 1

Image 5.2: Dolphin House regeneration 2

From community work to policy and academia

I believed that the Dolphin House experience would give hope to other communities, and show wider Irish society the reality of housing inequalities and that this was not the fault of those in poverty but of failed policies. I wrote about Dolphin's experience in my book, *Public Private Partnerships in Ireland: Failed Experiment or Way Forward* (Hearne, 2011), and in the international academic *Journal of Human Rights Practice* (Hearne and Kenna, 2014).

Then in September 2013, after an emotional goodbye to my friends, colleagues and the community of Dolphin House, I took up a one-year academic lecturing post in the Department of Geography at Maynooth University. There I started to research and highlight the newly emerging housing crisis. I wrote an op-ed in the *Irish Times* in November 2014, which criticised the Fine Gael–Labour government's housing policy, and stated that:

> The Government's new Social Housing Strategy 2020 plan correctly identifies the underfunding of the provision of social housing and rising rents in the private sector as the principal causes underlying the housing crisis. Unfortunately, it continues this underfunding as the 2015 social housing budget will be just half of what it was in 2008. Furthermore, the strategy failed to radically reform the National Asset Management Agency, which is the largest housing body and property developer in the State. This leaves a fundamental contradiction. (Hearne, 2014)

Moreover, I went on to make the following point:

> When our financial system was in peril there was no obstacle too large for the State to overcome. Now we face an equivalent crisis in housing needs. It is legitimate to ask why the same radical approach is not applied to the housing crisis. It appears the Government is unwilling to stand up to the financial and property investors. (Hearne, 2014)

I got involved with grassroots housing groups and supported the development of a new social movement to campaign on the housing and worsening homelessness crisis. How that movement unfolded is further detailed in Chapter 10.

Around this time, my contract at the Department of Geography ended, and in view of ongoing austerity and the increasingly precarious job market, which affected contract staff and recruitment in academia, I took up a position as a senior policy analyst with the inequality think tank TASC. Another move, another short-term contract position. At TASC, I published reports on the escalating housing crisis, associated worsening inequality and the processes of financialisation.

In July 2016, I stood (unsuccessfully) for election to the Seanad Éireann, the upper house of the Irish parliament. I stood on the National University of Ireland panel, and put the housing crisis at the heart of my campaign, including the proposal of eight solutions to the housing crisis (see Box 5.1).

Box 5.1: Solutions to end the housing crisis

1. **Declare a national housing emergency** to give housing the political priority it needs
2. **Triple the social housing capital budget to fund a new Housing and Homes Agency** to lead the delivery of 10,000 new social and affordable housing per annum (including strengthening capacity of local authorities and housing associations)
3. **National Asset Management Agency to be directed to suspend selling its land and assets** to vulture funds and use its land and finance to build 10,000 social and affordable housing units per annum for families and low income households
4. **Introduce rent control** linked to inflation and provide tenants' rights to longer leases
5. **Suspend all housing evictions**: support people to stay in their homes through increasing Rent Allowance, writing off debt for those in mortgage arrears and forcing banks to accept solutions
6. **Compulsorily purchase land from vulture funds and developers** to use for social and affordable housing
7. **Allow local authorities to borrow from the Housing Finance Agency** to build affordable rental housing on their significant land banks

---

Participatory action research with homeless families

In early 2017, I took up a contract position as a postdoctoral researcher at Maynooth University in the Department of Sociology, under Mary Murphy. I researched the impact of the 2008 global financial crisis and subsequent austerity on vulnerable groups as part of the European Union (EU) RE-InVEST research project, a collaboration of social scientists, NGOs and trade unions, funded under the EU Horizon 2020 project. As part of this research, we co-developed a unique participatory action research methodology to understand and address issues of poverty, the Participatory Action Human Rights and Capability Approach.

We undertook participatory research with homeless families in Dublin on their experiences of the 'marketisation' shift in social housing policy and the private rental subsidy, the Housing Assistance Payment (HAP), and looked at the impact of the new emergency accommodation (Family Hubs) on their wellbeing. We worked to empower a small group of homeless families to undertake a dialogue with housing officials and the Irish Human Rights and Equality Commission whereby they outlined their experience and views. We published the research findings in a policy brief, *Investing in the Right to A Home: Housing, HAPs and Hubs* (Hearne and Murphy, 2017), to highlight the negative impacts of housing policy and to promote the voice of the families and our policy recommendations into the public sphere and influence policy. This resulted in national media coverage, discussion in the national parliament and a subsequent invitation to discuss the findings with the parliamentary committee on housing in September 2017. The families, pleased to see the research published in the public domain, felt it was an accurate portrayal of their views and experiences.

On the day of the launch of our policy report, the then Taoiseach (Prime Minister), Leo Varadkar, was asked in the Dáil (the lower house of the Irish parliament) about the findings of the report in relation to the problems we identified with emergency accommodation and the spiralling homelessness crisis. However, on the floor of the national parliament, the Taoiseach spoke about me personally on matters that were, as, journalist Mick Clifford wrote in the *Irish Examiner* on 7 July 2017, 'not relevant to whether children are being developmentally damaged in emergency accommodation'. Clifford asked in his article:

> How are other academics – or their bosses in third-level institutes – to interpret this response? Should they now pause to reflect before producing something that might embarrass or displease the Government? If they highlight deficiencies in governance are they exposing themselves to personal attack from the Taoiseach?… Mr Varadkar got away with it, not least because of the failure of either academia or those working in the area of housing and homelessness to call him out. One might well ask whether the silence is attributable to fear of displeasing a central government that tightly controls funding for such institutions and groups. (Clifford, 2017)

Those close to me personally and professionally were concerned that the Taoiseach's comments might affect my professional development, particularly given my precarious employment situation. I worried too and took some time to reflect. Later that year, I continued my commitment to public engagement and presented our findings to the parliamentary committee on housing in September, and in December I helped organised, with homelessness charity Inner City Helping Homeless and the MyNameIs campaign, the Songs and Words for a Home for All protest concert outside parliament. I continue to be active working with housing campaigns, supporting homelessness NGOs, housing associations and cooperatives to address and solve the housing crisis.

Image 5.3: Homeless and Housing Coalition protest, April 2018

Approaches to social change

Community workers, grassroots activists, NGOs, policy analysts, researchers and academics play a major role in social change, empowerment and participation in relation to social justice and housing issues. However, it is not generally accepted that academics play such a publically proactive role in both advocating, and campaigning for change and social justice.

In society today, academic social scientists are expected to play the role of 'experts' and 'technocrats' affirming the status quo, to confine themselves to the rules of the neoliberal game where the understanding of politics is confined to market-dominated ideologies, and to a managerial conception of politics that avoids the vocabulary of power and equality. Policy recommendations are expressed in terms of 'best practices', 'guidelines' and 'standards', thereby obscuring power relations and suppressing the possibility of 'deliberation about contesting visions of the good' (Brown, 2015: 4). The role of the neoliberal social science academic is to stay within the university, securing research funding for their austerity-ridden institution, researching non-contentious issues and entering the public sphere only to act as 'objective' commentator. Above all, the academic must eschew an overtly 'political' stance such as advocating ideas of radical transformation, or else face public opprobrium, lack of career progression, inability to secure funding and pariah status in the neoliberal university.

The important question to consider is the actual purpose of our research and knowledge production. Whose interests does it serve? How can it contribute to positive social change, for example in the area of progressing the right to housing? What principles should underpin our research, what strategies can we use, and how should they frame our work?

Bourdieu (1991) finds that – given its capacity to represent and to name social experience – research carries significant symbolic power, particularly when authorised by the academy.

Campus Engage, an initiative of Irish universities aimed at bringing researchers and communities together to address societal challenges in Ireland, promotes such engaged research, which is 'advanced with community partners rather than for them'.

Participatory action research is an approach to generate knowledge in partnership with communities to empower the socially excluded in order to co-produce new knowledge about the reality of the impact of social and economic policies based on their lived experiences. It includes taking constructive action to ameliorate difficult, often oppressive, situations. Therefore, it is also a method of 'action' that brings this knowledge into the 'public sphere' of academic, NGO, policy and media debates in order to challenge social injustice (Gaventa and Cornwall, 2001).

Brazilian community educator Paulo Freire argued that people have a universal right to participate in the production of knowledge and that action research involves a process whereby 'people rupture their existing attitudes of silence, accommodation and passivity, and gain confidence and abilities to alter unjust conditions and structures. This is an authentic power for liberation that ultimately destroys a passive awaiting of fate' (Freire, 1974: xi).

Freire highlighted the central role of the poor and oppressed in action research:

> The silenced are not just incidental to the curiosity of the researcher but are the masters of inquiry into the underlying causes of the events in their world. In this context research becomes a means of moving them beyond silence into a quest to proclaim the world. (Freire, 1974: 34)

Economist and philosopher Amyrta Sen also expressed this view when he wrote: 'It is, as we have tried to argue and illustrate, essential to see the public not merely as "the patient" whose wellbeing commands attention, but also as 'the agent' whose actions can transform society' (Sen and Dreze, 1989: 279).

The goal of research and policy analysis, therefore, is not only the interpretation of the world, but actively engaging in its transformation.

In the interregnum – neoliberalism is dying but new is not yet born

The Irish state and policy needs to recognise and accept that critical public academics, policy makers, NGOs and community and voluntary organisations have a vital role to play in raising awareness of issues affecting the most vulnerable, offering alternative knowledge and policy alternatives and thus enhancing democracy through empowering the most marginalised.

There is a vital role and obligation for academics to be part of Habermas' 'unruly public' – to draw on our time, skills, knowledge and role to critically engage in the public sphere (Fraser, 1990: 57). Academic researchers can have diverse roles and participate in forms of public engagement to ensure that co-produced knowledge contributes to society and social justice. Burawoy (2005) makes the case for a role for social scientists in promoting democratic solidarity to overcome neoliberalism – acting as 'public sociologists'. Social scientists can contribute to the public debate by providing information and knowledge, for example, highlighting the extent, causes and consequences of extreme inequalities such as housing exclusion. However, it is not only the social scientist's own knowledge that is relevant; the production of knowledge should be democratised, as with participatory action research, involving those affected as well as the public. The Italian political philosopher Antonio Gramsci provided a useful conception of the role of the intellectual in society, whereby all men and women are 'philosophers'. In this context, citizens' daily lived experience and social movements are treated as 'knowledge producers' and the aim is to systematically generate counter-knowledge as a fundamental step in the process of social change (Cox, 2014: 965).

Sen makes the important reflection, again drawing on Gramsci, that even if the goal is to change 'people's thinking and priorities' – as it was the case for Gramsci – this still requires 'an engagement with the shared mode of thinking and acting' (Sen, 2009: 121). This is a kind of a dual task, using language and imagery that communicate efficiently and well through the use of the existing 'common sense', while trying to make this language express proposals that would transform society (Sen, 2009).

Therefore, as an 'organic intellectual' – working within and among social actors engaged in transformation – the 'public sociologist' can play a key role in contributing to the co-construction of common values and identity across the diverse groups required to enhance their collective capabilities to transform society (Burawoy, 2005). Academic research, therefore, should not be separate from civil society, policy debates, movements and communities, but be part of them.

The current hegemonic 'common sense' ideology is neoliberalism – the belief in the primacy, infallibility and allocative efficiency of the market, the individual as utility maximiser, the commodification and monetisation of everything, and the removal of notions of a common society, solidarity and social support. However, this ideology has been deeply discredited because of the 2008 crash, rising inequality and its failure to deliver economic freedom and prosperity for everyone. We are in a period similar to that aptly described by Gramsci when referring to the 1930s, where: 'The crisis consists precisely in the fact that the old is dying and the new cannot be born; in this interregnum a great variety of morbid symptoms appear' (Gramsci, 1971: 275).

Neoliberalism is dying, but there is a battle of ideas, and politics, for what replaces it. In this interregnum, one morbid symptom is the current authoritarian, nationalist, racist, sexist, extreme version of neoliberalism and financialised capitalism, which is in the ascendency in some of the most powerful countries in the world. The question we must ask and answer is what can challenge it and provide an alternative. It is a politics of solidarity, of hope, and of freedom based on equality and social and environmental justice.

Academics have a key role in nurturing that solidarity and alternative value system and policies as public intellectuals and as organic intellectuals contributing to the 'War of Position', which aims to shift the 'common sense' within civil society to create a counter-hegemony of ideas and policies for a better, fairer and environmentally sustainable society. The current hegemony forecloses the possibilities of real social justice alternatives, and asserts that inequality and neoliberal policies are natural, the most efficient, and ultimately the only, way to do things.

Housing, asset-based home ownership and financialisation have been central to the rise and dominance of neoliberalism. It gained much of its support through the undermining of public housing provision (for example, the UK Prime Minister Margaret Thatcher's pointed attack on council housing in the 1980s) and the promotion of home ownership as the ideal for society. But housing is also a space where counter-ideas, movements and practices are undertaken by people based on cooperative, community, collective, equality and rights-based values, that fundamentally challenge the neoliberal order.

Housing systems result from the balance of power and influence of different sectors and forces in society: who controls it, who exercises their power and how. Academics, policy analysts, NGOs, trade unions, community workers and the wider public can all play a role in supporting those who are excluded and currently 'powerless' to exercise and realise their power and win the battle of ideas within civil society for an alternative 'common sense' based on the right to housing for all.

Academics and researchers can produce knowledge (like housing policy and analysis), but society and politics (social power) play a decisive role in whether or not that knowledge is used in a progressive, transformative way. If we want to see change in policy and practice, therefore, we have to engage with politics and power.

Based on my research and experience, I suggest five areas, outlined in Box 5.2, for the academic researcher (and this can be applied to policy analysts and researchers, NGOs, human rights organisations, trade unions and community activists) to contribute to achieving an egalitarian, socially and environmentally just, and rights-based housing system.

We can work to rupture silences about injustice and inequalities or we can allow hegemony of the common sense to go unchallenged. It is not just about identifying inequalities, but also challenging their persistence. It is not just about identifying solutions, but arguing for them in the public sphere.

Box 5.2: Strategies for engaged research and social change

1. Produce new 'knowledge', analysis and research of housing issues and policy, such as explaining the causes of housing crises and inequalities. Analysis from the normative framework of a human rights, social justice and environmental sustainability approach as an important counterbalance to the dominant market and neoliberal analysis. A rights and justice analysis should include policy alternatives aimed to empower, inform and inspire affected groups and the public, achieve cross-society solidarity and offer practical solutions to policy makers.

2. Work directly with vulnerable and excluded groups, communities and civil society to co-produce new knowledge and understandings of how social issues such as housing affect particular groups. A participatory action research approach is particularly effective. Existing policy and academic knowledge can be deepened and become more authentic through the direct experience of affected groups. Alternative policies can be co-constructed that better reflect the experiences and needs of those affected.

3. Engage with the policy process. Work with front-line workers and service providers, NGOs, state bodies, policy makers and elected representatives to gather their policy rationales and engage them in policy dialogue with those directly affected by social issues.

4. Be a public intellectual and advocate, bringing the voice of the excluded into the public political sphere along with new co-constructed knowledge and policy alternatives, through policy proposals, op-eds for the media, podcasts and speaking at public movement meetings.

5. Nurture solidarity across society. Facilitate and support the construction, in partnership with civil society, of structures and relationships of empowerment. Be part of social movements for housing affordability and rights, campaigns, and facilitating dialogue between diverse actors to develop common alternatives and action. Co-construct spaces for movements, civil society and wider public audiences, through which social solidarity can grow, for example by creating spaces for dialogue, policy development and strategy formation.

With the rise in the politics of fear and blaming the vulnerable, there is an urgent need to construct solidarity across society, rather than perpetuating division among disadvantaged groups, playing one against another such as home owner against social housing tenant, private tenant against home owner, locals against migrants, or environmentalists against those concerned with inequality. There is an absence of solidarity in society stemming from the tendency to treat crises in the realms of political economy, ecology and social reproduction as unconnected. This lack of solidarity is indicative of 'fragmented imaginations' and critical scholarship can play an important part in joining the dots and offering new possibilities for political imagination that might, in turn, trigger new solidarities and foster the critical consciousness necessary to help generate social change.

There is a need, therefore, to work on the connections between all those affected by the housing crisis (and its links to the climate crisis) so that the focus is on the policy failures and inequalities that cause the crisis. By educating people about the systemic causes and common solutions, we can create a stronger civil society to challenge dominant policy. It is through social divisions that a politics that protects the privileged continues to hold power.

6

The neoliberal roots
of the current crisis

Housing crises are not new

Ireland is an interesting case through which to understand housing, because of its particular history. It shows that housing crises are not new, nor are they universal, either within countries or across different countries. There were severe housing shortages due to rapid urbanisation and inequalities in the late 19th and first half of the 20th century. For example, Dublin and other Irish cities had some of the worst slum housing conditions in Europe in the early part of the 19th century. This was due to the lack of an independent government, the disinterest of the British colonial administration in providing housing for the Catholic majority in Ireland, discrimination against the Catholic population, and growing urban poverty and social class inequalities. In 1914, a local government committee tasked with investigating the living conditions of Dublin families with the lowest incomes produced a report entitled *Housing Conditions of the Working Classes in the City of Dublin* (Local Government Board for Ireland, 1914), which found private rented homes that were severely overcrowded, unsanitary, unsafe for children, and generally 'unfit for human habitation'. James Connolly, a leading socialist Republican and trade unionist, was one of the executed leaders of the 1916 Irish rebellion against the British Empire and signatory of the 1916 Proclamation of the Irish Republic. Writing in his newspaper, the *Worker's Republic*, he wrote in 1899 about the slum housing conditions in Dublin and describes it in a way that echoes through the century since they were written to resonate with today's housing crisis:

> The housing accommodation of the Dublin workers
> is a disgrace to the City; high rents and vile sanitary
> arrangements are the rule, and no one in the Corporation
> seems to possess courage enough to avow the truth, or to
> face the storm of obloquy which would be directed upon the

head of the councillor who would take the opportunity to expose on the floor of the City Hall the manner in which the interests of house landlords are protected. (Connolly, 1899)

He went on to describe the solutions to the crisis then, which also remain relevant as solutions today...

We pointed out that the Corporation of Dublin had it in its power to sensibly mitigate the sufferings of the industrial population in the City by a wise and intelligent application of its many powers as a public board. Among the various directions we enumerated as immediately practical outlets for corporate enterprise, there were two allied measures which, were they applied, might do much to at once relieve the most odious and directly pressing evils arising from the congested state of our cities. Those two measures were:–
- Taxation of unlet houses, and
- Erection at public expense of Artisans' Dwellings, to be let at a rent covering cost of construction and maintenance alone. (Connolly, 1899)

Sadly, James Connolly was shot under orders from the British administration and did not see the broad thrust of his recommendations put into practice. But they became the dominant approach to housing in the 20th century under the Keynesian period from the 1940s to the 1970s.

It was generally accepted in this period that the laissez faire (market) approach to the economy in the 19th century had failed, as it had left the housing market unregulated and allowed landlords engage in exploitative rack renting. Slums developed with terrible conditions for the poor and working households living there, with major public health issues. In the first decades of the 20th century, the issue of housing conditions and affordability was a central concern of working people and the poor, and taken up by trade unions and socialist political parties that demanded that the state must act where the market had failed.

Nascent welfare states began to intervene in laws that condemned unfit housing and entrusted local municipal governments with the direct provision of public rental housing to house those cleared from the slums and for workers. As the Fordist, or Keynesian period (post-Second World War to the 1980s) developed, the state, through national and local government, increasingly took the responsibility for, and played, a central role in building large numbers of decent quality and affordable and public (council/social) housing and financing affordable housing in Europe, the US and other regions across the world.

This was done through the construction of public housing, the regulation of the private rental sector through measures such as rent controls and the provision of grants and low-cost loans for house building and home ownership. It came to be accepted that the state must play a central role in housing provision.

Housing became a key pillar of the developing welfare state. The provision of affordable, good-quality, public housing was a central part of the 'social contract' between the state and its populations in the Keynesian period, although housing is also referred to as the 'wobbly pillar' of the welfare state in social policy, as the private market plays a major role in its provision. Throughout the 20th century, different countries developed various 'housing regimes' according to the balance of market and state provision.

The philosophy underpinning the approach to housing in most European countries during this period was that it should be delivered according to social need and as a social right – that is, it was provided to meet the population's requirement for affordable housing, through mainly non-market (decommodified) sectors such as local authorities and not-for-profit housing associations (Drudy and Punch, 2005; Madden and Marcuse, 2016). This 'non-market' or decommodified approach to housing treated it primarily as a home and as a basic necessity, as shelter, a place to stay, to feel secure, to build a base, to find an identity, and to participate in community and society. Access to housing was treated as a social good, and a 'social' requirement like education or public health. The 'use' values of housing as a home, shelter, security, community and neighbourhood were prioritised over its 'exchange' value as a real estate investment asset or mortgage commodity. Housing was produced in response to need and not just the ability to pay. Such a decommodified approach aims to take housing out of the market and protect households from market inequalities and exclusion.

Housing was placed as a central concern of social and public policy because of this fundamental importance in securing shelter, security, community and societal development and human dignity (Drudy and Punch, 2005). In the traditional public policy philosophy of 'public' – or as it is more commonly referred to nowadays 'social' – housing provision was part of local governments' redistributive role as a public housing authority and regulatory role as a planning authority. The priority within this policy approach was providing households with access to both decent and affordable housing. The acquisition of land by state bodies to build housing was also a central part of this approach.

However, since then we have been on an inexorable path back to the future – returning to the housing policies that lead to the tenements of the 19th century. We have gone full circle and forgotten the lessons from Connolly and others. But today's housing exclusion and distress take a new and extreme financialised form in a time of unprecedented wealth and, at the same time, unparalleled housing inequalities.

Ireland's housing history

Early state intervention in Ireland in relation to housing was linked to land reforms that gave tenants access to land and homes. The first local authority housing was provided in rural areas in response to agitation and protest from the Land League against evictions. In the 1870s to the 1890s, landlords (often absentee landlords who lived outside of Ireland) raised rents and evicted poor tenant farmers, recovering from the great Irish famine of the 1840s. As many as 100,000 families were in rent arrears by 1879. Image 6.1, of an eviction by armed police and British soldiers using battering rams leaving a family outside their destroyed thatched cottages, is an indelible cultural image in Ireland.

Image 6.1: Tenant farmer's home in County Clare destroyed by battering ram during eviction

Source: Reproduced by permission of the National Library of Ireland

The Land League organised a movement of resistance of tenant farmers to achieve the 'three Fs' (fair rent, fixity of tenure and free sale) by 'defending those who may be threatened with eviction for refusing to pay unjust rents', reducing 'rack-rents' (referring to unjustly excessive rents [the word 'rack' evoking the medieval torture device], often obtained from landlords by threat of eviction), abolishing landlordism in Ireland, and enabling tenant farmers to own their homes and the land they worked on. The so-called Land War involved rent strikes, with the Land League highlighting specific cases of eviction and placing pressure on landlords trying to remove tenants from their homes. One of the most high-profile of these campaigns led to the introduction of the word 'boycott' into the English language. In 1881, Captain Charles Boycott, a landlord who was evicting farmers, was ostracised by the local community in South Mayo in protest. This 'boycott' of landlords, along with the rent strikes, became one of the most effective methods of campaigning by tenants. The Land League was successful and the Labourers (Ireland) Act 1906 was passed, which funded county councils to build over 40,000 new rural cottages, each on an acre of land. The Land Commission also established a system of government loans to enable tenant farmers to buy their homes from their former landlords, and to build new homes. By 1921, 50,000 rural cottages had been built in this way.

In urban areas of Ireland, much of the first 'social housing' in the 19th century was built by private companies and philanthropic organisations to house their workers, for example Guinness's Iveagh Trust in Dublin. In the post-independence (1921) era, there was an increase in state intervention in housing. It became a key area of social policy activity, focusing on the provision of local authority housing and providing grants to support private ownership. The new Free State aimed its housing at aspirant home owners. For example, the introduction in 1922 of the Million Pound Scheme enabled local authorities to construct 2,000 houses in just two years, most of which were sold to middle-income buyers. Dublin Corporation built the famous Marino estate on the model of the garden city for workers in 1924.

One of Ireland's two largest political parties, Fianna Fáil and Fine Gael, both centre-right in political ideology, has led each government since Independence. Therefore, in contrast to other European countries, Ireland did not have a social-democratic or socialist government in power that developed Keynesian policies and a welfare state. The dominant political, social, economic and cultural perspectives in the Irish state in the first half of the 20th century were conservative, predominantly free-market oriented, nationalist and deeply influenced by the conservative Roman Catholic Church, and they reflected the rural, agrarian-focused, population (Bartley and Kitchin, 2007). Reflecting Ireland's particular post-colonial context and their resultant populist approach to politics, however, Fianna Fail's and Fianna Gael's brands of conservatism were complex, and both developed policies that spanned a wide range of ideological perspectives.

Housing, for example, was seen as an important area where the Irish state would play a uniquely important role, given its historical and cultural significance, the need for the new state to gain popular legitimacy, and the major housing problems facing the new state. The justification for extensive state intervention in housing was outlined in 1966 by Seamus Dolan, an elected member of the national parliament for Fianna Fáil, when speaking in a debate in the Seanad (upper house) on housing provision:

> 'We in Fianna Fáil have at all times laid great stress on the need for proper homes for our people. It is a well-known fact that because we were oppressed for centuries we inherited a great number of insanitary, unfit houses so that when we achieved independence the housing situation was deplorable. However, it was not until 1932 that a real start was made. The Government then decided to introduce measures whereby they would assist less wealthy small farmers and others in the country to provide their own homes out of their own meagre resources with assistance provided by the State.' (Dolan, 1966)

Local authority housing expansion

While central government departments including the Department of Environment, Community and Local Government were responsible for setting policy and law in relation to social housing provision and the standards for housing conditions, local government housing authorities were delegated, under the various Housing Acts, the day-to-day responsibility for the provision and maintenance of social housing. This involved local authorities directly designing and building housing stock. The units were then rented at subsidised low rates to tenants. New tenants were allocated units from the local authority's social housing waiting lists. Low-interest loans and grants were given for house purchase.

Local authorities became increasingly important providers of housing in Dublin and in other urban centres during the first half of the 20th century, producing high-quality homes and neighbourhoods (MacLaran, 1993; McManus, 2002). In just ten years, from 1932 to 1942, local authorities constructed 49,000 units, representing 60% of total housing output. During the Second World War, public provision represented 65% of the housing total and was as high as 70% in the year 1945/46 (Finnerty, 2002). During the 1950s, public provision of housing generally exceeded 50% of the total new build (Drudy and Punch, 2005). In just one year, 1950, for example, 7,787 houses were built by local authorities and 4,518 by private enterprise, that is, over four times the number of social houses built by the state in 2018. In 1950, the population of Ireland at the time was just 2.8 million. With a population of 4.7 million in 2018, Ireland would need to have built 13,000 social housing units to produce a similar level to that of 1950. There was a reduction in local authority house building in the latter half of the 1950s and in the 1960s. In 1963, for example, local authorities built just 1,856 houses and 5,578 were built by private enterprise (Hearne, 2017).

As a result of state policy, which included the building of homes to promote access to home ownership among middle- and low-income households and the sale of local authority homes to tenants, home-ownership levels increased dramatically from the 1950s to the 1980s. The level of home ownership increased from 52% in 1946 to 59% in 1961, and increased further to 68% in 1971. The proportion of households in rented local authority housing was 20% in 1946 and stayed at this level through the 1950s until the early 1970s. In 1971, 15% of households were in local authority rented housing. In 1946, 25% of households were in the private rental sector and this declined rapidly in the 1950s and 1960s to 17% in 1961 and just 13% in 1971 (Hearne, 2017).

In the 1960s, a government White Paper on housing highlighted that there was insufficient housing available and significant amounts unfit for human habitation. Inner-city homes collapsed, with tragic deaths as a result. This led to the establishment of the National Building Agency, which oversaw the building of local authority housing in suburbs such as Ballymun, Tallaght and Clondalkin.

Ireland also provided a form of 'socialised' home ownership through tenant purchase and cheap loans to promote the maximum uptake of private house purchase. By the early 1960s, the purchaser could recoup almost 30% of the cost of a standard suburban house from the government. Grants and government-backed home-purchase loans continued right into the 1980s.

The Irish state also supported home ownership as a way of creating 'model' citizens, thereby dealing with social unrest and reinforcing support for a conservative state and politics. As the Bishop of Cork stated in 1957:

> 'The man of property is ever against revolutionary change, Consequently a factor of the first importance in combating emigration and preventing social unrest and unemployment marches and so on is the widest possible diffusion of ownership....' (Quoted in McCabe, 2011: 11)

In the mid-1970s, there was another expansion of local authority house building, while the private sector also increased its output of housing. The Minister for Local Government, James Tully, a Labour Party member of the new Fine Gael–Labour coalition government, outlined in the Dáil in 1973 that:

> 'Housing is one of the key areas in my portfolio which the Government have singled out for special attention because they are satisfied that the approach to this major national problem has been half-hearted and inadequate, particularly over the past decade.' (Tully, 1973)

He went on to say that an average of less than 15,000 houses was built annually over the previous six years when the total required "to meet the urgent needs of families in unfit and overcrowded conditions, to replace condemned houses and to cater for new household formation should have been at least 20,000 a year". He stated that there was a "housing emergency" and that "the situation is particularly critical in the case of people waiting for rehousing by local authorities. House building in this sector has lagged far behind private building. Last year, for example, local authorities completed fewer than 5,800 houses, representing only one-quarter of all house completions." He noted that it would be difficult to bring about the necessary increase in output of local authority housing within the normal resources of local authorities. Therefore, he announced the introduction of "a special emergency programme, using the National Building Agency for the purpose, which aims to produce 10,000 houses over the next five years, additional to the normal on-going operations of local authorities". He outlined that he had "strengthened the resources of the agency to enable it to provide the necessary supplementary technical and management resources to get this programme under way" (Tully, 1973).

In this period, as the private sector increased its role and local authorities developed high-rise building projects, cities and towns became more clearly divided into public and private sector housing. Some public building projects were poorly planned and designed, and emphasised quantity in response to population growth rather than quality. Many public estates had limited physical access and few facilities such as shops schools and playgrounds and were isolated from surrounding areas.

In 1973, Tully criticised the practice of using local authorities and their tenants as "guinea-pigs for experiments with constructional methods and materials". He made the case that:

> 'The stigma attached to a local authority house or a county council cottage should be removed from the point of view of design, so that if the occupants later on decide to vest their houses or become the owners they will fit into the community without any stigma being attached.'

Tully outlined the intention that the houses to be built by local authorities into the future were to be "of a standard equivalent to that accepted as normal for private grant houses and will be in no way inferior in accommodation and amenities simply because they are part of the local authority housing programme".

Output increased in the early 1970s to reach a high point of 1975 (see Figure 6.1) when local authorities built 8,794 social housing units representing one third of total housing provision. Again, it is noteworthy that the population of Ireland at the time was 3.2 million. A new scheme for the sale of council houses to sitting tenants at a large discount was introduced in 1973. At the same time, private market provision also increased significantly.

The neoliberal housing shift

Internationally, a dramatic shift took place in the economic order in the late 1970s and the 1980s as the dominant economic approach of Keynesianism was replaced with what has come to be termed as the neoliberal approach. Neoliberal policies, a laissez-faire approach in a late 20th-century form, involved supporting 'free markets', competition and deregulation, and a smaller role for the state, achieved through privatisation and limits on the ability of governments to run fiscal deficits (Ostry et al, 2016). As part of the neoliberal policy direction in housing, governments and states shifted from being direct

Figure 6.1: Social housing completions in Ireland, 1970–2016

ESB connections (number) by housing sector and year (number)

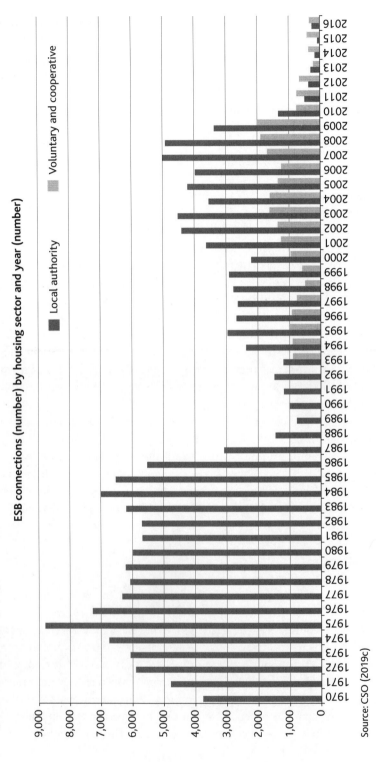

Source: CSO (2019c)

suppliers of affordable and public housing to facilitators of the private property market. This was underpinned by strong ideological support for home ownership as part of a promotion of the neoliberal values of individualism, private wealth accumulation, a reduced state role in regulating markets and providing services, and the establishment of the private market as the central mechanism for organising the economy and society (Kemeny, 1981).

Under neoliberalism, housing was commodified (Madden and Marcuse, 2016) and social housing was privatised and marketised (Hearne, 2011). The market, rather than the state or government, became the principal provider of housing. This meant that housing was primarily treated as a market commodity (like cars, televisions and so on) rather than a home meeting people's needs and rights. Housing increasingly became valued primarily for its 'exchange' value, as an investment asset providing capital appreciation, a return on investment, and a source of rental income and wealth generation rather than its use value as a home. This neoliberal approach was underpinned by the theory (and belief) that the market forces of supply and demand are the best determinants of supply and price of housing. Price settles or reaches 'equilibrium' when supply equals demand, and housing supply will respond to market indicators such as increasing demand. Housing as a commodity, whose price and provision is subject to laws of supply and demand of the market, has a very different relationship to its users from that which applies to housing provided as a basic human need and social right.

This neoliberal approach found its most pronounced expression in the Conservative governments in the UK in the 1980s under Margaret Thatcher. However, it has been pursued in various forms, and different extents, by governments across the world. As a political ideology, it viewed social housing as a failed form of housing for a lower class of citizen and which created a dependency culture. It dismissed the conceptualisation of social housing as an essential social need and public service for vulnerable people and those on low incomes. Promoting home ownership was also a way of undermining political support for the Labour Party (the proponents of social housing) and its control over local councils. The stigmatisation and undermining of social housing was part of a political and ideological project to dismantle the welfare state and the idea of rights to housing, health, education and so on. This ideology blamed and criminalised the poor for being in poverty, and placed the responsibility for poverty on the individual, rather than on the structural inequality resulting from capitalism.

Home ownership, long promoted as the ideal form of housing by conservative politicians because of its promotion of the 'diligent responsible man', was further promulgated as the cornerstone of unbounded neoliberal capitalism, which promised to make everyone an owner in 'shareholder capitalism'.

Financialisation

This idealisation of home ownership occurred in tandem with the expansion of financialisation through opening up mortgage lending to financial investments and the trading of such mortgages on the international financial markets, thus making housing and 'real estate' an important financial commodity in global markets. Housing was no longer geographically tied to one area but became part of global flows of finance seeking the most profitable investment opportunity. As a result, the tension between housing (and land) as a form of shelter (its use value) and housing as an asset class (its exchange value) grew significantly (Aalbers, 2015).

The expansion of financialisation has involved the increased dominance of financial actors (banks, lenders, private equity and hedge funds) and financial markets in the economy since the 1980s, when financial markets were deregulated, supported by tax incentives and facilitated by technological development. This deregulation of financial and mortgage markets turned housing into a liquid financial commodity. Madden and Marcuse (2016: 31) explain this process of financialisation of housing in the following terms: 'Managers, bankers and rentiers produce profits from real estate through buying, financing, selling, owning, and speculating.'

The first wave of financialisation took place from the 1980s up to the crash of 2008 and involved the expansion of credit for mortgaged home ownership and the investment purchase of housing to 'flip' or rent. The asset-based welfare state also promoted this discourse, whereby housing was viewed as an asset that could provide a future pension, as the welfare state and employers reduced their pension provision (Dewilde and De Decker, 2016). The financialisation of housing was also fuelled by the opening up of increased capital flows, as occurred in Ireland following the deregulation of the European financial system in the 1990s and 2000s.

This financialisation saw the creation of financial products such as mortgage securitisation, involving the bundling of risky and less risky mortgages into more profitable investment products traded on financial markets (Lowe, 2011).

The deregulation and expansion of housing finance also played a central role in the financialisation of the Irish and international economy. During this period, the financialisation of housing became central to debt-fuelled economic growth. Housing became a key business of banks and financial institutions, estate agents, solicitors, developers and wider parts of the economy. It also contributed to the growth in gross domestic product – anything between 3% and 15% annually. For home owners, rising house prices led to increased consumer spending/consumption (and increased borrowing, leveraging equity in housing). The dramatic expansion of household debt, a form of privatised Keynesianism (Crouch, 2011), was enabled through measures such as the removal of lending regulations and the introduction of subprime lending and equity release on homes, which provided a continued increase in consumption despite stagnant incomes and increasing inequality. Rather than the main consideration being one of access to a home, the financial, policy and political sectors encouraged people to get their 'foot on the property ladder', treating housing as an investment asset.

Marketisation

Harvey (2005) describes neoliberalism as a process of 'accumulation by dispossession'. It is about creating 'unlimited' market opportunities for the private sector (that is, entrepreneurs, mainly those with huge wealth, and corporations) within public governance, services and infrastructure through the privatisation and commodification of all public goods and infrastructure. The dismantling of the welfare state under neoliberalism was to be undertaken through a process of privatisation and the imposition of market mechanisms, ethos and disciplines on public services – in other words, the marketisation of public services. Marketisation would be done through, among other things, deregulation (introduction of a diversity of providers through competition between them at every level of delivery), the contracting out and outsourcing of public services to the private sector, and the transfer of assets and services to private ownership. The ideal neoliberal government would only regulate and monitor the private sector, which would deliver and operate public infrastructure and services. Private sector delivery, it was claimed, would improve service delivery, effectiveness and increase cost-efficiency.

The interrelated processes of financialisation, privatisation and marketisation opened up the public housing system and state mortgage lending, which had developed in a largely 'non-market' sphere, to private investment and private companies, thus providing new pathways and opportunities for capital accumulation (profit making). The withdrawal of the state from the large-scale, direct supply of public and affordable housing transferred the provision of housing to large sections of the working and poor populations on the basis of need to provision on the basis of market rules, where if you can afford it you get it, but if not, you don't.

Neoliberalism in Irish housing

While Ireland promoted a form of public, subsidised home ownership throughout the 20th century as part of the Irish 'social contract' and support for a conservative state, the neoliberal era involved government and the state making a marked shift in Irish housing policy towards commodification through financialisation and marketisation and the promotion of housing as a financialised asset. It involved handing over the provision and financing of housing from the state, which had provided affordable loans and grants to home owners, to banks and financial institutions, which made access to borrowing for home ownership much more expensive. Ireland thus shifted to promoting a housing model of heavily indebted, mortgaged home ownership and the withdrawal of the state from providing affordable ownership and a radical reduction in the role of local authorities in building public housing. The 'right to buy' for tenants in council housing, the effective sell-off of local authority housing, was extended.

Local authorities' ability and capacity to develop housing was radically reduced with the removal of their facility to borrow for building social housing and a reduced role in issuing mortgages in the mid- to late 1980s. The financing of public housing shifted instead to annual capital grants from central government; essentially, the power and control over public housing shifted from local to central government. This move was to have significant negative impacts on social housing provision in the following decades. The marked decline in direct-build social housing provision in the 1980s is illustrated in Figure 6.1, alongside the growing role of housing associations in the provision of social housing. The number of dwellings rented from local authorities in Ireland, which had steadily increased to reach 125,000 in 1961, dropped consistently thereafter to 88,000 units in 2002 (Drudy and Punch, 2005).

The challenges faced in the 1980s as a result of rising inequality, unemployment, drugs and poor local authority estate management in large public housing estates were exploited to develop a stigmatising discourse that all social and public housing was a 'failure'.

In 1961, 18.4% of housing stock was social housing but this reduced to 15% in 1971, 12.5% in 1981, 9% in 1991 and just 7% in 2002. The market became the dominant provider of housing, and in 2005, local authorities built 4,209 units, representing only 4.8% of housing provided (Drudy and Punch, 2005). Ninety-five per cent of housing was provided by the private sector leaving the non-market sector of public provision residualised.

Public–private partnerships

The shift to marketisation in Irish social housing policy and delivery accelerated in the 1990s through various mechanisms including 'entrepreneurial' planning, public–private partnerships (PPPs) between local authorities and private developers, the sourcing of social housing from the private rental sector and purchase of social housing from the private market.

Apart from the supposed financial benefits to the state, the PPP model was also designed to fulfil the government policy aim of a mix of housing tenures (social and private ownership and private rental) in areas that had a high concentration of local authority housing. The assumptions of the benefits of 'mixed tenure' were underpinned by an anti-public housing bias and based on the residualised social housing approach, rather than mixed-income public housing. Policy viewed large-scale, social rented housing as problematic and undesirable, while Dublin City Council expressed its desire to transfer responsibility for managing social housing to housing associations, and policy promoted home ownership as the ideal tenure, whereby most people would have their housing needs met from the market, with a residualised form of social housing meeting the needs of the extremely disadvantaged.

Unsurprisingly, then, PPPs were used as a key mechanism to regenerate disadvantaged, run-down social housing estates. These new PPP regeneration plans involved demolishing existing social homes and replacing them with largely private housing on these former public housing estates. In some cases, this meant a four-to-one ratio of private to public housing in the new developments.

The PPP model required the development of regeneration plans that suited the requirements of the private developer and financial capital and not those of communities or social housing provision. As the property market boomed, the number of projects being planned expanded rapidly. By May 2008, Dublin City Council was engaged in, or planning, the regeneration of at least 12 large local authority estates in the inner city through this mechanism. The ensuing projects would involve the privatisation of valuable public land, the dislocation and destruction of inner-city communities housed on the estates, and a reduction in the quantity of social housing units located within those communities. The communities and thousands of social housing units were razed to the ground, and the land that had housed thousands of low-income families was to lie idle for well over a decade to come.

From bricks to benefits

A further example of marketisation of public housing was the increasing use of income support subsidies (housing benefit) to assist tenants in the private rented sector (Drudy and Punch, 2005). As state investment into building local authority housing waned, housing need was growing during the 1990s and 2000s with increasing numbers of low-income households unable to afford rising housing prices. Without the availability of public council housing, these households had no choice but to access housing in the private rental sector. The proportion of households living in private rented accommodation increased for the first time since records began from 8.1% in 1991 to 11.4% in 2002 (Drudy and Punch, 2005).

These low-income households in the private rental sector required support to cover rising rent costs. A housing benefit, the Rent Supplement, was introduced in 1987 as a rental subsidy for private rental tenants unable in the short term (due to unemployment, underemployment or illness) to afford to pay private rent. This rental supplement scheme was administered through the Community Welfare Service as a form of temporary income support and was not understood when it was introduced initially as meeting a social housing need. In the decade from 1994 to 2004, Rent Supplement claimant numbers increased by 101%, from 28,800 households in 1994 to 57,874 households in 2003, whereas the number of mainstream social housing tenants increased by just 15% in the same period. Thus, subsidised private rented housing became a crucial substitute for social housing in the 1990s and 2000s. By the height of the 2000s housing boom, the number of households living in government-subsidised private rented housing had reached half the number living in mainstream social housing (60,694 compared with 130,300) (Hearne and Murphy, 2017).

Part V, Planning and Development Act 2000

Part V of the Planning and Development Act 2000 required, as a condition for planning permission, that up to 20 per cent of private land zoned for housing development can be obtained by a local authority towards the delivery of social and affordable housing through the transfer of lands (at existing use value rather than development value), the build and transfer of houses (for which the local authority must pay to purchase), or the private developer paying an agreed amount to the local authority. However, even this limited intervention in the market was resisted hugely by the developer-finance-construction industry and in 2002, the government amended the Act under pressure from lobbying by developers. The change allowed local authorities to opt out of enforcing the onsite 20% rule and instead allow approval of Part V status if the developer gave the local authority land elsewhere or the financial equivalent of the value of the land transfer. Many local authorities used the amendment to opt out of enforcing the 20% per cent social housing rule, and Part V therefore had a lower than expected impact on the provision of social housing. Between its introduction in 2000 and 2011, nearly 13% of additional social housing was procured using Part V, with most of it transferred to and managed by voluntary housing bodies rather than local authorities, which saw themselves as 'getting out' of the management of social housing.

Table 6.1: Social housing in Ireland: from direct state provision to privatisation and marketisation

1930s–1970s	Significant direct role of state in delivery of social housing, and state support for affordable home ownership and tenant purchase	18% of total housing stock is social housing
1980s	Removal of local authorities' ability to borrow and build, reduction in capital funding for new build, extended tenant purchase and 'surrender' grant	12.7% of housing stock is social housing in 1981
	Financialisation of mortgage markets	
1990s/2000s	Shift to reliance on private rental accommodation (Rent Supplement), Part V, acquisition, PPP	6.9% of housing stock is social housing 2002
	A third of new social housing purchased from private market, 40% of the additional social rented dwellings provided between 1990 in 2007 were sold to tenants	

Expansion of home ownership under neoliberalism

Throughout the 1990s, a wide range of measures such as government grants, tax incentives and mortgage interest relief, aimed at supporting private housing development and promoting owner-occupied housing, and were provided to home owners, investors and developers. Local authorities and semi-state development agencies also undertook 'fast-track' planning permissions and rezoning to facilitate private housing development.

The promotion of mortgaged home ownership and the purchase of additional property through 'buy to lets' as an investment was supported and justified by policy makers under the discourse of the asset-based approach to the welfare state. This involved individuals being encouarged to accept more responsibility for satisfying their own welfare needs by investing in financial products and assets expected to increase in value and be realised in times of need, for example as a future pension. As housing assets became main mode of asset accumulation in the late 20th century, asset-based welfare became increasingly mainfest as a form of 'property-based' or even 'home ownership-based' welfare. It has been argued that there is likely to be a policy trade-off between home ownership and welfare state development.

Home ownership, therefore, was particularly important in liberal welfare state regimes such as that Ireland, with its minimal welfare state. Those who can afford to buy a house seek to use it to compensate for the deficiency of pensions, healthcare and elderly care. Home ownership is understood as a hedge against income insecurity in old age. As a result, home-ownership levels increased in Ireland from 68% in 1971 to reach 80% in 1991, one of the highest rates of ownership in Europe (Norris and Redmond, 2005).

However, the reduction in social housing availability and its residualised restriction to groups with the lowest incomes, combined with the lack of a secure and affordable private rental sector in Ireland, meant people had little choice but to try to get a mortgage and purchase a home. This then added to increased demand for purchases through the private market, and when this was backed by excessive credit lending, it led to increased and ultimately unsustainable house prices. Thus home ownership (and the aspiration to achieve it) was not, in many instances, a choice, but a necessity, to access a secure home. And many of those who bought a home in the 1990s and 2000s as a result of the lack of an option of social or secure private rental housing, became 'subprime' borrowers who took on unsustainable levels of debt and were hit hardest when the housing bubble burst in 2008 and resulted in the mortgage arrears crisis.

The bubble bursts

From the 1980s to the 2000s, rising house prices and asset values were viewed as a political triumph by the centre-left and centre-right governments. They all supported the financialisation of housing and saw it as key to political support among the high- and middle-income voting classes, but also among working-class people who wanted to 'better themselves'. However, the extension of home ownership required a huge expansion of credit – to many for whom it was unsustainable. The dramatic rise in credit enabled the deepening indebtedness of mortgaged home owners and a significant increase in buy-to-let mortgages for property as an investment, all of which further fuelled price increases. These were facilitated by the increased flows of capital and finance among financial institutions and global financial markets that poured into 'hot' housing markets seeking huge returns and were underpinned by the belief that house prices would just keep rising.

However, inevitably the bubble burst, with devastating consequences for citizens, cities, economies and states. As the global economy slowed and the subprime banking crisis worsened (triggered by low-income households defaulting on mortgages acquired from subprime lenders in the US), house price rises in Ireland started to slow in September 2006, levelling off in March 2007 and remaining static until November 2007. By the beginning of 2008, it was clear that the promise of a 'soft landing' was empty and all of the issues built up over the course of the Celtic Tiger boom years – massive growth in housing and land prices, household and bank debt, overzoning and overbuilding – exploded into a new set of crises as the property bubble burst.

From the peak of the housing boom in 2008 to its nadir in 2012, house prices fell by 57% in Dublin and 48% in the rest of the country. Ireland experienced one of the deepest house market collapses on record. The economy and house prices went into serious decline, resulting in the Irish bank guarantee of September 2008, the creation of a state-owned National Assets Management Agency (NAMA) in September 2009 (which utilised €34 billion of public funds to purchase €74 billion of distressed property loans from the Irish banks), and an €85 billion bailout by the International Monetary Fund and European Central Bank in November 2010. A period of harsh austerity cutbacks in public expenditure was enforced. The costs of the housing boom and the failure of the neoliberal housing policy regime were to be borne by Irish society and ordinary people across the world, with future generations laden with permanent austerity when private financial institutions were bailed out and states took on their debt. The austerity and deepening marketisation in social housing policies, combined with the Irish state's response to the crisis of facilitating a second wave of financialisation in order to attract global investors to buy up distressed assets from NAMA and provide private rental housing, was to have profound implications for the Irish housing system, and for housing need and inequality, which is the subject of Chapter 7.

Ireland's market-dominated housing system, and alternative cost rental housing systems, can be usefully understood and explained using Kemeny's concept of dualist and unitary rental systems.

Cost rental housing: unitary and dualist housing systems

A very useful framework for understanding different 'housing regimes' or housing systems and their effectiveness is that provided by Kemeny (1981, 1995). Kemeny makes the case that different housing models result from the various constellations of power relationships, ideological beliefs and cultural patterns in how a country treats housing. Different housing regimes vary in terms of the emphasis placed on market or non-market provision, the predominance of home ownership or rental options, the role afforded social or non-profit housing, and the level of financialisation. These various models have different outcomes in terms of efficiency, equity, quality, cost and security. In countries where financialisation and market provision are dominant, inequality is exacerbated.

Kemeny points out that as vested market interests are more prominent in housing than in other welfare sectors, the housing market is likely to reflect the power balance between different interest groups. Kemeny discusses the place of housing in the welfare system, emphasising this dimension of power. Ideological factors are therefore crucial in understanding the long-term approach towards housing in any one country. This is not just the politics of particular governments and their policy decisions, but rather a more general societal ideology, which influences attitudes and expectations about welfare, states and markets.

Kemeny (1981) draws on Esping-Andersen's (1990) varieties of welfare states, where different configurations of class power produced different welfare states characterised by degrees of decommodification (a greater role for non-market public provision, people protected from the market), stratification and universality (universal availability of public services and income supports rather than a system based on means testing). All other things being equal, more power for labour (trade unions, left-wing political parties) should produce a correspondingly higher level of decommodification and universality. Using this framework, Ireland's highly commodified housing system can be seen to reflect the low level of labour power and left-wing political ideology in government, and the dominance of centre-right conservative politics and ideology.

Kemeny (1995) distinguished between different rental systems. First, the 'dualist' rental system is one where the state controls and residualises the social (non-profit) rented sector, and thus protects the unregulated private (for-profit) renting sector from competition from a mixed-income public housing alternative. This dualist regime is evident in liberal welfare states such as the UK, Ireland, Spain, Portugal and Italy. Table 6.2 provides examples of dualist countries which are marked by high levels of owner occupation (around 70%), a for-profit rental sector (private rental sector) ranging between 10% and 25% of households, a restricted means-tested social housing sector of between 5% and 20%, and no cost rental or not-for-profit private rental sector.

In contrast, in the 'unitary' rental system, social and private renting are integrated into a single rental market where social rental ('cost rental') housing is available to all households regardless of income, and is thus allowed to compete for tenants with the for-profit rental sector. The unitary system derives mainly from a social market strategy where the social or non-profit rental sector (principally cost rental housing) is accessible for all social groups. In addition, the private for-profit rental sector is strongly regulated. To maintain fair competition within a unitary system, the state delivers a tenure-neutral subsidy system by distributing housing benefit across all tenures. Examples of countries with a unitary system are shown in Table 6.2, and are marked by lower levels of owner occupation (between 35% and 55%), higher levels of for-profit rental sectors ranging between 20% and 40% of households, and a cost rental or not-for-profit private rental sector of between 18% and 25% of households and no restricted means-tested social housing sector.

In the unitary, or integrated, housing system, the social or non-profit rental sector tends to reduce rents in the private sector, thus increasing the affordability and accessibility of the whole rental and housing market across all income groups. Proportionally, by keeping rents lower than mortgage outgoings, this system lessens pressures and demand for owner occupation and moderates real estate speculation, thus making

Table 6.2: Housing tenure in various European countries and their capital/large cities

Country	City	Social housing as % of total housing stock	Universal/generalist or targeted/restricted eligibility social housing	Home ownership as % of total housing stock	Cooperative housing as % of total housing stock	Private rental
Netherlands		30%	Universal	59%	2%	9%
	Amsterdam	42%				
Austria		24%	Universal	50%	11%	15%
	Vienna	43%				
Denmark		21%	Universal	52%	10%	17%
	Copenhagen	28%				
Sweden		18%	Universal	42%	23% (tenant ownership/cooperative)	17%
UK		17%	Targeted	65%		18%
	Manchester	30%				
	Belfast	27%				
France		16%	Targeted	58%	5%	21%
	Paris	19%				
Ireland		10%	Targeted	69%		21%
	Dublin	13.2%				

Source: Housing Europe (2019)

home ownership more affordable. Low-income groups have access to high-quality rental houses and the middle-income groups can choose between home ownership and public or private renting. In general, the high-income groups are in home ownership and low-income groups are predominantly in the rental sector, while the middle class is divided among these two tenures providing a socio-tenure mix.

Dualist housing systems, therefore, result in artificially induced housing shortages. This is because 'profit renting has never in any period of history been able to satisfactorily meet the demands for rental housing and when cost renting is structured in such a manner as to limit its availability then rental housing shortages are almost inevitable' (Kemeny, 1995: 152).

The choice that is made available to the vast majority of households is that between owner occupation and for-profit renting. The latter, with its high insecurity of tenure, rents that gravitate towards a return on the current market value of property, and often high levels of landlord selectivity from among potential tenants and interference in domestic matters, creates a housing system in which the only form of housing that offers security of tenure, and at least an element of non-profit extraction, is owner occupation. Dualism therefore channels demand into owner occupation (Kemeny, 1995: 152). Kemeny also hypothesised that the total cost of housing in a society is higher in dualist systems as housing provision is more commodified (for example, through mortgaged home ownership and private renting), as more players in the chain of housing provision need to make a profit (for example, through capital gains, trading up, overconsumption and debt maximisation).

In a unitary housing system, by contrast, a 'social market' is encouraged, wherein both profit and non-profit provision meets general needs, and the cost rental affordable housing model ensures a steady, stable supply of affordable housing (Drudy and Punch, 2005).

The Irish housing system was, and continues to be, a textbook example of the dualist model identified by Kemeny (1995).

7

The new waves of financialisation: vultures and REITs

The Irish state's strategy to overcome the global property and financial crash of 2008 and achieve the recovery of financial institutions and the wider economy was based on the sale of 'toxic' and 'non-performing' loans and associated land and property, at a considerable discount, to international 'vulture funds' and property investors via the National Asset Management Agency (NAMA) and domestic banks. Central to this approach was supporting rental and house price inflation to bring about a recovery in the property market and therefore asset prices, and thus increase the attractiveness of these loans to potential vulture and investor fund purchasers, and improve the balance sheets of the bailed-out Irish banks. The strategy was based on a deepening of the financialisation of the Irish housing (and wider property) system. Irish governments enticed the 'wall of money' of private equity, global investors and vulture funds into Ireland to buy up the toxic loans and assets from NAMA, from the liquidators of the Irish Bank Resolution Corporation (IBRC, the former Anglo Irish Bank) and from the other Irish banks. In 2013, an emerging housing shortage became a further rationale of the government to justify incentives for global property funds that it was hoped would contribute to increasing the 'supply' of housing.

This chapter explains how this policy approach, enacted by the Irish state and the Fianna Fáil- and Fine Gael-led governments over the period 2008–19, but in particular during the Fine Gael–Labour government of 2011–16, has resulted in 'non-bank entities' such as vulture funds and international financial institutions purchasing large bundles of mortgages at a discount from Irish financial institutions, the hoarding of land bought at discount from NAMA and the banks by foreign investors, the increased purchase by investors of new and existing housing pushing out prospective home owners, a massive inflation in rents fuelled by Ireland's new investor landlord class, the real estate investment trusts (REITs), and increasing repossessions of homes and buy-to-let property. Through NAMA and the sale of assets from the winding-up of the former Anglo Irish Bank and other Irish banks, vulture funds had bought up to 90,000 properties and held at least €10.3 billion worth of assets in Ireland by 2016 (RTÉ One, 2017).

The US global equity funds, vultures and real estate giants are in the process of transforming the Irish housing system, especially in Dublin, making it less affordable and more unequal. These are the new property moguls, the new developers, the new landlords – and they have very little connection to, or interest in, the homes and the people that live in them, or the cities in which they invest, other than the maximisation of the return and profits on their investment. Just like the Irish developers in previous decades, the new global property finance cabal has formed a close relationship with politicians, civil servants and government, and has had growing influence on housing and economic policy. The current housing crisis results, in large part, from the orientation of housing policy towards their interests, visible in the reluctance of government to intervene in rising house prices and rents during the period 2013–17. This chapter shows how these policies were promoted to entice global investors to buy up NAMA properties and land, while rising house prices and rents were also viewed as necessary for rehabilitating the balance sheets of the banks, a core aim of all policy after the 2008 global financial crisis. The other aim was to bring home owners out of negative equity, the core key Fine Gael and Fianna Fáil voter base. The impact on the wider housing system and homelessness, on Generation Rent, on inequality, on the economy and society, was not considered to be important.

NAMA, the state's 'bad' bank, creates a second wave of financialisation

The launch of NAMA was announced by the Minister for Finance, Brian Lenihan, in the government's emergency Budget in April 2009. The Irish banks – Allied Irish Banks (AIB), Bank of Ireland, Anglo Irish Bank and Irish Nationwide – transferred toxic loans to the value of €72 billion to NAMA, thus removing them from the banks' balance sheets to enable them lend again to the wider economy. NAMA purchased approximately 12,000 loans, belonging to 850 debtors, including around 60,000 properties as security, at the discounted rate of €32 billion. This was part of the €64 billion in public funds transferred by the Irish state to the various banks to bail them out and enable them to recapitalise following the crash. While initially promising to 'chase developers to the ends of the earth' (*Irish Examiner*, 2019b) to get them to repay their loans and recoup taxpayers' bail-out costs, over time NAMA became more focused on just selling off its assets and loans as quickly as possible at a discount. Following its election to government in 2011, Fine Gael subsequently encouraged NAMA to 'wind up early', offload its loans and associated property and land assets, and pay off the €32 billion debt. There was little attention given to alternatives such as a long-term role for NAMA in using its land and property to provide affordable housing and inclusive, sustainable urban development. NAMA officials (operating under direction from the Minister of Finance) prioritised Section 10 of the National Asset Management Agency Act 2009 to 'obtain the best achievable financial return for the state'. NAMA's aim was to achieve maximum commercial return for the state through optimising the 'income and disposal value' of its assets to 'sustain the strong performance of the Irish property market' (Daly, 2014: 2). NAMA thus played a central role in implementing the state policy of reigniting the Irish property market through selling off toxic loans and assets at a considerable discount to international vulture and property investors. Through 2013 and 2014, as rents and house prices increased rapidly, NAMA's strategy was 'to increase significantly the flow of assets to the market to tap into the increased international – and increasingly domestic – investor interest in Irish real estate' (Daly, 2014: 3).

NAMA argued in 2015 and 2016 that prices needed to rise further in order to attract further foreign capital into the market, stating that 'many of those who are interested in buying development land in the Dublin area at the moment will have rate of return targets of 15%-20% and realistically those targets are unlikely to be met unless market prices rise significantly from current levels' (Daly, 2014: 3).

NAMA sold off its residential and land assets in the form of packaged 'portfolios' of property to international investors. Ninety per cent of assets sold by NAMA went to US equity and vulture funds. NAMA was the key driver of sales of portfolios of loans to global investors in Ireland in this period. It explicitly stated that 'certain assets were sold early in the cycle to drive market recovery and to attract international capital willing to invest in Ireland' while claiming it was 'doing all we can to support the recovery of the country's property markets ... and to channel investment into the Irish economy' (NAMA, 2017: 2).

The problem with this approach was that while it might have appeared that NAMA was maximising the commercial return to the state and taxpayer, this was a very short-term and narrow lens of analysis. I pointed out at the time that NAMA was playing a major role in worsening the housing crisis and thus adding to the long-term economic and social costs to the state and Irish people.

NAMA sold off loans, land and property to foreign vulture funds that then evicted tenants and raised rents to unaffordable levels. It sold portfolios of residential property on the basis of continued rising residential rents into the future. For example, it sold its Orange portfolio (including 761 residential apartments in the Greater Dublin area) for €211 million in 2014 to Irish Residential Properties Real Estate Investment Trust (IRES REIT). NAMA advertised the portfolio as providing a residential rental income of €10.6 million. Selling to investors with this expected rate of return placed huge upward pressure on rents for these apartments and the wider market.

Selling to the vultures

Vulture and private equity funds that have purchased assets from NAMA and other Irish banks include Deutsche Bank, Cerberus, Barclays, CarVal, Oaktree, Goldman Sachs and Apollo. These acquired in excess of €2 billion of portfolios each between 2015 and 2018. Cerberus has so far been the largest purchaser in the Irish market, having purchased assets worth more than €15 billion. There were non-performing loan sales worth €39.7 billion between 2015 and 2018, and NAMA alone sold loans worth €11 billion between 2016 and 2018.

The US real estate giant, Hines, worth €93 billion, bought the Project Cherry portfolio from NAMA for €270 million in 2014, along with another American fund, King Street Capital Management. This portfolio included the largest development site in south County Dublin – the 166-hectare Cherrywood site. Hines plans to invest €2 billion creating Dublin's newest suburb in Cherrywood. In a joint venture with Dutch pension investor APG Asset Management, Hines has developed plans for 1,221 build-to-rent apartments in Cherrywood. Hines and King Street also sold 47 hectares of the development land in Cherrywood to US vulture fund Lone Star for a reported €140 million. This shows how real estate vulture investors are making hundreds of millions in profits (which will be paid for through rising house prices and rents) from the Irish housing market by flipping land and properties, facilitated by the Irish state by acquiring the assets at discount from NAMA.

US property fund Marathon Asset Management purchased Project Plum from NAMA in 2015, including 588 apartments, for a reported €120 million. It then sold the apartments in 2019 to IRES REIT, as part of a larger portfolio of 815 apartments for €285 million, in the largest single disposal of buy-to-let properties to take place in the Irish market. Bidders for the portfolio were told that they could take advantage of the rental shortage and increase rental income from €14.7 million to €17.7 million per annum, a 20% increase in rents. Marathon is likely to have made tens of millions in profit from this one sale alone. This gives an indication of the type of super-profits being made by these large global funds on the backs of the Irish taxpayer and Irish people.

Oaktree, a US equity fund worth €97 billion, and its subsidiary Mars Capital, bought from NAMA the Project Emerald and Project Ruby portfolios, which included commercial and residential property loans worth €4.7 billion, for just €800 million. There were approximately 900 apartments and residential units in this portfolio, including the Limerick Strand apartments where tenants faced eviction in 2017. Blackrock, the world's largest asset management agency, bought commercial and student housing units in Dublin Docklands from NAMA in 2016.

Kennedy Wilson, another large US real estate investor, has also bought sites and developments from NAMA, with which it has partnered in a joint development venture. Kennedy Wilson has bought €1.5 billion of assets in Ireland, including more than 1,300 new residential units in various stages of development. These are part of prominent Dublin projects such as Clancy Quay, The Grange, and City Block 3. Kennedy Wilson also bought the iconic Gasworks building in the Dublin 4 high-tech area, in 2012. Ireland is set to become the biggest EU market for Kennedy Wilson.

Lone Star, the multibillion US private equity firm that invests in distressed assets internationally, owned by American-Irish billionaire John Grayken, has also purchased assets from NAMA, the Irish Bank Resolution Corporation (IBRC) and other banks. Grayken was ranked Ireland's third richest person in the *Sunday Independent* 2018 rich list, with a fortune of €5.8 billion. The newspaper stated that Grayken made his fortune by making a 20% return on his investment in 'buying distressed assets in bombed out economies and flipping them as markets improved' (Sunday Independent, 2018). Lone Star bought 60% of all assets sold by the IBRC. In 2014 and 2015, Lone Star bought (as a minority partner with Cairn Homes) a portfolio of Ulster Bank loans worth €5 billion that included 687 hectares of prime residential land in Dublin, as well as office and retail blocks.

Goldman Sachs, another multibillion-dollar US multinational investment fund, bought mortgage loans in 2014 from Ulster Bank and AIB via its Beltany Property Finance subsidiary. In 2016 there was major controversy when householders in the Tyrrelstown development were issued notices of eviction after Goldman Sachs bought the loans. In March 2016, it was reported that up to 200 families from the estate could be evicted as a result of Goldman Sachs taking over the loan (*Irish Mirror*, 2016).

Corporate welfare for REITs and vulture funds

To make matters worse, REITs and vulture funds receive subsidies ('corporate welfare') from the Irish state, which worsens the housing crisis. Between 2010 and 2019, the Irish state, through NAMA in particular, but also via IBRC and other banks, played a pivotal role in selling a huge swathe of Irish property, homes and land at a discount to REITs, vulture funds and global property investors. It was an example of corporate welfare from the Irish state to the global wealth funds. NAMA provided the asset sales to start what was to become an avalanche of investor landlords and vulture funds in Ireland. IRES REIT is explicit about how NAMA, by providing them with these assets, transformed the Irish rental market: 'With the closing of this transaction, our property portfolio will grow to a total of 1,202 apartment suites, transforming IRES into Ireland's largest non-governmental residential landlord' (IRES REIT, 2014).

NAMA has also been involved in financing and developing (with funds such as Oaktree and Kennedy Wilson) its assets in the most profitable forms of property development, providing office (commercial) real estate, and luxury prime residential apartments and expensive homes, rather than affordable housing. A fifth of all the homes built using NAMA funding have been sold to corporate investors and 40% of NAMA homes were sold for over €400,000.

Between 2010 and 2015, NAMA sold development land (sites) to investors that had the potential for up to 20,000 housing units. However, most of this land was hoarded, as investors watched land prices (and their future profits) rise with no concern for the impact on the housing market in Ireland. Just 1,100 (5%) of the land bought from NAMA was developed by 2016.

The speculative purchase of land by these investors also enabled them to exert considerable control over the production and prices of housing. The availability of land is a prerequisite for the provision of housing and therefore those who own or control it can exercise what has been called a 'double monopoly' (Yamada, 1999). First, there is obviously a relatively fixed supply of land. Second, land for housing depends on the willingness of landowners to release and sell for such purposes. When there is excess demand for housing, the inevitable outcome is an upward pressure on the price of land. This creates an artificial scarcity and in turn encourages more hoarding.

NAMA's approach has thus contributed to the worsening housing crisis. NAMA has played a significant role in initiating a second wave of financialisation of housing and land in Ireland, especially in Dublin, by developing land and housing according to its highest 'exchange' value rather than prioritising its most needed social 'use' value (that is, for affordable housing).

I commented on NAMA's problematic approach in an article in the *Irish Times* (Hearne, 2014):

> The uncomfortable truth is that those who will benefit most from Government housing policy, and NAMA in particular, are international wealthy investors and banks, developers and landlords – and not the ordinary Irish people who have paid dearly for the write-downs on development loans transferred to Nama. The reality is that Nama is playing a significant role in worsening the housing crisis through its sale of assets.... Nama is facilitating a massive transfer of wealth created by the Irish people to foreign and domestic capitalist investors.... By pushing for maximum commercial returns, Nama is working against the interests of those looking for an affordable and secure home. It is continuing the speculative-asset approach to housing that fuelled the crisis. This promotes residential property as a commodity rather than a social good.

NAMA has given wealthy investors and global property funds a major opportunity for massive wealth accumulation at the expense of the Irish people. These investors have gained from purchasing NAMA land and assets at a discount and then selling them for higher prices, or from developing the assets and then charging escalating rents and house prices. They are making hundreds of millions in super-profits on their investments. For example, Blackstone, the world's biggest private equity firm, is said to have made in the region of €40 million profit from the sale of buildings it bought from NAMA in the Dublin Docklands area. Similarly, it has been speculated that Cerberus, the US company that bought the Project Eagle loans from NAMA, a deal which was subsequently subject to controversy (*Irish Times*, 2017b), made hundreds of millions in profit on the transaction. These profits do not come from thin air – they are paid for by the Irish people through the ongoing repayment of the bail-out debt, and especially renters and home purchasers through escalating rising rents and house prices. This clearly contributes to rising inequality.

The Irish public has lost billions of euros from the sale of massively discounted assets by NAMA and bailed-out banks, is losing out as a result of the higher prices and rents being charged by real estate investors, and is losing out further as the potential to use NAMA's assets to provide a social return in the long term through the provision of social and affordable housing is handed over to investment funds.

Unfortunately, Section 2 of the National Asset Management Agency Act 2009, which states that NAMA has a mandate 'to contribute to the social and economic development of the State', has been given very little priority within NAMA's activities. NAMA continues to worsen the housing crisis by pushing for 'maximum return' in the sale of the 20,000 houses it is selling over the coming years. Some NAMA developer-built, two-bed apartments are being currently advertised for sale at €500,000. This is a far cry from the promise of NAMA 'starter' homes made by the former Minister for Finance, Michael Noonan. Receivers acting for NAMA have even sought a reduction in social housing requirements as part of NAMA-partnered developments in Dublin's Poolbeg pensinsula. NAMA still has significant land and property assets that could be developed with Section 2 as its priority.

A tsunami of repossessions as vultures move in on home mortgages

'Non-bank entities', such as vulture funds and international financial institutions, have also purchased large bundles of mortgages at a discount from Irish financial institutions. These non-bank entities have dramatically increased their holding of the total Irish mortgage accounts since 2013. In the six years from 2013 to 2019, they went from holding just 2% of the total accounts in 2013 to 6% in 2016, reaching 14%, or one of seven, of all mortgage accounts in 2019. This equated to 118,448 mortgages and 18% (almost a fifth) of all mortgages in value terms in 2019. Non-bank entities held 13% of all primary dwelling houses (PDHs), that is, 92,413 home mortgage loans, and a quarter (24%) of all buy-to-let mortgages (26,035 accounts). They held 38% of all PDH mortgages in arrears, 44% of all PDH mortgages in arrears over 90 days, and almost a half (49%) of all PDH mortgages in arrears over 720 days. Of those non-bank entities, unregulated credit servicing firms held 2% of all PDH mortgages, and 22% (a fifth) of all PDH mortgages in arrears over 720 days. They also held a quarter of all buy-to-let mortgage accounts (in value terms). By 2019, non-bank entities held 20,357 restructured PDH mortgage accounts and 4,036 restructured BTL mortgage accounts (Central Bank of Ireland, 2019a).

Again, it is large US vulture and private equity firms that are purchasing these loans. For example, in 2019, the Permanent TSB (PTSB) bank, which is 75% state-owned, sold a portfolio of non-performing mortgage loans of 1,422 home mortgages and 510 buy-to-let mortgages, with a value of €274 million, to retail credit firms Start Mortgages and LSF Irish Holdings, both affiliates of Lone Star. In 2018, PTSB sold the Project Glas portfolio to an affiliate of Lone Star for around €1.3 billion. Within that portfolio, a total of 7,400 loans were owner-occupier mortgages, while 3,300 were buy-to-let properties. Project Glenbeigh, with loans worth €1.3 billion including 6,139 home mortgages, was also sold in 2018 through a securitisation agreement, which involves the loans being serviced by Pepper Finance Corporation (Ireland) DAC on behalf of vulture funds. Pepper now manages over 8% of the outstanding residential mortgages in the Irish market.

In other examples, Ulster Bank sold 5,200 non-performing mortgages (2,300 relating to homes and 2,900 covering buy-to-lets) in 2019 for €1.4 billion to a purchaser managed by affiliates of US vulture firm Cerberus Capital Management, and the nationalised bank AIB sold a €1 billion portfolio of 2,200 non-performing loans (of which 10% were family homes) to affiliates of Cerberus in 2018. AIB wrote to 1,500 customers in arrears, stating:

> We believe that we have gone to great lengths to contact you but you are still not in an arrangement to solve your mortgage problem…. If your mortgage loan remains in default with no arrangement in place, this leaves us very few ways to resolve the problem. Typically, in line with the bank's publicly stated position, mortgage loans like these end up with the loan being sold to a third party, or the home being repossessed.

The mortgages attached to thousands of family homes and rental buy-to-let properties (some in arrears, some restructured and some performing) are due to be sold by the various Irish banks to vultures in the coming months and years in order to reduce the levels of bank's non-performing loans (NLPs), under pressure from the European Central Bank.

Some of these NPL sales have involved customers who had been engaging with the banks and were fulfilling their restructuring arrangements but whose loans were still classified as NPLs. There was a strong narrative within the public debate put across by the banks, and supported by some politicians and high-profile economic commentators, that most of those in arrears were 'strategic defaulters' who had refused to engage with the bank and were opportunistically taking advantage of the crisis to stop paying their mortgages. However, research (CAN, 2018) into the lived experience of those in long-term arrears found high levels of anxiety, stress and ill health among people in arrears, which, coupled with a lack of financial capacity, advice and support, led to them 'giving up' and being left in a state of terror, waiting for repossession to take place. These people were living in fear of aggressive legal action. Kenna, who undertook a comparative study of evictions across Europe, explained to the *Irish Times* (2019) that discussion of strategic default is 'a diversion' and 'the reason for arrears is, by and large, people lost their incomes'.

There has been a growth in 'credit servicer' firms such as Pepper, Hudson, Finance Ireland, Magnetar, Link and Lapithus, all of which are owned by funds that have previously invested in the loan portfolio transaction market. Lone Star owns Hudson, Apollo owns Lapithus and Link manages distressed mortgages for Cerberus Capital. Surprisingly, the Irish State Investment Fund is a part-investor in Finance Ireland, a debt servicer of mortgages in arrears. The concern is that these servicer firms will ignore attempts by mortgage holders to meet their restructuring arrangements, and instead try to gain the property to sell or rent out.

One of the credit servicer firms recently described Ireland as 'the gift that keeps giving', stating that Irish lenders had lined up three loan portfolios with par values (face values) of between €4.5 billion and €5 billion each for sale before the end of 2019 in order to reduce the number of NLPs in its portfolio to less than 5% of its total loans. It expected the Irish banks to outsource the distressed mortgages remaining on its books to credit-servicing specialists. It also predicted that the vulture funds would resell some of the portfolios bought from Irish lenders to other private equity buyers, leading to an even greater likelihood of repossession in order to cover the return made by this speculative investment.

There is a severe inequality here: vulture funds buy the loans at a discount of up to 70%, but the mortgage holders in arrears are expected to pay back the full loan or face repossession.

Vulture and equity fund strategies to profit from distressed housing

We can see then that these private equity and vulture funds have a diversity of strategies to deal with these assets and loans. The vulture and investor funds, tend to make significant profits from buying the 'toxic' or 'distressed' loans at discount prices and then selling them on when the markets rise – as is going on now in Ireland. Some go about selling or flipping the properties in a short time frame, others wait for prices to rise before selling (hoarding), some develop them, and some repossess homes in arrears. But underpinning all the strategies and intervention by these international vulture, real estate and equity funds in the Irish residential system, is the drive to maximise the return on their investment from the assets and loans. And these large (mainly US) investment funds are not here to extract just small profits. They are investing on behalf of pension funds, high net worth individuals, shell companies (related to money laundering and criminal funds), global wealth funds, and private equity, all expecting massive returns. We can see then how this financialisation and vulture and equity fund takeover of the Irish property market and homes by vultures and giant US equity funds, is worsening inequality – by making generation rent and those being repossessed in Ireland pay for higher returns to the extremely wealthy US billionaires, wealth funds, and pension funds. It is a form of re-colonisation of Ireland, only this time the new landlords and masters are US funds.

Third wave of financialisation: build-to-rent investors squeeze out the home buyers and choke Generation Rent

The wave of global real estate and vulture investment in distressed assets and loans, highlighted in the preceding sections, can be described as the second wave of financialisation of residential property (housing), following the first wave of financial market and equity involvement in mortgage lending and securitisation from the late 1990s to 2008. A third wave of financialisation is evident in the post-2010 period as global institutional investors have increasingly invested in the private rental 'build-to-rent' sector. This third wave is a further development in the restructuring of the finance–real estate relationship through the increased role of large-scale corporate finance and global private equity funds (pension funds, hedge funds, wealth funds, shell funds, private equity) in the provision of rental residential property. It provides another important vehicle for investing the global 'wall of money' searching for higher returns in a context of reduced profitability and rising risk in the wider 'real' economy.

The increased interest in real estate and increasing inflows of equity from sovereign wealth funds and wealthy individuals (high-net-worth individuals) into real estate funds stems from its high rate of return in contrast to other sectors of economies like bonds or production. As one equity investor explains, "We're seeing an increased flow from high-net-worth or super-wealthy individuals who view the equity and bond markets as no longer offering them return and are therefore looking at real estate as a place to get return. It's pretty significant." However, residential homes as a form of real estate investment is also about wealthy individuals acquiring 'trophy assets'.

Property consultant Cushman & Wakefield's 'The great wall of money' report (2017) showed that in 2015 total trans-border real estate investments were valued at a record $443 billion, with investors 'particularly attracted to the supply/demand imbalance driven by population growth in many residential markets across European capital cities'. A report by PricewaterhouseCoopers (PwC) and the Urban Land Institute (2017) on emerging trends in real estate in Europe claimed that the 'build-to-rent' sector is seen as a 'compelling opportunity' because of the 'limitless demand' from private renters needing homes. Investment in real estate funds is also a way for global investors to minimise and avoid tax bills, and route funds from tax havens, and even criminal activities, into high-return, structured, legitimate areas of investment. REITs play a key role in opening up housing as an investment asset for global capital and equity.

REITs in Ireland: facilitating tax minimisation and property speculation

In order to further attract international investment into the Irish housing and property market, the government introduced a favourable new tax regime in 2012 to allow for the introduction of REITs in Ireland. This made rental profits arising in REITs exempt from corporation tax and other taxes. The then Fine Gael Minister for Finance, Michael Noonan, proclaimed in 2013 that the REIT framework was intended to "facilitate the attraction of foreign investment capital to the Irish property market". He further argued that "the acquisition and management of properties by professional REITs is part of a more sustainable, long-term property rental market for both investors and property tenants". He said REITs were set up "to facilitate collective investment in rental property by removing a double layer of taxation which would otherwise apply on property investment via a corporate vehicle" (Noonan, 2016b).

REITs have since expanded rapidly, with three REITs currently operating in Ireland with a market capitalisation value of €2.3 billion. For example, IRES REIT was set up in April 2014 as a subsidiary of CAPREIT (a Canadian REIT) and became the state's largest private landlord, owning 3,600 rental properties in Ireland. US real estate fund Kennedy Wilson has become one of Ireland's largest landlords, owning 2,100 residential units in Ireland, and is planning a further

1,300 new units in Dublin. In 2016, the chief executive officer of Kennedy Wilson stated that "Dublin is the most attractive property market in Europe".

Moreover, in 2016, in its key action plan for housing, *Rebuilding Ireland*, the government encouraged REITs and other institutional investors to develop in the build-to-rent residential sector:

> It is envisaged that Real Estate Investment Trusts (REITS) and other institutional investors which have been successful at raising development finance and investing in the commercial office sector, have the potential to begin significant investment in build-to-rent projects. (Department of Housing, Planning and Local Government, 2016b: 75)

Michael Noonan further extolled the virtues of the REITs, in the Dáil (lower house of the Irish parliament) in May 2016, when he said: "I introduced the real estate investment trusts, REITs, tax regime in the Finance Act 2013. This intervention has been successful in encouraging large scale investment into the commercial and residential property markets" (Noonan, 2016a).

The Department of Finance, in its 2013 document Tax Policy Rationale for REITs, explained that before the introduction of REITs, 'investment in property via corporate vehicles was not generally a tax-efficient option, due to the double layer of taxation that applies to profits earned in a company and then paid out to shareholders in the form of dividends' (Donaghy, 2013). Furthermore, it noted that prior to REITs there was a 'lack of a suitable avenue for collective investment, particularly for the smaller investor' in commercial and residential property. It also noted structural issues such as risks in the small landlord buy-to-let sector, manifest in the arrears crisis, and issues of standards in the private rental sector and the restricted availability of investment capital from the banking sector due to the financial crisis. It noted, therefore, that 'attracting alternative sources of investment capital to the property sector therefore has the potential to provide benefits' such as 'to facilitate investment into NAMA'. It also stated that 'by removing this double layer of taxation, REITs provide a framework for collective investment in property assets'. Instead of purchasing a single entire property, investors can buy shares in a REIT that holds a diversified property portfolio. Ownership of REIT shares, the document explains, 'also allows an investor to participate in returns from the property market without the need to manage and maintain a property personally'. According to the Department of Finance, the REIT model is also recognised and understood by large and institutional investors throughout the world and is therefore more attractive to these investors than specific 'Irish products' that would require 'due diligence work on the part of large investors before they feel sufficiently comfortable to invest'. A REIT vehicle, it states, 'would also provide a mechanism for property specialists to assemble a portfolio of investment property assets and then float that portfolio to retail and institutional investors worldwide'. Furthermore, the document asks if REITs can 'help Ireland become a hub for the financing and management of tax-efficient cross-border investment in rental property assets'. It points out that 'source-country taxing rights in multiple jurisdictions create difficulties in developing cross-border REITs' but that 'this problem is not insurmountable'. Essentially, it outlines the role of Irish REITs in the financialisation of housing globally (both extending investment into Irish residential property and using the Irish taxation regime to facilitate the development of cross-border real estate investment) and in aiding tax minimisation strategies of funds and equity investors.

Along with the REIT tax exemption, various other types of 'tax-efficient structures' and collective investment special purpose vehicles have been set up in Ireland, such as qualifying investor alternative investment funds (QIAIFs), Irish real estate funds (IREFs), Irish limited partnerships and Irish collective asset-management vehicles (ICAVs), and are used by non-resident foreign investors to invest in Irish property.

These investors hold funds' investments and assets to radically reduce the tax liability of the investments and profits made. The government has introduced legislation to enable these structures, such as the Irish Collective Asset-management Vehicles Act 2015 and Finance Act 2016, which contains legislative measures relating to the IREF regime.

As a representative from one tax firm explains, there are a range of tax 'incentives' available for REITs, ICAVs and QIAIFs: "In general depending on how the vehicles are constructed they can legally avoid tax on their rent roll, on capital gains when they sell and if their investors are non-residents they can avoid dividend withholding tax."

Since the introduction of the Irish Collective Asset-management Vehicles Act 2015, more than 400 ICAVs have been established and registered with the Central Bank of Ireland, generating around US$100 billion in assets under management.

Davy Stockbrokers, which manages over €1.7 billion in real estate assets, describes QIAIFs as 'an Irish regulated fund structure and the vehicle of choice for private and institutional investors who are undertaking large scale investment in real estate' (cited in *The Journal*, 2016b). For example, Kennedy Wilson Europe Real Estate, a property investment fund with assets in Britain, Italy, Spain and Ireland, manages its Irish property portfolio via two separate QIAIFs.

Such tax exemptions and incentives, along with the structure of the tax and fund industry in Ireland, have ensured that investors pay minimal, if any, tax on the huge profits made from investment in the residential sector, both in Ireland and other countries. Ireland's low tax and tax minimisation regime is another factor in attracting vulture funds and REITs to Ireland. This has resulted in the loss of billions in taxes, and the hyper-commodification and financialisation of housing and land. It's a Bermuda triangle of disappearing taxes on a significant scale. The low tax regime costs the taxpayer twice, as it represents a tax subsidy to investors (a form of corporate welfare) – it is not 'zero cost'. As the Department of Finance itself accepts, 'the tax "cost" of any new tax exemption measure (i.e. the amount of any reduction in potential tax revenue to the Exchequer) must be paid for by raising additional tax revenue from another source' (Department of Finance, 2019: 27).

8

Inequality and financialisation

REITs and 'cuckoos' come home to roost: private equity takes over the Irish housing market

The 'success' of government policy in making Irish property an attractive asset for global investors, equity and wealth funds has resulted in a dramatic increase in investor flows into real estate in Ireland. The total assets in real estate funds in Ireland (about two thirds of which are held in property in Ireland) almost doubled from €6.9 billion in 2014 to €12 billion in 2015, and then increased by over 400% to reach €27 billion by the third quarter of 2018 (Central Bank, 2018).

The PricewaterhouseCoopers' 2017 report on emerging trends in real estate in Europe noted that alongside 'established multi-family markets in Germany, Denmark, Sweden and the Netherlands ... an institutionally backed build-to-rent, or private rented sector (PRS), is beginning in Ireland', with investment in the private rental sector in Dublin referred to as 'a home run' by investors (PwC and Urban Land Institute, 2017: 13).

Figure 8.1 shows that the non-household sector (comprising private real estate funds and financial investors, charitable housing organisations and state institutions) significantly increased its role in buying residential property in Ireland from 2013 onwards.

Table 8.1 shows that by 2017 the non-household sector had become 'a significant actor in the Irish residential property market both in terms of purchases and sales' (CSO, 2019b). In 2017 alone, the non-household sector spent €2.1 billion on the purchase of 8,766 dwellings; this equated to 15% of the value of all residential purchases in Ireland in 2017. Apart from 2016, the volume of non-household purchases has increased every year since 2011, when just 760 non-household purchases were made. The number of purchases of dwellings by the non-household sector in 2017 was 11 times higher than in 2010. The value of non-household purchases has increased consistently from 2010, when the non-household sector spent just €171.9 million on dwellings. The number of sales from this sector also increased from 4,482 in 2010 to 16,031, and in value terms from €1 billion in 2010 to €4.3 billion in 2017.

Figure 8.1: Value of purchases of dwellings by non-household buyers in Ireland, 2010–18

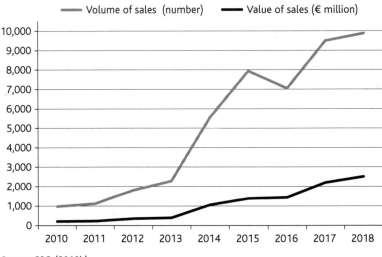

Source: CSO (2019b)

Table 8.1: Volume and value of non-household market dwelling transactions filed with Revenue, 2010–17

Direction	Indicator	2010	2011	2012	2013
Purchases	Volume	774	760	1,421	1,737
	Value (€ million)	171.9	176.2	297.0	325.3
Sales	Volume	4,482	3,153	4,109	4,819
	Value (€ million)	1,066.7	662.4	763.9	842.3
		2014	2015	2016	2017
Purchases	Volume	4,538	6,892	6,266	8,766
	Value (€ million)	913.5	1,274.2	1,360.5	2,079.2
Sales	Volume	8,788	13,263	12,590	16,031
	Value (€ million)	1,595.6	2,516.1	2,902.9	4,317.5

Source: CSO (2019b)

Within the non–household sector there are subsectors. Global equity, institutional investors and real estate funds are found in the financial and insurance subsector, which includes banks, holding companies, trusts, funds and similar financial entities, and the real estate subsector, which includes real estate management companies, companies buying, selling, renting or operating their own real estate, and so on. These two subsectors purchased dwellings in the residential market with

Table 8.2: Value of non-household sector market purchases filed with Revenue by sector, 2010–17 (€ million)

Sector	2010	2011	2012	2013
All	171.9	176.2	297.0	325.3
Construction	20.3	18.3	35.3	32.6
Financial and insurance	16.4	19.4	73.5	84.5
Real estate	7.2	14.4	46.3	23.5
Public administration/education	17.3	22.1	35.2	24.3
Human health and social work	69.6	49.2	30.7	50.0
Extra-territorial	8.0	16.6	41.3	48.0
	2014	**2015**	**2016**	**2017**
All	913.5	1,274.1	1,360.5	2,079.2
Construction	154.2	175.8	156.0	190.5
Financial and insurance	180.8	586.6	326.8	553.7
Real estate	369.7	139.9	171.5	386.4
Public administration/education	25.9	86.8	237.5	224.5
Human health and social work	37.7	76.5	196.1	253.2
Extra-territorial	63.4	69.2	99.6	276

Source: CSO (2019b)

a value of €939 million in 2017. This is almost half of all market purchases in the non-household sector, more than any other subsector. In contrast, in 2010, these two subsectors made up just 14% of non-household purchases. The amount spent by purchases from these real estate and financial sectors in 2017 was nine times that spent in 2011 (€107 million), representing a 43-fold increase on what these type of property investors spent in 2011 (CSO, 2019b).

Another major purchaser of property within the non-household sector includes the state via local authorities and not-for-profit housing associations. These are included in Tables 8.1 and 8.2 in the subsectors public administration, and human health and social work. This represents the shift away from the direct building of social housing to the marketised provision of social housing, via its purchase from the private market.

The extent to which private equity is engaging in the Irish housing market has begun to capture the media and public attention. In 2019, Ireland's largest daily newspaper, the *Irish Independent*, ran an article on the increase in property purchases by so-called 'cuckoo funds' (Weston, 2019). There was a fall of 6% in the number of new homes bought by households in 2019 but non-household purchases increased by 60%. In this period, households bought a total of 4,434 new homes while non-householders purchased 1,991. This means that one in every six of all home purchases in the Irish market was bought by cuckoo funds and local authorities.

The article stated:

> Property purchases by cuckoo funds and local authorities have surged, squeezing out first-time buyers.... Cuckoo funds have been heavily criticised. They tend to buy blocks of houses and apartments and are seen as elbowing in, and pushing first-time buyers out of the market.... The build-to-rent market is becoming increasingly popular here as institutional investors, dubbed cuckoo funds, radically change Ireland's traditional housing market by buying or building entire blocks of accommodation to be rented long-term.

The 'block sale' route has become an attractive option for developers as it removes risk and provides a quicker return on capital. This involves private housing developments that are ostensibly 'build-to-sell' housing for individuals, but are then sold in their entirety, as a block, to investors during the construction phase. Irish developers are also shifting to the 'build-to-rent' model and seeking institutional investors to forward purchase portfolios of thousands of new apartments. For example, one developer has reportedly sought institutional investors to forward purchase a portfolio of 1,695 new apartments at a price of €650 million (equating to an average price of €383,480 per apartment) that it plans to build across four landmark Dublin sites. The units are to be constructed in phases by 2022 and are set to be rented at between €1,825 and €2,725 per month. On completion, the portfolio is expected to have an estimated rental value of about €37 million per annum and to deliver €29 million in net operating income.

In another case, Irish builder-developer Cairn Homes sold 282 apartments at The Quarter in Citywest to institutional investor Urbeo. Urbeo has stated that it has 'ambitious plans' to expand its build-to-rent portfolio through further acquisitions and forward-purchase agreements. Urbeo is an affiliate of US investment giant Starwood Capital. Last year, it formed a €1 billion build-to-rent residential platform in Ireland. Of the €1 billion in funding, the Irish state's national reserve fund, the Ireland Strategic Investment Fund, is contributing up to €60 million. This is another example of the state investment fund engaging in speculative development of Irish housing, thereby contributing to the financialisation of homes.

New planning laws promote micro-apartments

In March 2018, new design standard guidelines for new apartments, *Sustainable Urban Housing: Design Standards for New Apartments*, were introduced by the Minister for Housing, Planning and Local Government Eoghan Murphy (Department of Housing, Planning and Local Government, 2018). The guidelines mean that developers who opt for build-to-rent planning designation specific to the private rental sector can benefit from avoiding local planning processes and submit their development to the national planning agency, An Bord Pleanála, for 'fast-track planning'. They can also benefit from reduced unit sizes and flexibility on internal storage, unit mix and minimum car-parking provision. This promotes, encourages and subsidises the development of co-living type housing, providing en-suite bedrooms for tenants with shared, communal living areas. Bartra Property is planning a series of Ireland's first co-living developments, dubbed 'niche living', including 222 co-living units in Tallaght, 208 in Dún Laoighaire and 100 in Rathmines.

Bartra Capital Property Group is an investment management vehicle founded by property developer and entrepreneur Richard Barrett. On its website (nicheliving.ie), Bartra explains the important role of the guidelines in co-living projects:

> Following the release of the Sustainable Urban Housing: Design Standards for New Apartments residential guidelines in Ireland, March 2018, Bartra are now able to introduce a fresh and innovative concept, delivering the first purpose-designed individual shared living suites in Ireland.

An Bord Pleanála refused planning permission for the Tallaght development, stating that the co-living spaces would 'fail to provide an acceptable living environment' and pointing to a 'notable shortfall in the provision of sufficient communal facilities' (*Irish Times*, 2019).

Eoghan Murphy has enthusiastically promoted this radical new approach to housing and living, describing it as an 'exciting' choice for young working professionals, stating that people should be 'excited' about a future of co-living where they will have 'less space for less rent' (*The Herald*, 2019).

However, the housing charity Threshold has labelled co-living as '21st-century bedsits with a glossy makeover', noting that co-living proposals involved 42 people sharing one kitchen with rents in excess of €1,300 per month. According to Threshold, this is 'a step on the road of tenements of the 21st century' (Threshold, 2018).

In 2019, one of the world's biggest co-living providers, Germany's Medici Living Group, announced that it had received the backing of Luxembourg-based Corestate Capital to build a massive €1 billion co-living portfolio around Europe. It stated that it was 'interested in expanding to Ireland after the positive ruling for co-living' (*Irish Independent*, 2019a), and intends to bring more than 5,000 new beds to Dublin over the next five years.

International property investors view co-living as one of the top new areas for investment and development prospects. However, even some private equity investors are becoming aware of potential downsides to co-living: "People are talking about shared serviced apartments, co-living, but that is only really for young, unmarried people. I think reducing the size of dwellings is a social disaster.... If you take a holistic view of the world, what pressure and stress does that then put on individuals, families and communities?" Another asked: "As an industry, we talk about building sustainable communities. But moving everybody into living in micro-apartments, is that really sustainable?"

Cushman & Wakefield property consultant points out that such new sub-sectors, such as co-living, have caused a blurring of residential and commercial boundaries, "resulting in some areas of the multi-family sector beginning to resemble hotels more than multi-let" (Cushman & Wakefield, 2017: 23).

So-called 'apart-hotels', serviced apartments for long-term stays that use a hotel-style booking system, are also expanding as a form of financialisation of housing. Formerly rented out homes are being converted into short-stay tourist accommodation via on-line platforms and property management companies. A majority of listings of short-stay accommodation in most cities are entire homes, many of which are rented all year round, reducing the supply of homes and disrupting communities.

The downsides of global investment and hyper-financialisation

Macro-level housing and economic policy in Ireland since 2008 has prioritised 'fixing' the banks through reinflating the property market and attracting foreign speculative investors into residential property, which has pushed up house prices and rents. This has further financialised housing and reduced its affordability for most of those who need it. An editorial of the *Irish Independent* in September 2019 highlighted the impact of cuckoo funds:

> They are not called 'cuckoo funds' and 'vulture funds' for nothing. But these entities are a continuing feature of our screwed-up property market, which is inflicting all kinds of injustices on people seeking a home at a tenable price…. Vultures and Cuckoo Funds … are an inevitable opportunity for entities with funds to enter a very dysfunctional market. Both continue to compound the difficulties faced by young people trying to find a home of their own. (*Irish Independent*, 2019b)

The ongoing facilitation of speculative (both global and domestic) property and financial investment in Irish housing – for example, through the National Asset Management Agency's (NAMA) practice of offering to sell loans at a discount to investors and vultures; real estate investment trust tax relief and various other tax incentives encouraging investors; and the failure to impose restrictions on profit seeking from residential property in Ireland through regulating rent, and taxing investment and land and property hoarding – is adding significantly to demand, thus inflating property prices and rents.

The Department of Finance produced a report on institutional investment in the housing market in 2019, which accepts that these investors are having an impact, noting that 'available evidence points to a significant role of institutional investors in certain segments of the residential property market such as the market for apartments' and 'some would-be purchasers have undoubtedly been displaced' (Department of Finance, 2019: 1).

The report also raises the issue of investor firms developing sufficient scale 'to have price (rent) setting power in certain locations' (Department of Finance, 2019: 1). It points out that over 40% of all new apartments are purchased by financial and insurance, and real estate companies, while over 50% of new apartments are sold intra-non-household and so are kept within the non-household sector. These corporate landlords are becoming a real force and have the power to set new (higher) market rents in certain areas. This has implications for the wider housing market, as landlords rent out new (built, refurbished or purchased) units at much higher than current market rents (as there is no cap on new units rented). This in turn raises, and effectively sets, the level of local market rents, thus allowing other landlords to raise rents and making housing more unaffordable overall. This embeds a permanent unaffordability into the housing market. This power is only going to grow as these corporate landlords continue to scale up over time, enabling them to develop monopolistic or oligopolistic price- and rent-setting power.

The Department of Finance report raises some very serious concerns about the long-term impact of investors on the housing market. It states that 'the activities of real estate investment trusts, funds and private equity firms poses broader long-term questions for policy makers in relation to tenure, affordability and the socio-economic make-up of urban areas' (Department of Finance, 2019: 4). Yet these concerns have been downplayed by government as it is more concerned with achieving the short-term political win of claiming an increase in housing supply irrespective of the implications for Generation Rent and affordable housing in Ireland in the future.

The government argues that because real estate investment trusts (REITs) 'are engaged in the development of projects for long-term rental', these investors are contributing to the overall supply of property and thus will help meet demand and reduce rents and prices. But the supply of high-end apartments that pushes up market rents does not contribute to reduced rents and prices. As explained previously, this practice actually serves to drag rents upwards. Investors supply apartments at the premium end of the market that are let out at the maximum rent the market will bear (thus forcing renters to pay the most possible and pushing up rents across the board). Such apartments are unsuitable for people on average incomes.

This trend has been found in other countries where the increased involvement of global equity real estate investors in residential property tends to reduce the supply of affordable, low-quality housing at the lower end of the housing market, and negatively affects security of tenure, housing quality and segregation. The investment strategies of equity real estate firms, for example 'upgrading', entails speculation on a rising market by exploiting opportunities to extract higher rents through renovation and modernisation – and as a result, low-income renters tend to be displaced (Dewilde and De Decker, 2016).

Financialisation has also increased the profitability of investment in commercial property, which has led to the increased real estate investment in commercial uses and thus raised the price of land, making it less likely that affordable housing is provided in these urban areas.

This reliance on global property investment also leaves Ireland and other countries deeply exposed to international property market cycles and the next global financial crisis, as highlighted in a recent report by the International Monetary Fund (IMF, 2016: 35).

Global investors move into student accommodation

Global real estate investors are also the major developers of new purpose-built student accommodation (PBSA). This is encouraged by flexible planning rules and a government subsidy that does not require investors to provide any social housing obligation (USI, 2019). The recent increase in student accommodation is another example of the way in which this influx of global real estate investors is reshaping the Irish housing system and making it more unaffordable. It also a useful example of the point that an increase in the supply of housing does not lead to an increase in the supply of affordable housing.

As explained in Chapter 2, private real estate investor developers have built most of the 6,000 PBSA units in recent years. An additional 15,000 units are expected to be built in the coming years, with global real estate investment funds playing a major role in delivering them. The government has welcomed this and has placed PBSA as central to its student housing strategy. The Minister of State for Higher Education, Mary Mitchell O'Connor, stated: 'I welcome the continued progress in delivery of student accommodation nationally. Increasing the availability of accommodation remains the most effective way to provide real choice to students and will act to moderate prices as the supply and demand near equilibrium in the future' (Department of Education and Skills, 2019). This reflects the dominant market ideology among the Fine Gael government, and the Department of Education and Skills when it comes to housing provision. The problem is that this approach will not provide affordable student accommodation. The first issue is that the existing units (many of which are 'luxury' student accommodation) are already too expensive for most students in Ireland; the rents being charged are unaffordable for the average student and the units are rented out instead to international students. Because these units are targeted at high-end students, and international students who generally pay fees, they are attractive for underfunded universities.

Second, all the new units being built will be able to set a new (and likely higher) market rent as they are exempt from rent pressure zone legislation that caps rents. So the 14,000 units coming on stream in next few years will be even more unaffordable and will mainly continue to house expanding numbers of international students accepted by Irish universities. An increase in this type of supply will not, as Mary Mitchell O'Connor claims, 'moderate prices' or lead to 'supply and demand' meeting equilibrium. Moreover, building PBSA that fails to provide affordable student accommodation does little to help the wider housing crisis, as most Irish students will still be seeking accommodation in the private rental sector. In fact, such PBSA worsens the wider crisis as it leads to the inflation of land values, and therefore, of wider residential prices and future student rental costs, as higher land costs feed into higher rents and prices. This type of global investor student accommodation will lock unaffordability permanently into Irish student accommodation. Most PBSA is developed by global investors and is dependent on profitability forecasts and the conditions in global finance, and so are an unreliable and a highly volatile form of supply.

Ireland is facilitating the global financialisation of housing

Ireland's role in setting up a facilitative tax and regulatory regime for REITs, global real estate investors and vultures is of international significance as it is both facilitates, and increases the profitability in, equity investment in residential property. It has helped investors overcome the challenge that 'real estate is the single largest asset class in the world but only a fraction of it is investable in any way for global capital' (PwC and Urban Land Institute, 2017: 13). Therefore, systems such as that in Ireland that provide potential for innovation, especially in the world of securitisation and REITs, facilitate the investment of the global 'wall of money' into property.

As a result of recent tax changes, the advantages in using a regulated fund structure to acquire Irish property assets have been somewhat eroded, although various loopholes still exist. As one tax firm representative explained, Ireland still provides "a favourable tax regime (especially when compared to other states who are also subjected to these international tax changes) and combined with a high demand and continuing high yields, Irish real estate remains a very attractive investment for international private equity". Therefore, Ireland's housing and economic policy of supporting REITs and investor equity funds since 2008 has also contributed to growing financialisation of housing and increasing housing exclusion globally, as Ireland has offered investment vehicles to enable the conversion of residential property and land into a financialised asset, from which funds can amass further wealth and enact further financialisation of housing and property across the globe. Ireland has intentionally become, through the REIT tax exemption introduced by the Department of Finance, a 'hub for the financing and management of tax-efficient cross-border investment in rental property assets' (Donaghy, 2013: 73).

Economist Dara Turnbull highlights the flows of investment from three British tax havens (the Crown Dependencies of Jersey, Guernsey and the Isle of Man) into Ireland in 2018 (see Figure 8.2), noting that overseas investors based in these three havens spent around €250 million on buying homes in Ireland, more than the rest of the world combined.

Figure 8.2: Flows of investor money into Ireland from British tax havens (€)

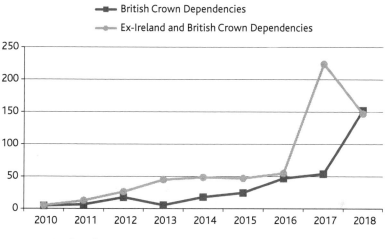

Source: Turnbull (2018)

Who makes housing policy? Housing policy driven by the priorities of cuckoo funds and vultures

Government support for real estate investors and vulture funds to solve the problems of the insolvent banks, mortgage arrears and NAMA's debt, and provide increased housing supply, has resulted in political resistance to implementing measures that could have immediately addressed the ongoing homelessness and housing crisis that began in 2013. The Fine Gael government refused to intervene in two of the key factors causing new family homelessness: rising rents and inadequate tenure security in the private rental sector. First, the government viewed rising rents as a positive way to attract investment (and therefore would not act to curb them). As Simon Coveney, the then Minister for Housing, Planning, Community and Local Government, explained in 2017:

'... we are starting to see an appetite for risk and investment in residential property in Dublin.... We have seen extraordinary increases in rent for residential properties which has changed that appetite.... We need to make sure the incentive remains in place to ensure that money is investing significantly in residential property.' (Coveney, 2017)

Second, increasing the rights to long-term security of tenure and protection from eviction for private tenants has been perceived by government as having a potentially negative impact on investor 'appetite' and related market supply. Such rent regulation and increased tenant protections would also limit the ability of buy-to-let investors in arrears, or banks repossessing such properties, to sell the properties with vacant possession, thus reducing potential sale value with knock-on effects for the potential attractiveness of the sale of non-performing loans to vultures, and the reprivatisation (sale) of the bailed-out nationalised banks such as Allied Irish Bank (AIB) on the private market. Thus the profitability of the banks' balance sheets continued to dictate housing policy.

The dominance of these policies is demonstrated by the following exchanges between ministers and opposition politicians in the Irish parliament in 2019. The opposition finance spokesperson for Sinn Féin, Pearse Doherty, asked the Minister for Finance, Pascal Donohoe, what he was going to do "to change the lucrative tax arrangements in place in order to disincentivise commercial investors from distorting the market for new housing in Dublin and nationally through the buy-to-rent model" (Doherty, 2019). Minister Donohoe responded:

'I am aware of concerns expressed in relation to purchases of residential properties by large-scale investors and the potential consequences for first-time buyers. However it is also acknowledged that insufficient supply is a primary driver of price pressures in the housing market and it is my understanding that REITs are engaged in the development of projects for long-term rental, thereby contributing to the overall supply of property. I therefore do not currently have plans to change the REIT tax structure'. (Minister for Finance, 2019)

The increasing reliance on a financialisation and marketisation approach to housing has meant the state is even more reliant on the private market to deliver both private and social housing.

Government is also increasingly turning to global investors to engage in the provision of social housing through various leasing schemes and new public–private partnerships, discussed in Chapter 5. This has given this new global property investor–vulture fund–finance nexus even more power over policy as government has hitched its policy wagon and political reputation to the investor built-to-rent and vulture model as a means of providing key solutions to the housing crisis outlined previously. Policy has been responsive to the requirements of global institutional investors over the needs of vulnerable families, children and workers, who have been made homeless or face huge rent hikes.

This suggests that many policy makers have been influenced by the demands of global equity funds, banks and the property industry. Housing affordability and security have not been prioritised by policy makers since 2008. The increasing power and influence of private equity investors over housing and economic policy is demonstrated in investors' intense lobbying over potential rent regulation and tax changes and the positive government response to that lobbying.

Officials in the Department of Finance met with private equity vulture firms 65 times in 2013 and 2014. The former Minister for Finance, Michael Noonan, attended eight of these meetings, including a meeting with the US vulture fund investors that bought loans from NAMA. In contrast, just five meetings were held with advocacy groups for mortgage holders, none of which Noonan attended.

Goldman Sachs, a US vulture fund investor that was charged by the US Securities and Exchange Commission for its role in causing the 2008 financial crisis – directly linked to its role in the subprime housing mortgage market – played a key role in advising successive Irish governments on the restructuring of the banks from 2008 to 2013 and it is still contracted by the Department of Finance to advise it on the potential sale of AIB. *Rolling Stone* magazine has dubbed Goldman 'the giant vampire squid' for its vampire-like practice of squeezing profit from economies and the consequent devastating impact on ordinary people's lives (*Rolling Stone*, 2010).

The positive attitude of the Irish government towards the role of vulture funds in solving the Irish crisis was most accurately expressed by Michael Noonan when he stated in the Irish parliament in May 2016 that:

> 'You criticise me for not intervening with vulture funds.
> Well, it was a compliment when they were so dubbed in
> America because vultures, you know, carry out a very good
> service in the ecology. They clean up dead animals that are
> littered across the landscape.' (Noonan, 2016a)

Worsening inequality from the latest waves of financialisation: winners and losers in the Irish housing system

Drudy and Punch (2002) showed that market-dominated housing systems like Ireland's result in a housing system with a division between winners and losers – those who gain from the market and those who do not. They pointed to winners such as speculators, investors, developers, landowners and landlords, and to losers, including a range of social groups disadvantaged in the market. In 2019, there are additional winners, including investor landlords, REITS, the global equity investors and vulture funds. The losers now include far more homeless people, particularly families and children on a significant scale. There has also been a dramatic increase in the number of households in the private rental sector who are affected by housing unaffordability and insecurity. The losers also include social housing tenants on state benefits in the insecure private rented sector as well as home owners in mortgage arrears and tenants in buy-to-let properties where the landlord is in mortgage arrears. The inequalities identified by Drudy and Punch (2002) have in fact worsened and deepened levels of housing distress, with additional new inequalities expanding to affect new groups in different ways.

As the Irish housing system shifts to a greater reliance on the investor build-to-rent private rental sector, more households are likely to be pushed into housing distress. This is why the collapse of home ownership and the increase in private rental housing in Ireland are so important and socially significant, as they have created new intergenerational housing inequalities with major implications for the future. This situation also suggests a growing inequality in relation to asset ownership between mainly low-income, young household renters and existing home owners, investors and landlords. The result will be growing inequality, as wealth is transferred from renters and the Irish state to global equity funds and speculative investors. The financialised approach to housing by the Irish state is turning housing into a wealth-generating asset for upper-income households and international equity and wealth funds.

The government takes the approach that this structural shift in the housing system to intensified financialisation through global equity funds and international investor landlords providing build-to-rent, luxury student accommodation and co-living is to be welcomed as it will help solve the crisis of a lack of housing supply. It facilitates rent increases and refuses to address the insecurity of housing or implement private tenant protection of security of tenure to allow private rental accommodation to be a secure home, as such measures are viewed as potential deterrents to investors. It is low- and middle-income households that will be stuck renting. The proportion of their income spent on rent will increase, which will lead to an increase in inequality as those stuck renting pay a higher proportion of their income on housing. Meanwhile those who will be able to buy their own home are those in upper-income households (who can be helped out by the 'bank of mum and dad'); they will be paying out a smaller proportion of their income as the cost of paying a mortgage is often less than renting, while they also accumulate an asset.

Inequality and new waves of housing financialisation

We can see then that, following the first wave of mortgage securitisation and credit extension, these second and third waves of housing financialisation involve further intensification of the process of commodification of housing that has been continued through the period of neoliberal policies in housing and the wider economy from the 1980s to the present. They help explain the rise in economic inequality in many developed countries.

Even within real estate, investors are turning from commercial real estate, which is viewed as having more 'cyclical uncertainty' to sectors where income is considered more resilient: residential private rental, build-to-rent, high-end, purpose-built student accommodation, and senior living accommodation. Investors talk of "a screaming opportunity for developers to provide more student accommodation". Cushman & Wakefield's (2019) report *Winning in Growth Cities* points out that 'multi-family residential assets' (rental properties for residential homes), having 'long been a traditional asset class in the Americas, have finally gained traction among investors in Europe' (Cushman & Wakefield, 2019: 39). They point to a growth of 14.2% year on year between 2017 and 2018, with a total of $215 billion invested across Europe and North America in 2018. Dublin is the eighth 'hottest' city in Europe for investment in this sector.

The financialisation of real estate has provided these new avenues (markets) for wealth accumulation for the growing 'wall of money', searching for higher returns in a context of declining returns and rising risk in the real economy. This wall of money came from institutional investors like pension funds, hedge funds and wealth funds, the growing trade surplus of emerging economies, quantitative easing, and the rise in profits of transnational corporations (particularly from tax havens). The financialisation process thus provided a 'spatial fix' to the 'over-accumulation' of capital from the 1980s onwards.

Thus housing and real estate more generally (commercial and residential/housing and land) helped manage the 'capital absorption problem' of capitalism in a state of over-accumulation. The resulting 'spatial fix', while trying to resolve the internal contradictions of capitalism, 'transfers its contradictions to a wider sphere and gives them greater latitude' (Harvey, 1985: 60). It is perhaps better characterised as a 'financial fix': an emergent financial landscape in a permanent state of instability that enables a continuous circulation of capital outside the sphere of production.

Madden and Marcuse (2016: 3) emphasise that: 'Housing and urban development today are not secondary phenomena. Rather, they are becoming some of the main processes driving contemporary capitalism.'

This latest transformation to financialised capitalism is profound. The majority of workers are in a new relationship with capital – as financialised objects through which capital extracts its surplus value, not just in the workplace but through the continued commodification and financialisation of all aspects of life. It is important to recognise that recent changes in the nature of work – through precaritisation, digitisation and flexibilisation – reflects the changing impulses (nature) of financialised capitalism. Surplus value is no longer principally extracted from the worker in the factory or office, but from the sphere of financialisation of everyday life and every 'body' in healthcare, housing, care work, education and so on. This is the new expanded base of capital accumulation and wealth extraction.

Under financialisation, housing systems have become part of a process of redistribution to the wealthy and capital – a form of 'accumulation through dispossession' whereby the gains (such as social housing) achieved by workers and the poor have been erased through new ways of profit making in areas of the economy formerly excluded from the market.

The (global and Irish) wealthy 'rentier class' and vultures have increased their wealth exponentially at the expense of poor people, young people, and low- and middle income workers, first, in the labour market through low wages and precarious work, second, in the sphere of 'social reproduction' through higher rents and mortgages, and third, from the state in the form of lower taxes and higher subsidies. Financialisation has thus resulted in increasing economic inequality as it has generated an increased return to capital/wealth extracted from the housing system while simultaneously (and causationally) increasing the housing 'costs' of workers/ and low- and middle-income households. There has been an increase in profits for investors extracted from the housing system, thus increasing the capital share. Low- and middle-income households lose access to affordable housing as wealth is transferred from the majority of citizens to the wealthy (Harvey, 2005). Housing systems are therefore reproducing and worsening inequality, as the increased value of housing and real estate assets have become key drivers in the creation of greater wealth inequality. Those who own property in prime urban locations have become richer, while low-income households confronting the escalating costs of housing become poorer. Surveys of ultra-high-net-worth individuals show that more than half have increased the proportion of their investments allocated to residential properties, with the most common reasons being to sell at a later date and to provide a safe haven for wealth. The 'economics of inequality', in fact, may be explained in large part by the inequalities of wealth generated by housing and real estate investments.

Housing wealth – housing valued at current market prices minus mortgage debt – has risen to historically unprecedented heights, implying that real estate has become more important as store-of-value for households in the age of financialisation. Thomas Piketty has described the rise of housing-based wealth in the last four decades as a 'metamorphosis of capital'. While economies in Europe were characterised by a large stock of agriculture-based capital in the 18th and 19th centuries, the stock of capital relative to income declined from the First World War up until the 1970s, only to return in the shape of real-estate-based wealth (Piketty, 2014).

Because housing is most households' largest asset, a liberal housing finance system that permits high levels of mortgage debt also permits households to leverage their investment in housing. If housing prices are rising strongly, these households can accumulate assets much, much faster than unleveraged households. Wealth inequalities thus cumulate more rapidly. In an economy with unevenly distributed ownership of assets, sharply rising housing prices exacerbate existing inequalities of wealth (Schwartz and Seabrooke, 2008). Rising house prices affect housing wealth inequality by generating capital gains (losses) for housing market insiders who bought at the right (wrong) location at the right (wrong) time, and through more restricted access to home ownership for lower occupational classes due to higher housing costs. Strong house price inflation tends to advantage housing market insiders and wealthier households, exacerbating existing inequalities. Gains and losses of home ownership have become skewed, with early home buyers (both older generations and higher-income households) generally better off and more recent ones (younger generations, middle-income households and minority ethnic households) worse off.

Home ownership in lower occupational classes is also more precarious than 'mainstream home ownership'. Such home owners are found to accumulate less housing wealth (that is, have larger debts), fall out of this tenure more often and own houses of lower quality (Schwartz and Seabrooke, 2008).

Housing and land wealth is highly concentrated in Ireland, with 72.7% of net wealth held by the top 20% and the bottom half of the distribution with just 4.9% of wealth (Hearne and McMahon, 2016). The top 10% owns 82% of all land (by value) and just 10% of households own 28% of the total housing in the country. Moreover, 175,000 people own two or more properties – covering 552,000 properties, and a mere 6,400 people own 156,500 properties, which means that 0.004% of the population owns 8% of the houses (Hearne, 2017). Home ownership in the top three deciles is at or close to 90%, and around 50% in the lower income deciles, while for lower income groups, such as lone parents, the home ownership rate is 26.3%, which is less than half the rate for couples with children and single adults (Hearne, 2017).

Rising house prices and rents in Ireland will therefore further exacerbate inequalities; in particular, as funds and investors acquire more property and ownership among young generations declines, the inequality in housing wealth and profiteering from the Irish housing system will become even starker.

Housing financialisation has played a key role in the growing wealth of the 1% and the re-emergence of 'rentier capital'. Massive investment of capital into housing markets and rising prices should not be confused with the production of affordable housing and the benefits that accrue from it. The bulk of real estate transactions of that sort do not create needed housing or long-term secure employment. When rented homes or mortgages are owned by remote investors, money mostly flows out of communities and simply creates greater global concentration of wealth.

Housing as real estate has become a major contributing factor, if not the key driver, of the problem of growing inequality. The current housing crisis results from, and contributes to, growing inequality in our societies and economies. There are strong links between the precaritisation of the labour market and precarious housing, and new forms of inequality resulting from the changing housing system, with growing wealth transfer from renters to investors, as well as huge corporate welfare transfers from the state to private landlords and investors via marketised social housing provision, rent subsidies and PPPs.

Richard Florida from the University of Toronto's School of Cities describes the fundamental contradiction in today's housing systems as follows:

> Housing is at once a basic mode of shelter and a form of investment. As this basic necessity has been transformed over time into a financial instrument and source of wealth, not only has housing inequality increased, but housing inequality has become a major contributor to − if not the major overall factor in − wealth inequality. When you consider the fact that what is a necessity for everyone has been turned into a financial instrument for a select few, this is no surprise.... The rise in housing inequality brings us face to face with a central paradox of today's increasingly urbanized form of capitalism. The clustering of talent, industry, investment, and other economic assets in small parts of cities and metropolitan areas is at once the main engine of economic growth and the biggest driver of inequality. The ability to buy and own housing, much more than income or any other source of wealth, is a significant factor in the growing divides between the economy's winners and losers. (Florida, 2018)

The housing crisis and shifts in the Irish housing system are producing new housing inequalities, but are also contributing to exacerbating wider economic and social inequalities at scale and impact beyond anything seen before in contemporary societies.

9

The lost decade of social and affordable housing: austerity and marketisation

The continuing homelessness crisis reflects the failure of Ireland's social housing policy over the past twenty five years to ensure an adequate supply of appropriate and secure accommodation for the various types of households in need. At the same time there has been an increasing reliance on procuring social housing by subsidising an insecure private rented sector. (McVerry et al, 2017: 9)

Austerity and marketisation in social housing

In her book *The Shock Doctrine*, Naomi Klein (2007) shows how, at times of major crises, neoliberal governments implement policies that would not be tolerated by the public in 'normal' times. Such 'shock doctrine' policies were evident in Ireland during the global economic crisis of 2008 and subsequent austerity period. The Fianna Fáil-led government of 2008–11 implemented austerity in order to bail out the collapsing financial institutions and enforce the cost of recession, adjustment and financial losses on to the state, public services and the public. Both that government and the subsequent Fine Gael–Labour government (2011–16), implemented austerity measures involving cumulative cuts to public spending and social welfare, and raised taxes of over €30 billion (over 20% of Ireland's gross domestic product). The social housing capital investment budget (the budget for building new social housing stock) suffered the second-highest proportionate budget reduction of any area of public spending during this period. It was reduced by 88% from €1.46 billion in 2008 to €167 million in 2014 (Byrne and Norris, 2017). This reflected the government, state and political bias against social housing investment and the placement of the largest burden of austerity on to the most vulnerable (including young people, those with disabilities, lone parents, disadvantaged communities and low-income households, all of whom suffered huge cuts to welfare and supports during austerity with consequent detrimental impacts on their housing situations). Table 9.1 shows the

Table 9.1: The lost decade of social housing provision in Ireland: social housing building, 2009–19

	Local authority new build	Housing association new build	Total new-build social housing	Reduction in new build on 2009 baseline
2009	3,362	2,011	5,373	0
2010	1,328	753	2,081	3,292
2011	486	745	1,231	4,142
2012	363	653	1,016	4,357
2013	293	211	504	4,869
2014	158	357	515	4,858
2015	75	401	476	4,897
2016	320	337	657	4,716
2017	1,014	761	1,775	3,598
2018	2,022	1,388	3,410	1,963
2019	858	622	1,480	3,893
Total 2010–19	6,917	6,228	13,145	40,585

Source: Department of Housing, Planning and Local Government, Housing Statistics (various years)

effective cessation of the social housing building programme in Ireland during the austerity period. This resulted in a 'lost decade' of social housing provision. This is one of the main reasons the Irish housing system suffered such a major shock with the emergence of a new homelessness crisis in 2013. The output of new-build social housing fell from 5,373 units (3,362 local authority units and 2,011 voluntary and cooperative units) in 2009 to 1,016 in 2012, and just 476 units in 2015 (Department of Housing, Planning and Local Government, 2019b). The governments used this period of austerity to attack and undermine social housing in Ireland. A gradual reinvestment took place in 2016 and 2017, in response to public concern and anger and the escalating housing and homelessness crisis. This was reflected in the output of 1,857 units in 2017, 3410 units in 2018 (although the accuracy of these official figures in recent years have been questioned with accusations of over-inflation of numbers), and 1480 in 2019 (Department of Housing, Planning and Local Government, 2019b).

Austerity measures involved an intensification of the ongoing neoliberal shift from the direct building of social housing by local authorities to the marketisation of social housing provision through the private sector. Marketisation involved the increased use of the private rental sector for social housing (via subsidies and leasing), but also the purchasing of units from the private market and the requirement for developers to include 20% (reduced to 10% in 2016) of social housing, which would be purchased by local authorities or housing associations, within new private housing schemes under Part V of the Planning and Development Act 2000. The austerity policies, therefore, reflected the ideological view of policy and government that sought a radically reduced role of the state in building and managing social housing. Austerity was the mechanism through which the intensified neoliberal shift of marketisation was implemented in Irish social housing.

The human impact of austerity was visible at a local level in some of the country's most disadvantaged social housing estates. After the collapse of public–private partnership (PPP) plans for the regeneration of inner-city estates in 2008, any regeneration was dependent on funding from the central state. However, the National Regeneration Programme, which provided funding for post-PPP plans, was part of the same social housing capital budget being decimated by austerity cuts. This resulted in Exchequer funding for the National Regeneration Programme being reduced by 34%, from €121 million in 2008 to €80 million in 2013 (Hearne and Redmond, 2014). As a result, there was very little regeneration of the most disadvantaged communities during this lost decade.

These disadvantaged areas were also affected by the dramatic reduction in government funding for community development projects. By the end of 2013, the voluntary and community sector was reduced by 35% on its 2008 level, leading to a loss of 11,150 jobs in the sector (Harvey, 2012). This undermined the centrality of community development in the promotion of social inclusion, capacity building and empowerment in marginalised communities (Harvey, 2012).

We can assess the impact of austerity and marketisation on social housing at the national level using a calculation of the 'opportunity cost' of austerity cuts, that is, how many social housing units would have been built if austerity had not been implemented. This shows how many potential new-build social housing units were 'lost' during this period. By using the 2009 social house-building output as the baseline of 5,373 units per annum, it shows that a total of 53,730 social housing units would have been provided over the ten-year period 2010–19. However, only 13,145 units were actually built over the period. This means that austerity and marketisation resulted in the loss of 40,585 permanent social housing units that would have otherwise been built in that period (Hearne, 2017). We can also compare the lost decade of social housing (2009–19) to the ten-year period prior to that. Over the period 2000–09, when social housing was being residualised under neoliberalism, there were still approximately 53,000 new social units built (40,000 by local authorities and 13,000 by housing associations). In contrast, in the ten-year period of austerity and deepening marketisation of social housing (2010–19), just 13,145 new social units were built – a 75% reduction on the output of social housing from the previous pre-austerity decade (Hearne, 2017).

This is clearly a lost decade of social housing in Ireland. The halting of the social housing construction programme also led to a major reduction in the capacity of local authorities, which led to a loss of key skills and personnel such as engineers, architects, planners and so on. This in turn led to the decimation of the social housing provision infrastructure in local governments and housing associations.

The radical reduction of direct social housing building was a key contributory factor in the homelessness and housing crisis that emerged in 2013. The resultant lack of social housing meant that low-income and vulnerable families who previously would have received secure long-term council housing, were instead forced into the private rental sector from 2010 onwards. As rents started rising in 2013, they were increasingly unable to afford the rent. In many cases, they also suffered income reductions from cuts to social welfare, lone-parent benefits, wages and so on, and some were evicted into homelessness. The loss of social housing also means there is very little alternative accommodation available for those families and individuals who are evicted from the private rental sector, and have therefore been forced into emergency homeless accommodation. The austerity and marketisation policies that caused the radical reduction of social housing provision, therefore, has led directly to the growing crisis of family and individual homelessness since 2013. These twin policies acted both as a cause (forcing low-income families into the private rental sector, and leaving them with reduced income to cover rising rents) and as a failure to offer a remedy after eviction and homelessness (the absence of social housing for those evicted). This demonstrates the destructive social fall-out from austerity and marketisation policies in Ireland. In terms of housing policy and outcomes, austerity and marketisation have failed as a policy in Ireland and are the major contributory factors in causing the ongoing homelessness and housing crisis.

Shift to private rental sector

From 2010 onwards, the provision of social housing via subsidies to the private rental sector almost entirely replaced direct building of social housing. As explained in Chapter 5, this move towards providing subsidies to private landlords had commenced as a short-term measure with Rent Supplement in 1997, but expanded to a form of 'social housing' in the Rental Accommodation Scheme (RAS) in 2004 and the Housing Assistance Payment (HAP) scheme in 2014.

Under the RAS scheme, the local authority sources accommodation in the private rental sector for qualifying tenants, directly contracts with landlords to lease their properties for a minimum of four years and rents the accommodation to the tenant under the differential rental scheme (which enables the tenant to work without losing benefit payments). In the event of a landlord exiting the scheme, under RAS the local authority is responsible for finding an alternative RAS property for the evicted tenants. The Housing Act 2009 officially defined in the legislation that 'institutionalised rental accommodation schemes with private providers', such as RAS, is a form of social housing support.

In the context of the marked decline in social housing finance, output and building during the economic crisis, rising unemployment meant that reliance on private rented 'quasi social housing' increased even further. The total number of Rent Supplement claimants increased from 79,960 households at the start of the financial crisis in 2008, to a peak of 96,803 households in 2011. Expenditure on Rent Supplement increased from €388 million in 2006 to €502 million in 2011 (Department of Public Expenditure and Reform, 2019). The government's 2011 *Housing Policy Statement* detailed 'a restructuring of the social housing investment programme', with private rental benefit schemes, such as the RAS, being prioritised as 'long-term social housing support'. This meant that RAS recipients, unlike those on Rent Supplement, were not entitled to be on the social housing waiting lists (Department of the Environment, Community and Local Government, 2011: 2). The 2011 statement also announced the effective cessation of major social house construction schemes: 'The financial parameters within which we will be operating for the coming years rule out a return to very large capital-funded construction programmes by local authorities' (Department of the Environment, Community and Local Government, 2011).

This shift from 'bricks to benefits' identified by Minton (2017) in the UK, is also evident in Ireland. Both Table 9.2 and Figure 9.1 show the trend in the collapse in direct completions of social housing by local authorities and voluntary bodies from 2010 to 2015 and the increased reliance on private rental benefits schemes such as the Rental Accommodation Scheme (RAS) and the Social Housing Current Expenditure Programme (SHCEP), whereby local authorities undertake long term leases with property owners. It also shows the introduction of HAP in 2014 and its rapid take-over as the principal form of social housing provision in 2015.

Table 9.2: The shift to a marketised social housing regime in Ireland: number of recipients of private rental subsidy schemes, 2008–18

Year	Rent Supplement	RAS	HAP	Total
2008	74,038	NA	–	74,038
2009	93,030	NA	–	93,030
2010	97,260	NA	–	–
2011	96,803	16,815	–	113,618
2012	87,684	17,386	–	105,070
2013	79,788	20,173	–	99,961
2014	71,533	20,473	–	92,006
2015	61,247	20,834	–	82,081
2016	49,735	20,306	16000	85,735
2017	34,378	19,756	31,200	85,334
2018	24,303	18,916	40,800	85,800

Source: Department of Housing, Planning and Local Government, Housing Statistics (various years)

Figure 9.1: Spectrum of social housing provision, 2004–15

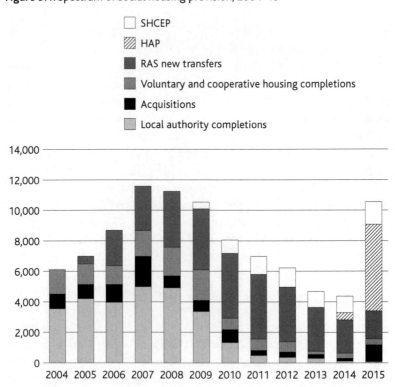

Source: DHPCLG (2016)

Rebuilding Ireland: embedding marketisation and austerity

In July 2016, in response to the growing housing crisis, public demands for action, and the work of the Committee on Housing and Homelessness set up after the 2016 election, the new minority Fine Gael government developed a comprehensive housing plan entitled *Rebuilding Ireland: Action Plan for Housing and Homelessness* (Department of Housing, Planning and Local Government, 2016b). This built on two earlier national plans for housing – *Construction 2020* and *Social Housing Strategy 2020* (Department of the Environment, Community and Local Government, 2014) – and on some of the recommendations of the report of the Committee on Housing and Homelessness (Houses of the Oireachtas, 2016). *Rebuilding Ireland* set out its proposals for dealing with the housing crisis under five 'pillars':

- address homelessness;
- accelerate social housing;
- build more homes (in the private sector);
- improve the rental sector;
- utilise existing housing.

A core commitment of the action plan was to invest €5.35 billion to secure the provision of 47,000 additional social housing units by 2021 by new construction, acquisition and leasing from the private market and utilisation of vacant social housing. A separate *Strategy for the Rental Sector* in 2016 announced the introduction of rent regulation where rents could not be increased by more than 4% in 'rent pressure zones' in the main urban centres (Department of Housing, Planning and Local Government, 2016c).

However, Rebuilding Ireland was the first government strategy for almost two decades that did not set out an aspiration of ending homelessness, or even long-term homelessness. All the targets were about 'inputs' of housing, not 'outcomes' of falling homelessness.

Rebuilding Ireland embedded the marketised provision of social housing as the central mechanism for the delivery of new social housing. It also changed the language and conceptualisation of what is understood as new social housing. Previously, new social housing delivery was considered to be the delivery of newly built local authority or housing association housing units. However, in the annual outputs of social housing under Rebuilding Ireland, new social housing provision has been redefined to include social housing 'solutions' such as tenancies in the private rental sector subsidised by the state, including through HAP.

An overwhelming majority, 112,700 (85%), of the total social housing provision (134,000 'solutions') planned to be delivered between 2016 and 2021 under Rebuilding Ireland was to be sourced from the private market (via rental schemes, long-term leasing, direct purchase and Part V requirements). Just 15% (21,300 units) was to be provided through non-market direct social housing building by local authorities and housing associations. Figure 9.2 shows that most (87,000 units, or 65%) of new social housing provision over the 2016–21 period of the plan was to come from HAP tenancies, while some 11,000 were planned to be purchased from the market, 10,000 units to be leased from the market, and 4,700 to be bought from the market via Part V.

Figure 9.2: The marketisation of social housing under Rebuilding Ireland: social housing provision forecast, 2016–21

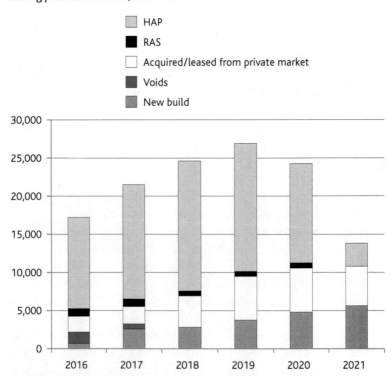

Note: This new social housing stock includes units and tenancies delivered through the HAP and RAS schemes on an annual basis. It should be noted that HAP is a demand-led scheme and it is envisaged that the transfer of those on rent supplement to HAP will be complete by 2020.

Source: Department of Housing, Planning and Local Government (2016b)

For example, for the year 2017, the Department of Housing, Planning and Local Government stated that 25,885 social housing 'solutions' were delivered nationally that year. However, 86% of this housing (22,353 units) was sourced from the private market (via rental schemes, long-term leasing, direct purchase and Part V), with the majority (17,916) provided via HAP-supported tenancies and 890 RAS tenancies in the private rental sector. A total of 2,198 were bought from the private market ('acquisitions'), 827 leased from the private market and 522 delivered via Part V. Therefore, just 7% (1,775 units) of additional social housing 'solutions' in 2017 were actually new-build social housing by local authorities and approved housing bodies.

For 2018, it was a similar story, with 85% of additional social housing coming from the private market. The Department of Housing, Planning and Local Government (2019a) stated that 27,103 social housing 'solutions' were delivered nationally. However, again the majority (17,926) were provided via HAP, 2,610 were bought from the private market, 1,001 were leased, and 841 provided via Part V.

By the end of 2018, there were a total of 85,000 households in the private rental sector in receipt of social housing supports, including 40,800 households in HAP tenancies, 24,303 households in receipt of Rent Supplement and 20,000 RAS recipients (Department of Public Expenditure and Reform, 2019). Expenditure on these schemes (€143 million on RAS, €277 million on HAP, €155 million on leasing, €132 million on Rent Supplement), together with expenditure on homeless services (€146 million), amounted to €835 million in 2018. This meant that the amount of current expenditure on housing comprised 45% of total housing expenditure in 2018, yet it went to private landlords and developers, and returned no housing asset to the state.

This shows that the Rebuilding Ireland figures are completely misleading because most of the 'new' units are not, in fact, new social housing stock, but just various forms of subsidised private rental housing. The headline social housing figures disguise the reality of the extremely low level of new-build social housing and the overdependence on the private market to provide social housing. The Rebuilding Ireland public relations spin disguises the ongoing dismantling of social housing from the provision of permanent social homes to new forms of marketised temporary 'solutions', deepening and enshrining the marketisation and privatisation of social housing. The government's housing policy manipulates the term 'new social housing' and misleads the public with the term 'social housing solutions' in order to give the impression that the government is building significantly more social housing than it actually is.

The impact of the marketisation of social housing: HAP

The development of the HAP scheme as the primary source of new social housing since 2015 marks a significant departure in the nature of social housing delivery in Ireland towards a privatised, market-oriented approach. HAP, including a specific HAP scheme for homeless people, does provide an important form of housing support to an increasing number of low-income households in Ireland and has the advantage of using a differential rent system, which enables full-time employment, a clear improvement over RS, which limited employment options for recipients and acted as a poverty trap. However, a human rights and capability lens of analysis reveals a number of fundamental problems with HAP. Drawing on United Nations housing rights indicators (UN, 1991), Table 9.3 provides an overall assessment of how different social housing mechanisms in Ireland enhance or diminish already meagre and limited housing rights. It is important to highlight that such housing rights do not formally exist in Irish law or policy, but the aspects of the right to housing are used here as a tool to provide indicators to assess current policy. Using this right to housing framework, a diminution of policies that previously delivered aspects of the right to housing, in contrast to traditional local authority and housing association provision, can be seen to take place under more marketised forms of social housing. The reduction in rights takes place most acutely under the HAP mechanism. The privatisation and marketisation of social housing provision through the private rental sector has meant greater housing distress for low- and middle-income households and a rising cost for the state. It has worsened the wider housing crisis by increasing demand and reducing supply in the private rental sector.

Insecurity of tenure

HAP leases are the same as other private rental leases in Ireland, which are predominantly short-term leases. Therefore, HAP recipients have little security of tenure and HAP social housing does not provide the resource of a home with long-term security of tenure that enables families to develop networks of support and provide stability and security for their children. Accessing housing with adequate security of tenure is a fundamental requirement for families with children,

Table 9.3: Assessment of housing rights indicators across social housing mechanisms in Ireland

Human right	Traditional social housing (local authority and housing association)	Rent Supplement (RS)	RAS	HAP
Adequate housing – legal security	Very good Life lease with inheritance	Poor – security of tenure is limited – Residential Tenancies Act 2004 exemption clause for landlord to sell or give to family member (+ three other reasons)	Good – local authority legally obliged to rehouse	Poor – security of tenure is limited – 2014 PRTA exemption clause for landlord to sell or give to family member (+ three other reasons)
Adequate housing – accessibility	Fair – access available for vulnerable households but insufficient stock available	Poor – discrimination and exclusion – tenant responsible to source and dependent on market supply	Fair – local authority obliged to source accommodation but dependent on limited market supply	Poor – discrimination and exclusion – tenant responsible to source and dependent on market supply
Adequate housing – affordability	Good differential rent, legislative controls	Rent review every two years Tenants paying 'top-ups' in competitive market where rent exceeds RS limits	Rent review every two years, differential rent	Rent review every two years, differential rent Tenants paying 'top-ups' in competitive market where rent exceeds HAP limits
Social housing list priority	Transfer available to other social housing stock	Yes – tenant can be on local authority housing waiting list	No, tenants must forgo place on social housing list	No, tenants must forgo place on social housing list

Source: Hearne and Murphy (2018)

and particularly for formerly homeless families in emergency accommodation that have already suffered the trauma of the loss of a secure base.

HAP, therefore, denies the achievement of ontological security to families and individuals, the fundamental need for human beings to have a secure, permanent home (Padgett, 2007). Ontological security describes the deep meaning that is attached to home as a place where a person can carry out their daily routine and normal functioning without fear of disruption. The issue of insecurity may escalate in coming years as more landlords exit HAP to sell, or re-rent their property to higher-paying tenants or let them out as short-term holiday lets, in a context of rising rents and house prices. This is a significant diminution of the human right to secure housing that previously existed in social housing provided by local authorities.

Housing assistance and discrimination

As explained in Chapter 4, tenants who qualify for HAP social housing supports have to find accommodation themselves from the private market and thus are competing with professionals and high-income renters in a tight private rental market. They therefore encounter housing disadvantage in terms of access, affordability, quality, administrative practices, discrimination, and increased vulnerability to homelessness. Research (Hearne and Murphy, 2018) reveals that low-income and vulnerable families experience structural exclusion from the private rental market. The already significant challenges and trauma experienced by homeless families are compounded by the sense of failure evoked by the inability to compete and access housing in the market.

The shift to HAP is part of an ongoing process of reducing state welfare entitlements while increasing the marketisation and financialisation of social housing provision in Ireland. For example, the use of private rental subsidies such as HAP contribute to the neoliberal transformation of how social housing is perceived by citizens. Rather than being understood as a social and human right that is provided by the state and ensures a permanent home or 'housing for life' for low-income and vulnerable households, marketised social housing is now a temporary 'support', with access and entitlement restricted. The removal of HAP recipients from social housing waiting lists is indicative of this process.

The transfer of responsibility for sourcing accommodation from a local authority to those in housing need such as homeless families reflects the values, ideologies and philosophy underlying neoliberal approaches (Brown, 2015). The placing of responsibility and blame squarely on the individual is a key feature of neoliberalisation in social policy, causing individuals to internalise market failures and inequalities (Brown, 2015). This affects parents, and mothers in particular, undermining their core identity as providers of fundamental needs for their children – such as a secure home. The transfer of responsibility for policy and market failure on to families (who are already vulnerable) worsens their sense of shame and stigma, leading to personal internalisation (private trouble) of market failure (public issue). It disempowers affected groups, as it contributes to a reluctance to speak publicly about issues they have now internalised as their 'own fault'.

Current marketised social housing policy, therefore, rather than protecting families from market failure, further exposes them to the social violence and inequalities of both austerity and of the private market. Households in receipt of HAP are still in housing distress and should be considered in housing need and remain on social housing waiting lists (Hearne and Murphy, 2018). Significantly, the failures of HAP and the marketisation of social housing also expose homeless female-headed families to new versions of older (now discredited) policies of institutionalisation – emergency accommodation in Family Hubs.

HAP, therefore, as a marketised form of housing support that cannot deliver access to housing or long-term housing security for those in housing need, should not be classified as a form of social housing.

HAPs political role in reducing waiting lists

The shift to the marketised private rental form of social housing provision also has political origins and implications. The removal of HAP tenants from social housing waiting lists enables a reduction in the official statistics on housing need. The designation of RAS and HAP as a form of social housing, and the associated removal of tenants in receipt these supports from social housing waiting lists as their housing needs are considered to have been met by the state, enables government and authorities to reduce social housing waiting lists, and therefore minimise the scale of the social housing crisis. They have used this to claim their policies are working. For example, the social housing waiting lists increased from 43,000 households in 2005 to 98,000 households in 2011 and then decreased (despite the worsening housing crisis) to 92,000 households in 2016 and 71,858 households in 2018 (Hearne and Murphy, 2018). However, if RAS and HAP recipients (who are in insecure private rental accommodation, and therefore without the protections of traditional social housing and an adequate right to security of tenure) are added to the 2018 waiting list figures, the list would increase to 131,574 households. This almost doubles the size of the waiting lists and clearly demonstrates the reality, which is a pattern of a worsening crisis of housing need and failing housing policy. In June 2019, Eoghan Murphy, the Minister for Housing, Planning and Local Government, used this manipulation of housing classification to claim that government policies were 'working' as the numbers on the housing waiting lists had reduced by 26% since 2016.

HAP and financialisation

Marketised social housing provision such as rental and leasing schemes, including HAP, also fit with wider state attempts to financialise the Irish housing system. Such schemes play an important role in acting as an economic floor for investors that see state housing policy expanding its use of the private market for the large-scale provision of social housing. This represents a guaranteed baseline return on future investment, thus reinforcing the profitability of the Irish private housing market as a site for international investors. With state-subsidised private rental tenancies now accounting for almost a third of all tenancies in the private sector, marketised social housing provision in Ireland provides a substantial guaranteed annual income to landlords and investors. The receipt of subsidies has also enabled some local landlords to survive high levels of mortgage arrears for buy-to-let investment properties, shoring up Ireland's financial institutions and economic model.

Furthermore, the strong institutional and state support for a deepening marketisation of social housing policy has been paralleled by reduced institutional support for local authorities to build social housing. For example, national targets for social housing provision through HAP have been exceeded every year since its introduction, but the amount of new social house building has been well below targets.

HAP is poor value for money

The Department of Public Expenditure and Reform (2019) determined that HAP does not return value for money in the context of tight housing market supply. HAP is actually a much more expensive form of social housing provision than direct-build social housing.

For example, the financing of a direct-build social housing unit in Dublin through state borrowing would cost approximately €800 per month (Reynolds, 2017). In contrast, the monthly payment for a HAP unit in Dublin is €1,244. This means that financing a HAP unit in Dublin is €5,328 more expensive to the state per annum than a new-build unit. Over a 30-year period, this equates to a HAP unit being €159,840 more expensive. Furthermore, if private market rents increase (as they have done in recent years), the cost of HAP necessarily has to increase over time. In addition, at the end of a typical 30-year borrowing period, the private landlord has accumulated an asset via HAP state payments. In contrast, in direct social housing building it is the state that has invested in, and accumulated, an asset. This asset can provide a future social housing home, through which the state gains an income in rent on the asset, and it can be used as collateral to draw down further borrowing for investment in social housing.

Rent subsidies and leasing also have major equity and distributional implications, with the transfer of significant amounts of public money to private sector landlords, who are among Ireland's wealthiest groups (over the 17-year period 2000–16, almost €6.1 billion was paid to private landlords via Rent Supplement alone) (McVerry et al, 2017). The *Rebuilding Ireland* strategy document estimates that in excess of 120,000 households will be in receipt of various private rental sector state subsidies by 2021 (Department of Housing, Planning and Local Government, 2016a). This will require state expenditure of approximately €1 billion per annum to private landlords (including, increasingly, real estate investment trusts and global investment vulture funds).

In contrast, an equivalent investment in direct building by local authorities and housing associations would provide a supply of approximately 55,000 new permanent social housing units over a ten-year period, and 165,000 units over a 30-year period. This suggests, therefore, that marketised provision of social housing through rental and leasing schemes such as HAP represent very poor value for money, and are an inefficient form of social investment.

Marketisation of social housing worsens the housing crisis

This form of marketisation of social housing worsens the housing crisis by adding to demand pressures in a market already affected by housing shortages. As referenced earlier, a third of all private rental tenancies are subsidised by the state, and therefore HAP, RAS and Rent Supplement inevitably push up rents, while the purchase and leasing of units by local authorities and housing associations adds to demand, pushing up prices and worsening the supply crisis.

Table 9.4 shows that from 2016 to 2019, the state bought 7,767 units from the private market, acquired 1,715 units under Part V regulations, and leased 2,949 units.

In 2017, the state bought 3,015 units – a third of the non-household purchases of dwellings that year (that is, about a half of what real estate investors bought that year). Rather than adding to the overall supply of affordable housing stock, as traditional direct-build social housing did, thus reducing rents and prices, the state's marketised social housing approach is worsening supply, as it reduces housing stock and thus has a major negative impact on the housing market. The housing crisis is a crisis of supply, but it is the lack of a significant supply of social and affordable that is at its heart. The absence of the state as supplier of such affordable housing is a large contributory factor to the crisis. While the purchase of housing from the market by the state for use as social housing is clearly a much better outcome than housing being bought by real estate investors and vultures, its impact on the housing market (through pushing up prices and pushing out home owners) is similar to that of investors.

Furthermore, Table 9.4 shows that just 1,715 units of social housing were provided from 2016 to 2019 through the Part V delivery mechanism. This equates to just one in ten units in the new social housing stock (build and purchase) provided in that period. Yet the Part V policy was supposed to be the cornerstone of new social housing provision under the shift to marketisation.

In order to comply with its Part V social and affordable housing obligations, one developer offered to sell to Dún Laoghaire–Rathdown County Council two-bed apartments at a cost of €583,000 per unit. In another proposed Part V deal, a developer offered to sell 40 units

Table 9.4: Marketised provision of social housing: state purchases and lease from private market, 2016–19

Year	Acquisition total	Leasing	Part V – new build
2016	1,957	792	37
2017	2,198	827	522
2018	2,610	1,001	841
Q1 2019	461	129	50
Q2 2019	541	200	265
Total	7,767	2,949	1,715

Source: Department of Housing, Planning and Local Government. Housing Statistics (various years)

from a 400-unit development to South Dublin County Council, at approximately €318,000 per social housing unit. These compare with an average cost of €200,000 per unit for building social housing on public land, thus demonstrating the poor value for money under Part V as it operates currently.

Part V adds to the evidence of the failure of the marketised and financialised approach to social housing provision in terms of a lack of delivery of real social housing units to the level required, and the poor value for money of the schemes. The effectiveness of Part V was reduced following its introduction in 2001 and further in 2015 when the then Labour minister responsible for housing, Alan Kelly, reduced the social housing requirement in private developments from 20% to 10% of units. This was done as a 'supply-side' incentive to developers and stimulated increased activity in the construction sector, another example of the interests of the private housing developers being prioritised over social housing policy.

And this is where the Rebuilding Ireland plan ultimately fails. Its output of social housing is dependent on a very significant increase in supply from a private housing market that is in a major crisis.

Despite this attempt to shift expectations and the stigmatisation and residualisation of social housing, the aspiration and desire for traditional forms of social housing remains strong among HAP recipients, with a majority opting to go on the social housing 'transfer' list. Similarly, the homeless families that we worked with in the ReInVest project expressed a preference for traditional local authority social housing as the means of providing a long-term secure home for their children.

HAP is now operationalised as the primary housing mechanism in Ireland, with permanent social housing only a secondary social housing investment. This suggests that low-income households will continue to be exposed to the private market and its multiple inequalities, insecurities and failures.

Marketisation of social housing: leasing

Ten thousand of the social houses to be delivered under the Rebuilding Ireland programme are to come from long-term leases of properties from the private sector by local authorities and approved housing bodies. The initial social housing leasing scheme involved the owner of the property being paid 80% (and 85% for apartments) of the market rent over the 25-year lease agreement with the state. However in 2018, after intense lobbying from private investors, the government developed the Enhanced Long Term Social Housing Leasing Scheme, which increased the rent payable to 95% of the market rate. The reason for this change was 'to facilitate larger levels of private investment in social housing while ensuring that the capital investment is off balance sheet in respect of Government expenditure' (Department of Housing, Planning and Local Government, 2019a) – that is, explicitly to increase the level of marketisation and financialisation of social housing. Under the enhanced lease arrangement, the private owner is responsible for both structural maintenance and day-to-day repairs. Furthermore, the new scheme stipulates that the lease cannot include an option for asset reversion to the local authority or approved housing body at the end of the leasing period. That means, as with HAP, the asset (property) is retained by the private sector, and the state left with no asset at the end of the lease. Private investors have heavily influenced the nature of these social housing schemes, which are being shaped not in the long-term interest of the Irish state and taxpayers, but according to the profitability requirements of private global investors and landlords. For example, lobbying returns show that in 2018, Bartra Capital Property lobbied for the 'inclusion of units developed under the Enhanced Long Term Social Housing Leasing Scheme as social housing for the purposes of development contributions' and 'to discuss Part V of the Planning and Development Act 2000 in the context of Social Leasing'.

Social housing leasing also adds to the core of our housing by taking supply away from the housing system that could otherwise be for private rental or home purchase. The state is taking from supply rather than adding to it.

Marketisation and financialisation of social housing: PPP redux

In 2015, a new form of PPP plan was redeveloped by Dublin City Council, including 'mixed-tenure development' to develop 1,300 housing units on 30 hectares of its vacant land. Some of this land included the communities of O'Devaney Gardens and St Michael's Estate that had been part of earlier collapsed PPP plans.

In February 2015, Dublin City Council invited the private 'market' (developers, financiers, equity funds and private sector housing providers) 'to explore options for developing some large Council owned lands'. From this consultation with private investors, the 'market' stated that it was 'nervous about becoming involved in mixed tenure private rental and below cost rental unless there is a safety net of guaranteed lease funding in the event of a shortfall in rental income to repay Return on Capital Employed to investors'

(Dublin City Council, 2015). This shows the importance of state-supported private rental schemes such as the leasing scheme and HAP to underpin the investment from equity and property developers. This is another example of state-promoted financialisation of social housing.

The council developed new plans for the land under the Lands Initiative projects that involved a PPP with private developers and investors with a plan of a mix of 20% social housing, 10% affordable and 70% private market housing. In 2019, it appointed Bartra Capital (the company developing the 'co-living' plans for various places in Dublin, discussed in Chapter 8) as the preferred bidder for the redevelopment of the O'Devaney Gardens site. The plan involves building 768 units on the site. There will be 411 private market housing units – which are likely to be unaffordable to home purchasers and bought instead by investor cuckoo funds and rented out at huge rents. The final deal also involved a 'commitment' by Bartra to sell half the private units for use as cost rental homes. But expecting this to be delivered is schoolyard naivety verging on idiocy. When it comes to the crunch, the developer will charge through the nose for any units it sells, be that to the council, a voluntary housing body, investors or home buyers. It is also poor value for money. The developer could make up to €50 million from it. This is corporate welfare – a huge transfer of public wealth to private investors.

Furthermore, 165 of the units will be sold under the government's new affordable housing scheme, which requires local authorities sell homes at 30–40% below the market value. But these so-called 'affordable' homes are being priced between €270,000 and €315,000 for a two-bedroom house and between €360,000 and €420,000 for a three-bedroom apartment. The new Central Bank of Ireland lending rules mean that first-time buyers can only borrow 3.5 times their salary and must have a deposit of at least 10% of the value of the house. This means that a household will have to earn almost €70,000 a year to buy the cheapest affordable house being developed on this public land, which is priced at €270,000. This excludes the majority of households from this 'affordable' housing scheme as nearly two thirds of households have a gross income of less than €60,000. Individuals or couples will have to earn at least €108,000 a year and have savings of €42,000 to buy affordable housing priced at €420,000. This restricts all but very high income earners as only 14.1% of all households have an income over €100,000. In addition, the unsubsidised housing that will be built on the site will be at least 40% more expensive than these prices, putting it out of the reach of all but the highest income earners and investor landlord.

As with previous PPPs (Hearne, 2011), the developers and investors will be focused on maximising their profits and thus pushing maximum levels of price and rent of private units (thus reducing the affordable housing provided, and increasing the cost to the state in private rental supports paid through HAP and so on).

Rebuilding Ireland extends the PPP model to all public land

The Rebuilding Ireland programme extended the failed PPP approach and applies it as the central strategy for state-supported social and affordable housing provision into the future. Rebuilding Ireland outlined plans of a 'new approach to housing provision' through 'mixed-tenure housing development on State lands' by either selling the land or redeveloping it in different forms with private investors (Department of Housing, Planning and Local Government, 2016b). It reflects the government's macro-level approach within housing and economic policy, based on a flawed market theory that has focused on providing an array of policy measures including 'supply-side' private market 'incentives' and 'demand-led' policies in the hope of increasing the profitability of house building for private finance and developers and thus expecting to increase housing 'supply'.

In April 2017, the government released a map of the land it was setting out for development. It includes 700 sites owned by the local authority or Housing Agency (totalling some 1,700 hectares), and 30 sites (200 hectares) owned by state or semi-state bodies in the Greater Dublin Area and other major urban centres. Architect Mel Reynolds has shown that the state controls 3,008 hectares of zoned residential land with the capacity for 114,123 dwellings – more than 17% of all zoned residential land by area and 25% of all potential dwelling capacity in the country. Of this, local authorities own 1,317 hectares of zoned residential land with capacity for 48,724 dwellings – and in County Dublin there is the potential to build 29,278 dwellings. Dublin City Council alone zoned enough development land for more than 18,000 dwellings (Reynolds, 2018). The National Asset Management Agency (NAMA) currently controls 1,691 hectares of zoned residential land with capacity for 65,399 dwellings, and in County Dublin it controls land with the potential to build 43,075 dwellings. Between NAMA and local authorities, the state appears to control more than one quarter of residential land capacity in Ireland. These sites were being offered to developers with the potential for 'up to 50,000 new-build homes'.

The emphasis in the Rebuilding Ireland strategy on the role of land in the cost of development and housing provision is correct as the role of land in housing development is fundamental – its use, control and planning. Land is a finite resource, although its uses can be changed and developed; it can be left derelict and idle, or intensified. Land costs are being inflated by hoarding by developers, vulture funds – and the state. For example, property investment firms own most of the vacant sites on Dublin City Council's register of vacant sites, while the state itself, via the council, owns seven sites on the register with a combined value of more than €27 million. Most of these are former PPP flat complexes. NAMA and the Health Service Executive (HSE) also own sites on the register.

Residential development land value in Dublin rose by 14% in 2016 and 15% in 2017. For every 10% increase in the price of new homes, land values increase by 35%. A 2017 report into apartment viability by the Society of Chartered Surveyors Ireland noted that 35% of a typical sales price was comprised of land value (Reynolds, 2018). Yet there is an abundance of zoned residential development land. There are 17,435 hectares of zoned residential land nationwide with the capacity to accommodate 414,712 dwellings. In County Dublin, there is currently enough zoned land to accommodate 116,705 dwellings.

However, Rebuilding Ireland takes the wrong approach to dealing with both publicly owned and private zoned land. Rather than reducing the price of land, for example through the use of Compulsory Purchase Orders to acquire private land hoarded for future development, or taxing it and making it available at a price that can deliver genuinely affordable housing, and using public (and NAMA) land for public housing, the government gives the public land to developers in the hope that they will provide affordable housing on it and also in the process support the resuscitation of the construction industry via profits from the development of social and private rental housing on the land. There is no evidence of how any of this will achieve an increased 'supply' and guarantee 'affordability'.

The vacant site tax, which should be forcing the sale of idle development land, has various exemptions that make it ineffective. Very few sites have been registered. If a developer files a commencement notice (which could involve putting hoarding up around a site), the site is no longer designated as vacant. A tiny proportion of zoned residential land has actually been registered. Furthermore, local authorities do not have the resources to assess the extent of vacant sites in their areas.

Subsidising the market

Another aspect of the government's strategy is demand-side policies to facilitate an increase in house prices by increasing the amount of money home purchasers can spend and thus the profitability of house building for private finance and developers, thereby increasing housing 'supply'. This was actioned through the Help to Buy scheme and the (successful) pressure applied to the Central Bank to change its rules in November 2016 (with the loan-to-value ratio for first-time buyers increased from 80% to 90% for loans above €220,000). This scheme was not subject to a cost–benefit analysis, in contrast to the process of cutting the funding of various social and community services that do not pass a rigorous cost benefit–analysis test.

However, in the real world of the housing market, as shown earlier, private speculative interests have significant monopoly control over major parts of the housing system, holding large amounts of land, controlling the building process and owning large numbers of buildings. They hoard land and allow asset price appreciation and they fix prices – so that even with 'incentives' they do not necessarily build and increase supply.

Stimulating the market and subsidising home ownership: no guarantee of affordable homes

The planned sell-off and privatisation on a mass scale of state-owned land is one the most serious mistakes (and indeed a tragedy) in the government's wider housing plans and policy. This is a shameful use of public land – selling to global vulture funds and investors to make huge profits while providing (un)'affordable' housing on public land.

It constitutes a massive loss (privatisation) of public land that should be used to provide predominantly state/public social and cost-rental housing and community facilities, and is a strategy that risks huge delays, and ultimately the collapse of the entire project, as was the case with the 2007 regeneration PPPs, because it is completely reliant on the profit viability of developers and financiers who can pull out at any stage. The most naive aspect of PPPs is that they are based on a 'zombie' approach. When house prices fall dramatically, as they inevitably will, and this could be sooner rather than later, the developers are likely to decide that the PPP is not 'viable' for them. The projects will collapse, again, just like in 2008.

The Land Development Agency, set up in 2018, is operating under the same failed PPP approach – it is about incentivising and making it financially viable for the private sector to get involved, using state land as a leverage, to deliver social housing at 'no cost' to the Exchequer. It's a myth. It's a massive transfer of wealth from the state and the Irish people to private sector, as was the case with the PPPs in 2008.

If the state just built on the land itself, it would have tens of thousands of extra social housing units now. As a result of the PPP/market-orientated approach, we have public land still lying idle in the midst of a crisis while the state engages in market speculation with its land. State land should be used completely for genuinely affordable housing. It is economically wrong, and morally and ethically unacceptable, for any market housing built on public land to be sold at an unaffordable rate.

The marketisation and financialisation approach to social and affordable housing delivery effectively hands the private sector a monopoly of housing provision in Ireland – with all the attendant risks (that are being borne out) such as supernormal profiteering, control of land and supply, and so on.

This is a question of what is the most efficient use of our national resources as a country – how can they best meet people's social needs and rights? This approach does not meet these needs – and behind the use of PPPs and HAP, and the leasing and selling off public land, lies an ideological aversion to the state playing a major role in ensuring that housing is genuinely affordable through provision and strong regulation of the private market. It is an approach held not just by government and ministers but deep inside our state institutions and local authorities. The core idea is that the state is not capable, and should not be the provider. Of course, this is a clever trick that suits wealthy investors and various financial interests because PPPs and social housing leasing are a form of corporate welfare – where the state is providing billions in hand-outs to the private commercial sector, wealthy investors and global finance. The state is focused as much on maintaining the current housing system and all the injustices and unaffordability within it, so that landlords benefit and house prices and rents remain elevated. Leasing, PPPs and HAP are all ruses – they give the impression the government is responding to social housing need and increasing social housing provision, but in fact they act as property investor and landlord welfare, propping up and propagating a deeply unjust and unaffordable housing system. They leave the structure of our deeply unequal housing system intact. Through their ideological opposition to social housing and their capture by investor interests, the government and local authorities enable private developers and global finance to develop public land.

Even if such policies lead to increased housing supply, 'market forces' will dictate that the new supply will comprise expensive homes for sale or high-end rental from investor landlords. The Irish and international experience shows that only 'non-market' (state and not-for-profit) providers guarantee a sufficient supply of affordable and social housing. The way this can be done in Ireland is outlined in Chapter 10.

10

The people push back:
protests for affordable homes for all

Housing has always been a deeply political issue given its centrality to people's lives. However, how it is politicised and treated, and its prominence in political and public debate, has changed over time. Housing is now becoming a political battleground of the 21st century between big finance, government and citizens seeking affordable housing. Cities are 'ground zero', the most advanced and intense front of the housing battle. As housing has become marketised and financialised by the global wealthy and investment funds, those excluded have become angry and are pushing back, asserting that housing should be affordable and available to all as a human right. From New York to Berlin, Barcelona to Dublin, protests are erupting, encouraging people to think differently about housing and forcing politicians to change policies. New housing movements highlight the human cost of the housing crisis, challenging global investors and proposing changes to local and national government policy. Ireland has been at the forefront of the new wave of housing campaigns. Irish people are angry at unprecedented levels of homelessness and the political failure to provide affordable homes. Housing has moved from being of peripheral concern to policy makers and government to becoming the number one political and public issue of concern, as growing sections of the population are drawn into a widening crisis, and new protests are putting housing to the top of the political agenda.

New housing protests are challenging evictions and rising homelessness, and the scandal of derelict properties and high rents, and are campaigning for the use of vacant public land for affordable homes for all and the inclusion of the right to housing in the Constitution and law.

New housing protests in Ireland

A housing movement has been increasingly active in Ireland since 2014, responding to growing homelessness, and rental and mortgage arrears crises. Activity initially involved a number of small grassroots groups working incrementally to develop strategies and tactics around how to tackle the housing crisis in Ireland. A larger housing social movement erupted sporadically in 2016 over plans to demolish and redevelop Apollo House, a former government office block, and then in a more sustained manner in 2018 with the Take Back the City and Raise the Roof campaigns. This chapter provides an overview and timeline of development of the main housing campaigns, movements and protests that have emerged in Ireland (particularly Dublin) since 2014. It focuses on those campaigns that have used a right to housing approach. There have also been sporadic protests against the eviction of home owners and business owners in mortgage arrears, but these have not explicitly sought to be part of wider right to housing movements. The chapter highlights the different actors involved, focusing on the issues and particular groups affected by the crisis, their strategies, demands and proposed alternative policies, as well as their forms of activist and public mobilisation, and subsequent impacts.

Table 10.1 provides a summary of the main campaigns drawing on a right to housing value framework in Ireland between 2014 and 2019.

2014 and 2015: years one and two of new housing movements in Ireland

In 2014 and 2015, locally based community housing action groups, such as Inner City Helping the Homeless, North Dublin Bay Housing Crisis Community (North Dublin Bay HCC) and the Dublin Tenants Association, were formed. These groups emerged at the grassroots level as a direct response to individuals and their families being made homeless, or facing the threat of homelessness, and sought to both provide support for each other and to take wider action to address the problem. Some developed as a result of the wider opposition to austerity campaigns in Ireland and experience of the 2014 Right to Water mass movement in Ireland (Hearne, 2015a).

One of the key grassroots groups was North Dublin Bay HCC. This involved a group of mothers and parents facing, or experiencing, homelessness getting together to support each other. Aisling Hedderman, one of the founders of the group, a mother with two children, had struggled to keep a home due to rising rents and the insecurity of tenants' leases in private rented accommodation. She explains that she "decided to do something, not just for her own family but for the hundreds of families who were facing a similar threat of homelessness". She set up the North Dublin Bay HCC as a housing action support group in Darndale (a strong working-class community with high levels of deprivation in Dublin's northern

Table 10.1: Housing and homelessness (right to housing) campaigns/protests Ireland, 2014–19

Name of campaign	Issue highlighted	Groups involved	Actions/strategy	Year/month of activity
2014: year one of new housing movements in Ireland				
Housing Action Now	The housing and homelessness crisis and alternative policies and European movements	Community workers, new housing activists	• Alternative policy manifesto • Public meeting with Spanish organisation Plataforma de Afectados por la Hipoteca (Platform for People Affected by Mortgages)	• 2014 (June) • 2014 (December)
2015: year two of new housing movements in Ireland				
North Dublin Bay Housing Crisis Community (North Dublin Bay HCC)	Evictions of families from private rental sector, lack of emergency accommodation for homeless, vacant social housing properties	• Local community activists from North Dublin City • Homeless Families and individuals in emergency accommodation	• Public meeting – Housing is A Human Right • Protest sit-in at Dublin City Council Offices (50 attend) • Housing and Homeless Pots and Pans protest march from GPO to Dáil (150 attend)	• 2015 (March) • 2015 (May) • 2015 (September)
Irish Housing Network (IHN)	Vacant buildings, homelessness, quality of emergency accommodation	Grassroots activists, North Dublin Bay HCC, local housing action groups	• 'Direct action', occupy vacant buildings, support services for those affected by crisis • Bolt Hostel occupation	2015 (July)
Dublin Tenants Association	Issues facing private rental tenants	Tenants in the private rental sector	Public meetings, individual tenant cases, local in Dublin 7, information	2015 (September)

(continued)

Table 10.1: Housing and homelessness (right to housing) campaigns/protests Ireland, 2014–19 (continued)

Name of campaign	Issue highlighted	Groups involved	Actions/strategy	Year/month of activity
2015: year two of new housing movements in Ireland (continued)				
Maynooth University academics/HAN/IHN	Supporting new housing movement, strategy development, alternative policy development	Housing activists, academics, concerned public, affected groups	• Towards a Real Housing Strategy conference • Peoples Housing Forums	• 2015 (October) • 2015 (November) and 2016 (January)
National Homeless and Housing Coalition	Build campaign calling on government to build social housing, rent controls, house homeless, right to housing	Left-wing political parties, trade unions, non-governmental organisations (NGOs), academics, grassroots activists	Protest march in Dublin (300 attend)	2015 (December)
2016: year three of new housing movements in Ireland				
Tyrrelstown Tenants Action Group	Opposing eviction of private rental tenants	Tenants of Tyrrelstown facing eviction	Protest at Dáil, public meetings	2016 (March)
Solidarity Housing	Alternative housing policy for public mixed income housing on public land	Workers' Party of Ireland	Policy proposal published and proposed in Dublin City Council	2016 (May)
Secure Rent Campaign	Secure rents and tenancies for private rental tenants	Uplift Trade unions: SIPTU, CWU, IMPACT, Mandate and Unite	Public meetings, press launch	2016 (October to December)
HAN/European Action Coalition	European housing crisis and supporting solidarity and resistance	Various European and Irish housing activist groups	Conference with activists from all over Europe in Dublin	2016 (November)

(continued)

Table 10.1: Housing and homelessness (right to housing) campaigns/protests Ireland, 2014–19 (continued)

Name of campaign	Issue highlighted	Groups involved	Actions/strategy	Year/month of activity
		2016: year three of new housing movements in Ireland (continued)		
Home Sweet Home	Rising homelessness, adequacy of emergency accommodation, use of vacant buildings, raising voice of homeless	Artists, trade unionists, IHN	Occupation of NAMA owned Apollo House (hundreds of activists and volunteers support the occupation, 600 attend solidarity protest)	2016 December/January 2017
		2017: year four of housing movements in Ireland		
Strandhill apartment residents	Eviction of private rented Strandhill apartment tenants, Limerick	Strandhill tenants	Protest, public meeting	2017 (January)
National Homeless and Housing Coalition, Inner City Helping Homeless and IHN	Conditions in emergency accommodation, opposing Family Hubs, ending of 'economic evictions', security of tenure and affordable rents, build social housing	Left-wing political parties, trade unions, NGOs, academics, grassroots activists	National homeless demonstration (400 attend)	2017 (June)
St Helen's Court residents	Opposing evictions of residents from St Helen's Court, Dún Laoghaire	Tenants of St Helen's Court	Public meeting, protest, Uplift petition	2017 (August) to 2019
My Name Is	Challenging normalisation of homelessness, highlighting impact of homelessness on children and their families	Inner City Helping Homeless and individuals	• High-profile posters, pickets at government offices • Songs and Words: A Home for All protest concert (500 attend)	• 2017–19 • 2017 (December)
Leeside Anti Eviction Group	Challenging eviction of private rental tenants in Leeside apartments, Cork	Tenants in Cork apartment complex	Protest march (250 attend), public meetings	2017 (December) to 2018

(continued)

195

Table 10.1: Housing and homelessness (right to housing) campaigns/protests Ireland, 2014–19 (continued)

Name of campaign	Issue highlighted	Groups involved	Actions/strategy	Year/month of activity
2018: Year five of new housing movements in Ireland			
Student housing groups and students' unions	Opposing rent hikes in student accommodation, for proper affordable student accommodation	Various student unions and student activists	Protests at student accommodation, colleges, and Dáil (hundreds attend), for example Dublin City University Shanowen Shakedown	2018
Irish Glass Bottle Housing Action Group	More social and affordable housing on NAMA owned Irish Glass Bottle site	Local community	Protest marches (hundreds attend)	2018–19 (March)
Fair Rent Homes campaign	For the development of public cost rental homes on public land of St Michael's Estate	St Michael's Estate Regeneration Team	Public launch, alternative plan, public meetings	2018 (April)
National Homeless and Housing Coalition	Build public affordable homes, make housing a constitutional right, end evictions, rent controls	Political parties, NGOs, trade unions, grassroots activists	Housing is a Human Right protest (10,000 attend)	2018 (April)
Take Back the City	Highlighting vacant buildings, homelessness, Generation Rent, impact of Airbnb	Grassroots activists, tenants	Occupation of vacant buildings and Airbnb offices (100s involved)	2018 (July to August)
Raise the Roof	Calling for building of social and affordable housing, legal right to housing, ending evictions, tenant protections	Irish Congress of Trade Unions, National Women's Council of Ireland, Union of Students in Ireland, NGOs, left-wing parties, grassroots groups	Policy conference, Raise the Roof – rally at Dáil, Homes for All and opposition motion to Dáil (10,000 attend)	• 2018 (January) • 2018 (October)

(continued)

196

Table 10.1: Housing and homelessness (right to housing) campaigns/protests Ireland, 2014–19 (continued)

Name of campaign	Issue highlighted	Groups involved	Actions/strategy	Year/month of activity
2019: year six of housing movements in Ireland				
Home for Good	Getting the right to housing enshrined in law in Ireland, referendum to insert right to housing in the Constitution	Mercy Law Centre, trade unions, Focus Ireland, Simon Community, Rory Hearne, Fergus Finlay, Senator Collette Kelleher	Developing proposal and campaign	2017–19
Raise the Roof	As above	As above	• Rally for housing – Homes For All – Dublin (15,000 attend) • Symbolic rally at Dáil (hundreds attend)	• 2019 (May) • 2019 (October)
Uplift and IHN	For O'Devaney Gardens to be used for public affordable and cost rental homes, not in the hands of public–private partnerships	Uplift members, IHN, Grassroots activists	Email/phone councillors to change plans, protest at Dublin City Council meeting (hundreds attend)	2019 (October)
Facebook group – Protest Against Homelessness in Ireland, Less Talk More Action	Ending homelessness crisis, homes not hotels and emergency accommodation	Grassroots homeless activists and support groups, homeless individuals and families	Protests in Dublin and Cork (2,000 and 300 attend respectively)	2019 (December)

suburbs) in 2014 to help people access emergency accommodation and keep them off on the streets. People are becoming homeless, she explains, "because landlords are selling their properties, banks are repossessing, the rent supplement is not enough to cover increases in the rent and tenants don't know about their rights or services that can help". That is why "community-based" action is needed, according to Aisling.

Another of the early campaigns to emerge was Housing Action Now (HAN). HAN launched its *Housing Action Now Manifesto* in June 2014, which highlighted 'the current crisis for mortgage holders, private rented tenants and those on the social housing waiting list', and argued that the crisis was 'a consequence of the promotion of housing as a commodity rather than as a social good'. It proposed that 'by creating a fair, balanced housing system which is affordable for all we can stop this – we can create a society where housing is a right'. HAN was formed by community workers and anti-austerity activists. They organised a protest in Dublin as part of the European Day of Action for the Right to Housing in October 2013, as "this housing crisis is not just Irish but taking place across Europe" (Housing Action Now, 2013). Some activists had been involved in the Unlock NAMA occupations of vacant buildings belonging to the National Asset Management Agency (NAMA) in 2012. In December 2014, HAN held a workshop with members of the Spanish housing movement campaigning against the eviction of home owners by banks, the Plataforma de Afectados por la Hipoteca (Platform for People Affected by Mortgages), to educate local Irish housing activists and nurture solidarity among European grassroots activists.

The growth of housing activism was well underway. Other groups included the Anti Eviction Taskforce, An Spreach, Dublin 8 Housing Action Committee, and Social Work Action Network Dublin. These groups were involved in supporting individuals and families in crisis situations and starting to explore the possibility of city-wide and national housing rights campaigns. Housing author and activist John Bissett explains that: "These groups sought to use methodologies of grass roots participation and education which are aimed particularly of those who are homeless or in need of housing. Their logic is that the people who are affected should be at the centre of the resolution."

As a supporter of the campaigns, I spoke at a public meeting entitled Housing is a Human Right, organised by North Dublin Bay HCC in a community hall in Darndale, and outlined a strategy and policies that could help to build a Right to Housing social movement (see Box 10.1).

Box 10.1: Strategies for a Right to Housing social movement, March 2015

1. Set out demands for no family home evictions/repossessions, expanding social housing (by local authorities and housing associations), rent control, supporting and empowering community cooperative housing, and putting the right to housing into the Irish Constitution.
2. Protest and mobilise affected people, supportive organisations (trade unions, NGOs and so on) and the public, in a Right to Housing public campaign, winning the hearts and minds of the public.
3. Develop alternatives – policy and long-term models.
4. Get political party buy-in to the campaign (and a change of government).
5. Start doing housing change in practice through cooperatives.

Source: Hearne (2015b)

These grassroots organisations responded to the rise in the number of homeless people by turning to more direct forms of protest, such as sit-ins, to try to get housing for those losing their home or stuck in emergency accommodation, and to highlight the crisis and increase political pressure.

In May 2015, around 50 people including activists from North Dublin Bay HCC and Housing Action Now along with families facing homelessness marched from the General Post Office (GPO) on Dublin's O'Connell Street to the head office of Dublin City Council. They marched into the council offices and began a 'sit-in'. They carried banners stating 'Housing is a Right Not a Privilege' and criticised the lack of available emergency accommodation, and the council's ineffective system of accessing hotel and rooms in bed-and-breakfast (B&B) accommodation. Later the council agreed to provide the families with long-term, secure accommodation. In September 2015, protest groups and homeless families, including parents and children living in emergency accommodation, organised a Housing and Homeless Pots and Pans march (where protesters bang pots and pans and other utensils in unison) that went from the GPO to the Dáil (the lower house of the national parliament). I was there supporting them, and was struck by the harsh reality of the growing family homelessness crisis when I saw children marching with their mothers. One girl was probably only around six years of age, wearing her school uniform, and had a poster stuck on to her bag saying 'In a hotel – I need a home'. The image of that girl has stayed with me, and I think about what she must have felt – a sense of fear, the stealing away of her childhood. Images such as this must push us all to continue to campaign, act and raise our voice until no more children are put through the trauma of homelessness.

Irish Housing Network

The Irish Housing Network (IHN) was formed as an umbrella organisation for grassroots housing action groups and emphasised the importance of campaigns being led by those affected by the housing crisis. Its activist strategy consisted of building a horizontal, activist-led network (excluding formal representation of political parties, trade unions and so on), promoting direct actions targeting particular issues, building capacity among communities affected by housing inequality, and creating a counter-narrative on the housing crisis. This has included the use of occupations to expose the paradox between high levels of housing vacancy and growing homelessness (Hearne et al, 2018). The aim is to show the public how authorities could use vacant buildings to respond to the emergency housing needs of growing numbers of homeless people, rather than relying on the unsuitable and expensive approach of emergency accommodation in hotels and B&Bs or in unsafe hostels.

In July 2015, the newly formed IHN occupied a Dublin City Council building in Bolton Street that had been a homeless hostel but then lay vacant for four years. The IHN tried to refurbish it as a homeless hostel. Dublin City Council responded by serving court injunctions to IHN activists. The occupation continued for a number of weeks, with rallies held in support of it, and it received significant media coverage. The IHN went on to organise a number of protests with families and individuals evicted from private rental and emergency accommodation.

In September 2015, the Dublin Tenants Association (DTA), a new, tenant-led group, was set up based on the idea that "organised tenants' organisations are one way to get our voices heard and shape a model of housing provision that puts human needs before profit" (Dublin Tenants Association, nd). It hosted a public meeting on forming a tenants' union in Ireland, given that "more of us are renting than ever before and the rental sector in Ireland is a mess". It highlighted the need to address insecurity of tenure, poor standards and crippling rent increases and asked: "We all need secure, affordable housing. Is it not a basic human right?"

DTA also invited representatives from the International Union of Tenants and UK tenants' organisations to Ireland to learn from their tenant-led campaigns, and set up a local support group in the Dublin 7 area to help take individual cases to the Residential Tenancies Board on behalf of tenants. The organisation found it challenging, however, given its status as a voluntary activist network with no paid staff, to develop a wider tenants' union beyond the local area (Byrne, 2018).

In the autumn of 2015, I contacted a number of housing and grassroots homelessness organisations with the idea of organising a housing conference that would bring together the diverse new groups emerging and provide a space to discuss the human impact of the crisis, and develop solutions and actions. It was aimed to pressure the government a week before the annual Budget. This conference brought together the public, charities, activists and academics to to develop a Real Housing Strategy based on people's housing needs and rights (Image 10.1).

Over 100 people attended and two documents were produced from the day: 'Strategies to end the housing crisis' and 'Solutions to end the housing crisis'. Two People's Housing Forums were subsequently organised in order to progress the issues, actions and strategies.

A new housing coalition, the National Homeless and Housing Coalition (NHHC), was also set up around this time to bring together various housing non-governmental organisations (NGOs), left-wing

Image 10.1: Towards a Real Housing Strategy poster

political parties, trade unions and grassroots housing groups to form a united campaign. Organised as a traditional political organisation alliance-type campaign, it called for the government to declare a housing emergency, build social housing, and introduce rent controls and secure tenancies. Its first Housing is a Human Right protest march was held in December 2015, with several hundred people in attendance. It was the first protest supported by homelessness NGOs such as the Peter McVerry Trust, Focus Ireland and the Dublin Simon Community. It was also the first of these housing protests to be supported by trade unions such as the Services, Industrial, Professional and Technical Union (SIPTU). The political parties that supported it included Sinn Féin, the Anti-Austerity Alliance (AAA), People Before Profit (PBP) and the Social Democrats. Addressing the protest, Peter McVerry, founder of the Peter McVerry Trust, stated that the government must declare a homelessness emergency.

2016: year three of new housing movements in Ireland

In March 2016, a group of 200 families facing eviction by a vulture fund from the Cruise Park estate in Tyrrelstown formed the Tyrrelstown Tenants Action Group to oppose the evictions. Notices of eviction were issued after Goldman Sachs purchased an €89 million loan from Ulster Bank that included the Cruise Park properties. The tenants' action group, supported by AAA–PBP politician Ruth Coppinger, refused to voluntarily leave their homes. Coppinger explained: 'These people have children in the school, on the GAA teams ... in the community. We're not breaking up the community for a vulture fund' (*The Journal*, 2016a). Some tenants wanted to be given the chance to buy the homes they were renting through an affordable mortgage scheme. The tenants successfully challenged the eviction notice via the Residential Tenancies Board. The government also subsequently bought 18 of the homes through the voluntary housing agency Tuath, securing the residences there.

The campaign also influenced a legislative change, the so-called 'Tyrrelstown Amendment', to the Planning and Development (Housing) and Residential Tenancies Act 2016, to prevent landlords with 20 or more properties from evicting their tenants at one time.

In early 2016, RTÉ One aired a documentary, *My Homeless Family*, that covered the life of homeless families over three months and showed the harsh reality of living in emergency accommodation like hotels and B&Bs (RTÉ, 2016). Erica Fleming, who had been living in a Dublin hotel room with her young daughter for over nine months, was one of the documentary's participants. In it, she explained: "I've always worked, I continue to work, but due to the difference between rent allowance and the actual rent I couldn't make up the difference and I ended up being homeless." Erica went on to speak in the media and public events in relation to her and others' experience of homelessness.

In May 2016, NHHC organised another march in Dublin. Approximately 300 people took part, including the residents facing eviction in Tyrrelstown. The protest, while small, provided these groups an opportunity to build support for their campaign and to feel solidarity as part of a wider housing movement. The IHN also supported an occupation of a homeless hostel that was being closed.

In October 2016, a group of trade unions (SIPTU; the Irish Municipal, Public and Civil Trade Union; Mandate; the Communications Workers' Union; Unite) set up a public advocacy campaign in partnership with the new online campaigning platform, Uplift. This Secure Rent Campaign called for rent certainty, security of tenure and long-term/lifetime leases for private tenants. Uplift organised a petition calling on the housing minister to regulate rent increases by linking rents to the Consumer Price Index (CPI), to revoke the right of landlords to evict tenants for the purpose of selling the property, and to move from current four-year leases to indefinite lease terms. Emily Duffy, a campaigner with Uplift, said 'tenants are being blackmailed into paying rents they can't afford' (Uplift, 2018: 1). This, along with the other housing campaigns, influenced the introduction of the government's *Strategy for the Rental Sector* (Department of Housing, Planning and Local Government, 2016c), which limited rent increases to 4% in the rent pressure zones of Dublin and Cork City.

Apollo House

On 15 December 2016, Apollo House, a large, vacant, NAMA-owned office building was occupied by Home Sweet Home, a newly formed coalition of activists from IHN, along with trade unionists, and supported by high profile artists and musicians such as Glen Hansard, Damien Dempsey and Hozier. Within two days the building was opened as a dry hostel for homeless people in central Dublin through volunteer work and donations from thousands of people across the country. Volunteers (of whom there were hundreds helping and thousands of others offering their help) included electricians, maintenance workers from the trade unions, doctors, nurses, social care workers, security workers, media experts and others providing cooking, cleaning, administration and other essential support. The Home Sweet Home campaign captured the public imagination and through its online funding page received almost €160,000 in donations.

Through fighting an injunction served by receivers appointed by NAMA in the courts, and through a media campaign in support of the occupation, Home Sweet Home was successful in making visible and politicising the homelessness crisis. During the occupation, the group put pressure on the Minister for Housing, Planning, Community and Local Government, Simon Coveney, to deliver new emergency provisions and address the housing crisis. After the minister made commitments to improve the amount and standards of emergency accommodation, the group left the occupation, almost a month after it started, on 12 January 2017 in compliance with a court injunction.

One IHN activist involved in Apollo said: "Apollo was a practical way in which ordinary people could show their solidarity with the homeless." It gave homeless people a sense of dignity and raised the bar of what is acceptable in terms of emergency accommodation. The activist further explained:

> 'The Home Sweet Home intervention allowed the homeless to have their voices heard and it allowed the public backing of them … it has given them a new chance at life…. The homeless in Apollo have smiles on their faces. They are different people – accessing education and looking to get jobs. They have been given a chance. They thought that society had forgotten about them but the campaign showed that we haven't forgotten about them.'

Apollo House with its single rooms and its provision of a 'home-like' building for homeless people aimed to highlight the inadequacy of some of Dublin's existing multi-bed emergency accommodation where there are issues of drugs, a lack of safety and a lack of accommodation for couples. As one activist told me: "The multi-bed (dormed) emergency accommodation treats homeless people worse than dogs. There is no dignity or decency in that. Here they are treated with dignity and respect – given their power to make choices – not treated like cattle put into a stall in a shed in Dublin city centre."

The Home Sweet Home campaign brought the homelessness and housing crisis to a political and public level way beyond what had been achieved up to this point.

After Apollo House there were calls for Home Sweet Home to convene a national housing conference that would bring together

Image 10.2: Apollo House occupation, December 2016

activists from all around the country and continue to grow the movement. However, there was a high level of burnout and exhaustion among activists who had been involved in Apollo, and disagreement about tactics used, methods of organising and strategies for future action meant that no further protests were organised by Home Sweet Home. In the following months, there was very little housing action at a national level.

2017: year four of new housing movements in Ireland

In January 2017, in Limerick, a city in the west of Ireland, 17 residents of the Strandhill apartments were informed that they were being evicted by their landlord, a US vulture fund that bought loans relating to the apartments from NAMA. Getting the tenants out meant that the landlord could sell with vacant possession, which would achieve a higher price. The online campaigning group Uplift worked with the residents to set up an online petition against the evictions targeting the Minister for Housing, Planning, Community and Local Government, Simon Coveney. In the online call for support, one of the residents who helped set up the petition explained the reasons for it: 'Over 90,000 homes in Ireland are owned by Vulture Funds, which makes many of us vulnerable to evictions and homelessness. Can you stand with us in our fight to stay in our homes and for the right to safe, affordable and secure housing? We also call on Minister Coveney to amend the Residential Tenancies Act to abolish sale of a property as a ground for terminating a tenancy.' As a result of the campaign, the minister intervened and contacted the owners to 'ensure that the existing tenancies are unaffected by transfer of ownership'. The apartment owners agreed to withdraw the orders to vacate the properties.

In August 2017, Inner City Helping Homeless (ICHH), along with the Irish Mortgage Holders Association and homelessness campaigners Michael Caul and Erica Fleming, set up a new campaign group, My Name Is, to try to change the perception of homelessness in Ireland, and make children and families the focus. ICHH started in 2013 when members of the local community organised a 'soup run', providing food for the increasing numbers of homeless people sleeping on the streets of the north inner-city area of Dublin. By 2014, ICHH was operating an outreach service across Dublin seven nights a week with 200 volunteers.

As part of the campaign, volunteers erected 400 posters of a child's face with the #mynameis hashtag across Dublin and Galway City. Passers-by were encouraged to share the hashtag as a way of creating a wider conversation around the issue. Over the following months, ICHH took the campaign across the country, including holding a candlelight vigil in Cork.

Image 10.3: My Name Is poster for Danielle Carroll Summer School 2019

As part of the campaign, in November 2017, the Irish artist Will St Leger recreated a typical emergency accommodation unit and placed it just off Grafton Street in Dublin's city centre. He constructed a room measuring 3.7m × 3.7m, containing bunk beds for a boy, a girl and their mother, a single chair and a cupboard for storing toiletries on which sat a kettle and microwave oven. Commenting on his action in the Irish Examiner (2017), St Leger explained:

'It's a ridiculous situation. The whole idea is to build this room and put it in the middle of the street and imagine there were no walls. If there were no walls in emergency accommodation [and the public could see into them], we wouldn't accept the status quo that we have now because we wouldn't accept that we put families into these rooms and accept that to be living because that's not living, that's endurance.'

On 12 December 2017, along with Clare O'Connor and Anthony Flynn from ICHH, and Michael Caul and Erica Fleming from My Name Is, I helped organised a protest concert outside the Dáil entitled Songs and Words: A Home for All. It was organised to appeal to a wider audience than traditional activists, and described as as a 'family-friendly event of hope'. The event was spurred by comments from the Taoiseach (Prime Minister) and other state officials that Ireland had a 'normal' level of homelessness and to mark a year since the occupation of Apollo House. Musicians and artists such as Glen Hansard and Frances Black blasted out their songs in front of the Dáil. On a bitterly cold day, hundreds of people turned up to hear spoken-word artists Emmet Kirwan and Erin Fornoff, poet Sarah Clancy, and homelessness

Image 10.4: Songs and Words: A Home for All protest poster

campaigner Peter McVerry. Glen Hansard sang a special song for the event, with the words 'a doorway's no place to be sleeping/a hotel's no place to raise your children'.

In August 2017, residents of a number of apartments in the St Helen's Court complex in Dun Laoghaire were issued with eviction notices to leave their homes within weeks by financial services firm PricewaterhouseCoopers, acting on behalf of the landlords – two global investment funds, Apollo Global Management and Deutsche Bank – which had bought the apartment complex from NAMA. The companies told the tenants that they needed to vacate the apartments so that the complex could be refurbished. The tenants stated that they had nowhere else to go and so would end up homeless, and that it would mean a major increase in rents when the units were re-let. A petition, supported by PBP politician Richard Boyd Barrett, was set up on the Uplift campaign site calling on the housing minister to stop the evictions. It stated: 'We need to stand up to Pricewaterhouse Coopers, Apollo Global Management and Deutsche Bank and tell them that they can't evict these people from their homes.' The petition went on to explain: 'Vulture Funds like Apollo Global Management are buying up more and more property in Ireland and this type of behaviour will become the norm unless our Minister for Housing steps in to stop it from happening.' Almost 7,000 people signed the online petition. In January 2018, the residents 'scored what could be a crucial victory against so-called vulture funds as the locals battle to stay in their homes' (*The Journal*, 2018). An adjudicator for the Residential Tenancies Board ruled that lease termination notices served on 17 households in St Helen's Court in Dún Laoghaire were invalid. A further effort was made to evict tenants in 2019, but the residents also successfully fought this attempt.

In December 2017, 23 households in the Leeside Apartments complex on Bachelor's Quay in the Cork in the south of Ireland were issued with eviction notices by a financial firm acting on behalf of a vulture fund, again to facilitate a refurbishment of the building. The residents set up the Leeside Anti-Eviction Group, and called for the government to close the loopholes that allow landlords to use refurbishment as an excuse to evict tenants and then charge higher rents when they put the property back on the rental market. In March 2019, a pioneering deal was agreed whereby the state, through the Cluid Housing Association, bought the properties for use as social housing for €15 million. The households issued with eviction notices will continue to live in the complex. Solidarity councillor Fiona Ryan, who had been supporting the tenants in their campaign against eviction, said the deal should serve as a template for other local authorities to follow:

> Evictions can be defeated by people power – that is the message that needs to go out now far and wide. It shows that public housing and public ownership are key to tackling this housing crisis. Where mass evictions are threatened by big landlords or vulture funds, the Government should take the properties into public ownership without compensation, halt the evictions and convert them to public housing. (*Irish Examiner*, 2019a)

This phase of newly emerging Irish housing movements from 2014–17 can be seen as an activist response largely shaped around homelessness and some localised action for private tenants, but it also expressed a wider vision for the right to housing. In part, the focus of this action on homelessness can be explained by the absence of national movements responding to the wider housing and property crash, and the mortgage arrears and rental crisis. With the homelessness crisis growing steadily worse from 2014 onwards, homelessness became a unifying signifier enabling broad unity among activist groups and concerned citizens. Homelessness became the point of antagonism around which broader political claims around housing were articulated.

2018: year five of new housing movements in Ireland

The Housing is a Human Right national protest march organised by the NHHC on 7 April 2018 was attended by 10,000 people, making it not only the largest housing and homeless protest in the current crisis (i.e. since 2014), but also the largest housing protest in Ireland in over three decades. The long lead-in time, and commitment and resourcing from trade unions, NGOs, political parties and grassroots groups, ensured that there was a large turnout. The material advertising the protest placed an equal focus on 'public and affordable housing for all' (aiming at a broader audience of those affected by the crisis) and 'an end to evictions and homelessness'. The protest was also strengthened by an increase in student activism at the time, such as Take Back Trinity and the Dublin City University Shanowen Shakedown student protests over rent increases in student accommodation.

In April 2018, community organisations in Dublin's St Michael's Estate Regeneration Team launched the Fair Rent Homes campaign. This opposed the Dublin City Council Housing Land Initiative, which

Image 10.5: National Homeless and Housing Coalition protest, April 2018

planned to 'give away our publicly owned land to developers' in new forms of public–private partnership (PPP), planned for vacant former social housing sites in Dublin City such as St Michael's Estate in the south of the city and O'Devaney Gardens in the north of the city.

> 'Dublin City Council is proposing to sell off three large areas of public land in O'Devaney Gardens (North Inner City), Oscar Traynor Road (North Dublin Bay), and St. Michaels Estate (Inchicore/Goldenbridge). The land will be parcelled up and sold to private developers to build a mixture of "affordable housing", retail units, and thirty percent social housing. We believe this plan will do next to nothing to provide housing for those who need it most, will line the pockets of private developers, increase rents locally and has the potential to destroy communities.' (Fair Rent Homes Campaign, 2018)

The St Michael's campaign sought 'the site at St. Michael's to be used to build new, affordable, safe, energy-smart public housing for families, young couples, and older neighbours who want to make Inchicore their home' (Fair Rent Homes Campaign, 2018). The St Michael's Regeneration Team spent two years researching the cost-rental model, including linking with the Nevin Economic Research Institute. It proposed a state pilot of a new cost-rental model of affordable housing provision – such as in countries like Austria and Denmark – on part of the St Michael's site that had been left vacant following an earlier failed PPP regeneration exercise. The proposal stated:

> All of the homes at the site at St. Michael's Estate would be completely affordable for a wide mix of people for their

lifetimes. The State will build the homes and continue to own them, renting them long-term to all residents at a cost that they can afford, weighted fairly according to their household incomes. This way the State never loses the value of its investment and will actually recoup the value in life-long, sustainable rent. (Fair Rent Homes Campaign, 2018)

The plan outlined that half of the homes would be reserved for households that currently qualify for social housing and the other half would be for people and households who are unable to afford high private rents and are not in a position to buy a home.

The campaign was successful, with the government launching a draft plan for St Michael's in July 2018 for 470 new public homes, including 330 cost rental and 140 social houses as part of Ireland's first-ever cost-rental housing scheme. In November 2018, Housing Action Now launched a similar campaign for public land across the country, Fair Rent Homes for Ireland: A National Campaign. It outlined a 'sustainable solution to the unjust Irish housing crisis based on a cost-rental housing model on a large scale including 70,000 households provided with a home, at a fair rent, for life' (Housing Action Now, 2018).

Take Back the City

In the summer of 2018, a new housing campaign, Take Back the City, was formed, and its activists occupied empty buildings in Dublin's north inner city including North Frederick Street, where a 12-day occupation was eventually ended by private security guards and the Gardaí (Irish police force). These protestors were more representative of Generation Rent – in their 20s and 30s, either stuck living at home with parents or paying huge rents; many were also students facing huge accommodation costs. One of the most shocking aspects of the state response to the occupation was that some of the security guards and the Gardaí wore masks, previously unheard of in Irish policing. The Take Back the City campaigners then occupied a third building in October, including the offices of the online accommodation platform Airbnb in Dublin's old docklands district, with the aim of highlighting the illogicality and immorality of buildings lying empty during a housing crisis.

As the housing author and activist John Bissett explains:

'There has been a steady growth of activism around the housing issue in Ireland in recent years. There have been high energy, high profile moments like the occupations of large buildings like Apollo House and the occupation of old tenement houses like one on North Frederick Street which ended with the bizarre situation of hooded Gardaí looking on while other hooded men from a "private security company" evicted the occupants of the house. Unlike many other European countries in Ireland housing occupations have tended to be short stay and temporary and driven more for symbolic value than by the primitive need for shelter by people who are homeless themselves.'

Raise the Roof campaign

A further attempt was made to bring the widest possible range of trade unions and civil society groups together into a housing campaign in the summer of 2018. The Raise the Roof campaign sought to communicate using language and policies that would appeal to the wider Irish public who were affected and concerned by the housing crisis, but had not previously attended housing protests. The Irish Congress of Trade Unions (ICTU) coordinated the new campaign, and produced a *Charter for Housing Rights* in March 2018 that set out five key principles to solve the housing crisis (Box 10.2).

Box 10.2: ICTU's five key principles for solving the housing crisis

- Declare a national housing emergency and begin a major public housing construction programme
- Establish a legal Right to Housing
- Take action to ensure security of tenure and rent certainty for tenants
- Stop evictions into homelessness
- Develop a national land management policy that will end speculation and hoarding and ensure that public land is reserved for public housing

Source: Irish Congress of Trade Unions (2018: 5)

Raise the Roof brought together a coalition that included, for the first time in housing protests, ICTU, the National Women's Council of Ireland, the NHHC, various NGOs, grassroots groups, the Union of Students in Ireland, and various left-wing political parties. A protest rally was planned for 3 October 2018 to coincide with an opposition party motion developed by Raise the Roof that was scheduled to be debated in the Dáil. The motion was proposed by Sinn Féin, People Before Profit, the Labour Party, Solidarity, the Social Democrats, the Green Party and Independents4Change, and called on the government to: declare the housing and homeless crisis an emergency; dramatically increase the supply of social and affordable (including cost-rental) housing by increasing capital spending on housing to €2.3 billion in the 2019 Budget; increase the requirements for the provision of social and affordable housing laid out in Part V of the Planning and Development Act 2000 to 20% in standard developments and 30% in Strategic Development Zones; prioritise the delivery of public housing on public land; aggressively target the return of vacant houses to active use; reduce the flow of adults and children into homelessness with emergency legislation to make it illegal for landlords, banks and investment funds to evict tenants and home owners in mortgage distress into homelessness; provide real rent certainty by linking rent reviews to an index such as the CPI; introduce a target for ending long-term homelessness and the need to sleep rough; and hold a referendum to enshrine the right to housing in the Constitution.

The national newspaper the *Irish Times* published a letter that I wrote and got 50 other academics to co-sign including myself, which outlined support for the motion and for the 3 October rally (*Irish Times*, 2018).

Image 10.6a: Front banner at Raise the Roof rally, May 2019

Image 10.6b: Human rights placards at Raise the Roof rally, May 2019

The 3 October demonstration was a huge success, with over 10,000 people attending the lunchtime protest and a majority of elected representatives in the Dáil subsequently passing the motion. The protest was, as Patricia King of ICTU, explains, "instrumental in ensuring that the motion was subsequently passed by the Dáil". The demonstration had a wide spectrum of people in attendance, a fact noted by the media and politicians.

Speaking at the rally, ICTU President Sheila Nunan said:

> 'This crisis is an issue for everyone. It is now almost impossible for workers, young families and students to secure decent, affordable accommodation and this has put intolerable pressure on living standards across all sectors. We need to see a dramatic increase in the supply of quality, affordable public housing. Housing is a human right and should not be the plaything of speculators.'

Síona Cahill, President of the Union of Students in Ireland, said at the rally: "This is the social justice issue of our generation, the locked-out generation." It is worth noting that as a result of the students' action in 2018, purpose-built student accommodation was included in legislation on rent pressure zones (which restricts rent increases to 4% per annum) in the Residential Tenancies Bill 2018.

Another demonstration was organised by the NHHC in December 2018, also with around 10,000 in attendance. Raise the Roof also organised a successful housing policy and rights conference in January 2019 and another national housing demonstration in Ireland in May 2019, with 15,000 attendees, the largest number to date. On

2 October 2019, Raise the Roof held a symbolic rally at the Dáil, with a declaration signed by over 50 trade unions, political parties, housing agencies, students' unions, women's organisations, Traveller groups, children's rights organisations and housing experts to demand that the government enact the Raise the Roof motion on housing overwhelming passed by the Dáil. It also got similar motions passed by Dublin's four local authorities, along with Galway, Cork and Waterford City Councils.

Conclusion: what have these housing protests and movements achieved?

These housing protests and campaigns, which together have created a new housing movement, or movement with many campaigns, in Ireland, have played a central and necessary role in bringing the unacceptable human impacts of the housing crisis to the attention of the public and government. This public action made visible what had been invisible. Take Back the City and Raise the Roof have involved new groups and young people. The protests and movements have played an important role in articulating alternative policies and building a public concern and consensus.

It is very difficult for those most affected by the crisis – homeless people – to actively engage in campaigns themselves. As one parent faced with possible eviction explained: "People are exhausted and depressed and all our energy is devoted to trying not to drown." Notwithstanding this, many homeless people have actively participated in protests, often leading them.

There remains a major challenge to those campaigning on the housing crisis to connect with the large bulk of the population, increasing numbers of whom are affected by the crisis but do not see a common link with others affected, such as homeless people.

Many commentators have asked why citizen action on housing has been slow to develop compared with other movements such as protests over water charges, privatization and austerity (Hearne, 2015a). There are myriad explanatory factors to why wider society has not stepped up, including government and state agencies blaming the victims, such as homeless people and those in mortgage arrears, themselves. The dominant view has been that people become homeless as a result of personal circumstances such as addiction, family breakdown or mental health issues. Little focus is put on the structural inequalities in the rental and home-ownership sectors and the huge negative impact of government housing policy. Society-wide solidarity, however, is seriously undermined when the causes of homelessness focus solely on personal circumstances and ignore the underlying policy and systemic issues.

The past decade has seen a doubling of the number of households in the private rental sector, and the increased duration of such tenures, along with unprecedentedly high rents and frequency of evictions, which means that there is a much larger section of the population – private rental tenants – who are affected by such issues. Ireland, however, lacks the infrastructure of other countries where people have rented for life and there is a long history of organising social movements and tenants' unions.

There is nothing inevitable about protests or social movements emerging. And in this case, the worsening crisis could have been met with rising despair and apathy. However, the opposite has happened and the action of activists and civil society has been a decisive factor. There are also other forms of important political action that have taken place in the past decade, such as the development of legislation to protect home owners in mortgage arrears from repossession from banks and vulture funds. Focus Ireland developed a specific piece of legislation that was tabled in national parliament by opposition parties to make it more difficult for professional landlords to evict tenants when they want to sell the house, and opposition parties such Sinn Féin, the Green Party, Social Democrats and PBP–AAA have proposed motions to implement the right to housing, introduce cost-rental schemes, freeze rents, and increase social and affordable house building.

The links between different groups who are affected by this crisis, from workers to migrants, Travellers to lone parents, and elderly people to students, need to be nurtured and people brought together. There is a need to connect with the climate movement and the Green New Deal, to bring climate activists and their demands into the housing campaigns, and housing justice into the environmental discussion. We need a movement for a right to a home – a home in which we can nurture ourselves and our family – and the right to a planetary home nurtured by humanity.

Informing and educating people about alternatives is vital, as is the necessity of working and campaigning together, of developing messages and language that connect with a much wider audience, of thinking about how we can mobilise and convince our friends and neighbours and work colleagues to get involved and push for a right to housing for all in Ireland. There is clearly a window of opportunity now and in the coming years to push for a radical people-centred housing policy built around the right to housing. Can we take it?

11

The right to an affordable, secure and decent home for all

The centrality of housing as a home for human dignity and wellbeing

A safe, secure home, built to a decent standard, is central to our very existence, our physical health and psychological wellbeing. It is necessary to facilitate child development and full citizen participation in society and the economy. A home is central to the dignity of each and every person and is the foundation of every person's life. It provides the secure base from which to carry out all of life's function. The importance of a home is shown most clearly by what happens to people when they don't have one. It is visible in the devastating physical and mental health impacts on those who are homeless, in particular on children.

A social justice, human rights and psychological approach to housing emphasises and understands its primary function as meeting the fundamental need of shelter and the secure ontological base of a home. In a widely accepted psychological theory on human motivation, Maslow's 'hierarchy of needs' identifies the most fundamental of human needs as 'physiological needs', which include shelter (Maslow, 1943). These are considered the main physical requirements for human survival.

Using Amartya Sen's capability approach, housing can be viewed as a 'basic capability' that provides 'a real opportunity to avoid poverty' (Hearne and Murphy, 2019). Housing that is decent and affordable allows people the freedom to focus on activities other than just survival. Housing enables people to be socially included: it provides an address, which enables access to education, employment, social services, community life, and political and civic participation such as voting; it enables people to form social relationships; and good quality, safe, and secure housing contributes to health and wellbeing.

When control over our housing situation is low (such as being in housing financial stress or living in fear of eviction from rented accommodation), ontological security is reduced, which can result in chronic stress responses. Therefore, access to adequate, affordable and secure housing is important not only for security and shelter but also for good health and wellbeing, and is central to family life and child development, as the home is the place where children grow up and the arena in which the most fundamental social relationships are formed and sustained.

The impact of homelessness and housing insecurity on child and family wellbeing

Child development experts explain that the lack of an adequate home can have detrimental impacts on children's physical, cognitive and emotional development. Take emergency accommodation or severely overcrowded housing where space is limited, for example; this can have a detrimental impact on babies, as lack of space impedes their natural curiosity for exploration and thus delays or inhibits meeting developmental milestones such as crawling. It can also affect toddlers and school children who have no suitable place to play or complete homework, as well as older children who have no privacy for sleeping or study.

In such circumstances, members of a family unit have no place to come together after a day at school or work, even for the most basic aspects of family life such as a shared meal. Children are unable to have their friends over for play dates or birthday parties. In primary schools, whole strands of curriculum deal with the child and the home, as a recurring theme for lessons. It shows the central importance of home, which cannot be overestimated. Just imagine what it is like for a child without a secure home living in emergency accommodation, and the shame that child feels trying to cover up their circumstances when their peers are talking in class about the colour of their bedroom walls, their toys, how many rooms they have in their house, the colour of their front door, or what games they play in their garden. You can see how a simple question in a maths class, such as 'How many steps are there from your front door to your back door?', can leave a homeless child traumatised.

A child needs a place to go where they have personal belongings that give them comfort and enjoyment and where they can develop a self-identity. In emergency accommodation settings, children's capacity to express themselves and be themselves is limited. They are unable to bring with them their treasured belongings, and must curtail their personal expression and development.

The problem of trying to find of a home, or being in fear of the loss of your home in an insecure or unaffordable housing situation, can become a dominating feature of a family's life. Trying to find secure affordable accommodation becomes an all-consuming activity. The seriousness of the impact of the experience of homelessness on a child's life can be appreciated when viewed through the lens of the trauma-informed theory of adverse childhood experiences (ACEs). A child who has experienced homelessness is significantly more likely to experience negative outcomes in adulthood, including mental health difficulties, unemployment, substance abuse and so on. The concept of ACEs is logical: if you experience significant trauma/adverse experiences in the formative years of childhood, your health and wellbeing are likely to be adversely affected for the rest of your life. Significant childhood trauma affects cognitive, social and emotional development at a stage when a child is developing an internal model of themselves and the world they live in. A child's resiliency skills can be extremely challenged if the family is under huge stress in insecure housing or in emergency accommodation. There are very limited supports for such children. It is easy to appreciate the negative impact on children's wellbeing of living in unsuitable settings for extended periods of time, and how the experience would result in significant challenges in leading a healthy and well-adapted life in the future.

Around 12,000 Irish children have experienced homelessness since 2014. These children are enduring traumatic experiences, and their resulting emotional and developmental impacts. This constitutes a form of structural violence caused by the housing crisis and government policy failure. Structural violence takes place when social structures such as poverty and inequality harm people (in terms of higher death rates, increased physical and mental illness and so on) by preventing them from meeting their basic needs. It is the avoidable impairment of fundamental human needs, a violence that results from society's structures.

In recognition of the fundamental role that housing plays in our lives in terms of providing a decent standard of living and enabling us to live with dignity, housing is considered a fundamental human right and has been an integral feature in the development of international human rights since the United Nations adopted the Universal Declaration of Human Rights (UDHR) in 1948.

Housing as a human right in international law

Despite opposition by various governments and public commentators to the concept of housing as a human right, international human rights law makes it clear that housing is a fundamental human right. Article 25 of the UDHR states: 'Everyone has the right to a standard of living adequate for the health and wellbeing of himself and of his family, including food, clothing, housing and medical care and necessary social services....'

The 1966 International Covenant on Economic, Social and Cultural Rights (ICESCR) has been ratified by almost 150 states including Ireland. Article 11 states: 'The States Parties to the present Covenant recognize the right of everyone to an adequate standard of living for himself and his family, including adequate food, clothing and housing, and to the continuous improvement of living conditions.' All the States signed up to this Covenant agreed to 'take appropriate steps to ensure the realization of this right'. International housing law expert Padraic Kenna has explained that:

> In terms of housing rights the minimum core obligations of States would involve a guarantee that everyone enjoyed a right to adequate shelter and a minimum level of housing services, without discrimination. Appropriate policies and laws geared towards the progressive realization of housing rights, form part of the obligation 'to recognize' the right to housing. Progressive realization involves meeting the rights obligations to a higher standard to the maximum of its available resources. (Kenna, 2005: 3)

Another international treaty that includes housing rights is the United Nations (UN) Convention on the Rights of the Child (1990, Article 27).

The UN further defines states' housing obligations under the ICESCR in General Comment No. 4 of the Committee on Economic, Social and Cultural Rights, a monitoring body of 18 independent experts. The UN's definition of adequate housing is set out in Box 11.1.

Box 11.1: UN definition of adequate housing

1. **Legal security of tenure** All persons should possess a degree of security of tenure which guarantees legal protection against forced eviction, harassment and other threats. Governments should consequently take immediate measures aimed at conferring legal security of tenure upon those households currently lacking such protection.

2. **Availability of services, materials and infrastructure** All beneficiaries of the right to adequate housing should have sustainable access to natural and common resources, clean drinking water, energy for cooking, heating and lighting, sanitation and washing facilities, food storage facilities, refuse disposal, site drainage and emergency services.

3. **Affordable housing** Personal or household costs associated with housing should be at such a level that the attainment and satisfaction of other basic needs are not threatened or compromised. Housing subsidies should be available for those unable to obtain affordable housing, and tenants should be protected from unreasonable rent levels or rent increases.

4. **Habitable housing** Adequate housing must be habitable. In other words, it must provide the inhabitants with adequate space and protect them from cold, damp, heat, rain, wind or other threats to health, structural hazards and disease vectors. The physical safety of occupants must also be guaranteed.

5. **Accessible housing** Adequate housing must be accessible to those entitled to it. Disadvantaged groups must be accorded full and sustainable access to adequate housing resources. Thus, such disadvantaged groups as the elderly, children, the physically disabled, the terminally ill, HIV-positive individuals, persons with persistent medical problems, the mentally ill, victims of natural disasters, people living in disaster-prone areas and other vulnerable groups should be ensured some degree of priority consideration in the housing sphere. Both housing law and policy should take fully into account the special housing needs of these groups.

6. **Location** Adequate housing, must be in a location which allows access to employment options, health care services, schools, child care centres and other social facilities.

7. **Culturally adequate housing** The way housing is constructed, the building materials used and the policies underlying these must appropriately enable the expression of cultural identity and diversity.

Source: UN (1991: 5)

States parties are accountable both to the international community and to their own people for compliance with the obligations under international covenants such as the ICESCR. This shows that the concept of housing as a human right is internationally accepted and permeates international and national legal arenas. However, the fact that many people experiencing poverty and social exclusion are unaware of their rights or have problems enforcing them restricts the realisation of rights in many countries. Furthermore, as Kenna highlights: 'Without a remedy there is no right ... the legal dictum *ubi jus ibi remedium* – where there is a right, there is a remedy – is a basic principle of law' (Kenna, 2005: 19).

The right to housing is also recognised at European level in the European Social Charter (ESC), to which Ireland is a signatory. This treaty, drafted by the Council of Europe, establishes a set of human rights and freedoms and a supervisory mechanism aimed at guaranteeing compliance among member states. Article 31 of the treaty specifically addresses housing, stating that 'everyone has the right to housing', and that signatory states must ensure 'the effective exercise of the right to housing' and must take measures designed to: promote access to housing of an adequate standard; prevent and reduce homelessness with a view to its gradual elimination; and make the price of housing accessible to those without adequate resources. However, successive Irish governments, reflecting their opposition to the principle of a right to housing, have refused to ratify Article 31, although Ireland has accepted Article 16, which overlaps with 31, thus providing coverage of some aspects of the right to housing under the ESC. European Union (EU) instruments that address housing include the Charter of Fundamental Rights (CFR), which is part of binding EU law. Article 34 of the CFR states:

> In order to combat social exclusion and poverty, the Union recognises and respects the right to social and housing assistance so as to ensure a decent existence for all those who lack sufficient resources, in accordance with the rules laid down by Community law and national laws and practices.

Furthermore, the EU European Pillar of Social Rights, developed in 2017, provides for 'housing and assistance for the homeless'. Kenna and others make the case that EU law is increasingly relevant to housing in Ireland and confers significant aspects of the right to housing.

Many European countries, such as Finland, Belgium, Portugal and Sweden, include the right to housing in their constitution. In the Constitution of Finland, both the democratically elected legislature and an independent judiciary are entrusted with a shared duty to protect constitutional rights. Article 19 of the Constitution of Finland includes the right to social assistance, the right to social security, the right to social and medical services, and the right to housing. The right to housing provides that: 'The public authorities shall promote the right of everyone to housing and the opportunity to arrange their own housing.' Another clause relevant to the provision of housing and shelter provides that: 'Those who cannot obtain the means necessary for a life of dignity have the right to receive indispensable subsistence and care. These clauses are primarily implemented and fleshed out through the enactment of ordinary legislation. However, they are also considered justiciable by the courts.

The uniqueness of the Constitution of Finland originates in its combination of ex ante review (before a draft law is passed) by a Constitutional Law Committee of Parliament, and a limited form of ex post judicial review (after a law is passed) by the courts. Ultimately, the Finnish judicial approach to economic, social and cultural rights has taken the form of individual rights and individual remedies being enforced through judicial review of the decisions of public bodies. While some cases may have system-wide implications, the courts have restricted themselves to deciding individual cases without speculating on such broader effects. Thus, it can be said that the rights to basic levels of social assistance – including housing assistance – have been used as a modest floor of individual legal protection for people in vulnerable situations.

Scotland's devolved parliament has also introduced policies and legislation widely regarded to provide comparatively broad legal protection for those who are homeless or at risk of homelessness. The measures adopted by the Scottish Executive and Scottish Assembly have contributed positively to combating and preventing instances of homelessness.

A statutorily enforceable right to housing in Scotland is grounded in the Housing Acts (1987 and 2003) which makes local authorities responsible for the long-term rehousing of homeless persons. This provides that in cases where local authorities are satisfied that an individual is unintentionally homeless, 'they shall ... secure that permanent accommodation becomes available for his occupation' (section 24 of the Housing [Scotland] Act 1987, as amended in 2003). In the interim, the local authority has a duty to provide temporary housing until suitable permanent accommodation is available. There is also a legal requirement that places a duty on all landlords, and creditors, to notify the relevant local authority when proceedings are raised for the possession of a dwelling house. This is a way to prevent homelessness as local authorities are alerted to households at 'risk of homelessness due to eviction or property repossession at an early stage' so that they 'may be able to respond on an individual basis to prevent homelessness occurring' (section 24 of the Housing [Scotland] Act 1987, as amended in 2003).

Making the Shift: housing strategies based on human rights

The Shift is a new global movement to reclaim and realise the fundamental human right to housing initiated by the UN Special Rapporteur on the Right to Housing, Leilani Farha, in partnership with United Cities Local Government and the Office of the UN High Commissioner for Human Rights. The Shift calls for a change in the way we think about and interact with housing and home. It affirms housing as a vehicle for equality, dignity and inclusive community, rather than for inequality and the concentration of wealth. It understands homelessness as a systemic failure to effectively and fully implement the right to housing and rejects the criminalisation of homelessness. While it acknowledges that the right to housing does not mean that everyone is entitled to a government provided home immediately, the Shift to a rights-based housing strategy means governments must ensure that everyone – particularly the most disadvantaged groups – has access to housing that is adequate (affordable, secure, and of decent quality).

The Shift calls for participatory human rights-based housing strategies that include those affected in making their claim to their right to housing. Through the Sustainable Development Goals, a collection of 17 global goals set by the UN General Assembly and designed to achieve a sustainable future, states have committed to ensuring access for all to adequate, safe and affordable housing and basic services by 2030. To do this, each state must design and implement a human rights-based housing strategy. The UN Special Rapporteur on the Right to Housing has set out the detailed principles for what should be in such a strategy.

Generally, a housing policy is composed of a number of programmes that address current housing issues, including homelessness, social housing supply or access to housing in the private market. Housing programmes are often operated by a single authority, a statutory agency or different levels of government. Housing strategies operate at a higher level than housing policy and programmes and are based on a vision of structural change that is required over time. A strategy coordinates a wide range of laws, programmes, policies and decisions to address housing needs that, when taken together, create a housing system. The aim of a housing strategy is not only to provide housing, but also to address gaps and inequalities in existing systems. It provides opportunities to review and change policies and programmes to ensure their efficacy and challenges the stigmatisation, marginalisation and discrimination that lies behind failures of housing systems. A housing strategy must aim to change societies in which significant numbers of people are deprived of the right to adequate housing, into societies in which everyone has access to adequate housing and in which housing is a means to ensure dignity, security and inclusion in sustainable communities. Rights-based housing strategies should draw on the right to housing not only as a set of legal standards, but also as a transformative vision for society and a call to action. This vision motivates local and national governments, social movements and communities around the world to act.

The Special Rapporteur has identified ten key principles for making effective human rights-based housing strategies. Box 11.2 provides a summary of some of the most relevant aspects of these principles. These provide a comprehensive outline of what governments and local authorities should include in their housing strategies and policies.

Box 11.2: Highlights of key principles of a human rights-based housing strategy

Principle 1: based in law and legal standards
- The right to housing should be recognised within housing strategies as a legal right, subject to effective remedies. Rights-based housing strategies should be based in legislation that recognises the right to adequate housing in all of its dimensions. In addition to relying on constitutional or legislative recognition of the right to housing, strategies should reference and adhere to the right to housing as it is guaranteed in international human rights law.
- Strategies must map a process through which the right to housing will be fulfilled within a reasonable time frame. Provisions are required to ensure not only entitlements in the present (immediate obligations) but also action-oriented obligations over time (progressive realisation obligations).
- Strategies must eliminate homelessness.
- Strategies must outline the obligations concerning the right to housing. These include the obligations of states to respect (not to encroach), protect (prevent interference by third parties) and fulfil (promote and facilitate access to and provide housing or assistance where needed).

Principle 2: prioritise those most in need and ensure equality
- Strategies must prevent housing systems themselves from sustaining and increasing socioeconomic inequality and exclusion. For housing strategies to be effective, they must address not only housing need, but also the structural causes underlying the need.

- Housing strategies should identify groups that suffer housing disadvantages and should address the particular barriers they face. These groups include: women; persons with disabilities; people living in poverty; migrants; racial and ethnic minorities; indigenous peoples; young people; older persons; lesbian, gay, bisexual, transgender and intersex persons; and people who are homeless or living in informal settlements.
- Women's equal right to housing must be ensured in all aspects of housing strategies.

Principle 3: comprehensive, whole-of-government strategies
- Strategies should address all issues that have a significant impact on the right to housing, including land-grabbing, speculation, privatisation, predatory lending and environmental degradation.

Principle 4: rights-based participation
- Rights-based housing strategies must firmly commit to ensuring meaningful participation of affected persons at every stage, from design to implementation to monitoring. Participation is central to human rights-based housing strategies because it challenges exclusion and silencing. Strategies must recognise that violations of the right to housing and other human rights emanate from failures of democratic accountability to people.
- Housing strategies should include specific participatory mechanisms to oversee their implementation, such as housing councils, commissions, committees or panels.

Principle 5: accountable budgeting and tax justice
- Strategies will not be successful if governments fail to allocate reasonable budgets and resources for their implementation. Housing strategies must include both short- and long-term commitments of adequate resources.
- Strategies must commit to addressing tax avoidance and loopholes in the housing and real estate sectors. Tax avoidance in housing systems constitutes a massive loss of revenue that should be made available for realising the right to housing.
- Housing strategies should commit to carrying out the necessary taxation reforms to ensure that taxation promotes rather than undermines the fulfilment of the right to housing.

Principle 6: human rights-based goals and timelines
- Rigorous human rights-based goals and timelines are required to ensure that housing strategies move as expeditiously as possible toward the goal of adequate housing for all and realise the right for every individual in the shortest possible time in accordance with the maximum of available resources.

Principle 7: accountability and monitoring
• Effective monitoring of the implementation and outcomes of housing strategies is a firm obligation of states. A designated monitoring body should be mandated to assess the ongoing effectiveness of the housing strategy, identify failures or shortcomings, recommend necessary changes and hold governments and other actors accountable. Whether it is a commission, a housing ombudsperson, a housing advocate or a national or regional human rights institution, the designated body must be independent of government, provided with adequate financial resources and free to express opinions and make recommendations on policy and legislation.

Principle 8: ensuring access to justice
• Rights-based strategies must include effective claiming mechanisms for the right to housing that guarantee access to remedies where a violation is found such as through courts and other means, including where violations result from failures to progressively realise the right to housing.

Principle 9: clarify the obligations of private actors and regulate financial, housing and real estate markets

Principle 10: implement international cooperation and assistance

Source: UN (2018: 5)

The right to housing in Ireland

While Ireland has ratified treaties such as the ICESCR that include the right to housing, and as such is subject to monitoring under the UN mechanisms, these treaties are not justiciable in any court of law and there is no legal right to housing in the Irish Constitution or other Irish law or legislation. Since there is no legally enforceable right to housing, there is no recourse available to those in need if the state fails to ensure they have access to affordable secure quality housing. Of course, in the absence of legally enforceable rights, legislators and policy makers can still draw on international human rights standards. Where there is an EU law connection with a housing issue, such as discrimination, the courts must apply the CFR, and some EU consumer law also provides elements of housing rights. Irish legislators could enact legislation to bring housing rights into enforceable Irish law, but have not done so. Advocates and non-governmental organisations (NGOs) can use international human rights mechanisms under the UN and Council of Europe systems, which, although non-justiciable, are potentially politically effective. These include the collective complaints mechanism of the Council of Europe, which has been utilised by social housing communities in Ireland, as well as the civil society role in providing input into UN monitoring of Irish housing policy and outcomes. The Equality Act (Miscellaneous Provisions) 2015 introduced 'housing assistance' as a new discriminatory ground, which means that discrimination in the provision of accommodation is against the law

The right to housing is not once mentioned in the government's principal housing policy plan, *Rebuilding Ireland* (Department of Housing, Planning and Local Government, 2016b), or any other housing policy statement, and successive Irish governments have actively opposed the creation of a legal right to housing. This has contributed to government policy failing to address the growing housing crisis, while local authorities are not legally obliged to provide adequate housing to homeless families.

Economic, social and cultural rights, such as the right to housing, are protected in a very limited manner in the Irish Constitution. Article 45 of the Irish Constitution, entitled 'Directive Principles of Social Policy', outlines that the state should protect the welfare 'of the whole people,' that 'justice and charity' inform all the institutions of national life, and that citizens 'have the right to an adequate means of livelihood'. It further states: 'The State pledges itself to safeguard with special care the economic interests of the weaker sections of the community, and, where necessary, to contribute to the support of the infirm, the widow, the orphan, and the aged.' However, these provisions are for the 'general guidance' of parliament and are not cognisable in any court. Articles 40–44 of the Irish Constitution recognise 'fundamental rights' that are justiciable. These include the right to primary education, and, importantly in the context of housing, Article 43 states that 'man, in virtue of his rational being, has the natural right, antecedent to positive law, to the private ownership of external goods'. As a consequence, the state is prevented in the Constitution from passing 'any law attempting to abolish the right of private ownership or the general right to transfer, bequeath, and inherit property'. These are some of the strongest property rights in the world. Article 43 does go on to say that these rights ought to be 'regulated by the principles of social justice' and may on occasion limit the right to private property in order to 'reconcile their exercise with the exigencies of the common good', although there is no definition of what is meant by the 'common good' or 'principles of social justice.'

As the housing and homelessness crisis has continued to worsen, there has been growing public momentum for Ireland to adopt a legally enforceable right to adequate housing. An opinion poll carried out in 2018 for the Irish Human Rights and Equality Commission found that 82% of people generally in Ireland, and 89% of 18- to 24-year-olds, believe that housing should be considered a human right. Very significantly, a large majority, 63% of Irish people, believe that a right to housing should be entered into Ireland's Constitution. Just 24% opposed it. Across age, class and geography, there is a majority in favour in all categories, although the strength of support does vary. In terms of age groups, 78% of 18- to 24-year-olds, 64% of 35- to 44-year-olds and 51% of over-55s were in favour of including the right to housing in the Constitution. In terms of social class, a majority (58%) of those in the higher AB socioeconomic grouping and 67% of the lower C grouping were in favour, showing the understandable stronger support among low-income groups for the right to housing, given that they suffer much more from the lack of housing and from violation of the right to housing. Interestingly, a majority of Irish people (over 60%) were in favour across all the regions in Ireland.

Homelessness NGOs such as Simon Community and Focus Ireland, religious organisations, political parties, academics and grassroots movements such as the Irish Housing Network and Housing Action Now, have campaigned for a legal right to adequate housing as a necessary response to the housing and homelessness crisis.

Convention recommends the right to housing

A Convention on the Irish Constitution was set up in 2012 to discuss proposed amendments to the Constitution. The Convention had 100 members, including 29 members of the Oireachtas (parliament) and 66 randomly selected Irish citizens. The government committed to respond formally to the recommendations of the Convention. The Convention recommended the inclusion in the Constitution of a provision for progressive realisation by the state of economic, social and cultural (ESC) rights, subject to maximum available resources, and for that duty to be cognisable by the courts. The Convention specifically deliberated on the issue of the right to housing and an overwhelming majority (84%) of attendees at the Convention recommended the inclusion of the right to housing in the constitution, showing significant public support for it following an informed debate.

The report on the Convention's deliberations highlighted that a concern was raised by some delegates that the insertion of ESC rights such as housing into the Constitution would 'bankrupt the State' (Convention on the Constitution, 2014). However, this was countered with the point that the ICESCR (ratified by Ireland in 1989) includes the principle of 'progressive realisation', acknowledging that states are subject to resource constraints. In other words: 'States are expected to act as best they can within the means available to them, a concept perfectly in accordance with any constitutional obligations on ESC rights. The same principle would apply in the case of the Irish Constitution' (Convention on the Constitution, 2014: 10).

Arguments made in favour of inserting the right to housing 'consisted of the idea that the new rights would lead to, or would allow the creation of, a fairer and more equal society, particularly if they were to be justiciable rights. The rights in question would be made inalienable if inserted into the Constitution, it was argued. Some members supported the idea as a means of pressuring the government to fulfil the rights in question, and to change the culture of public administration, as it would represent a framework for government accountability' (Convention on the Constitution, 2014: 11).

It is an anomaly in the Irish Constitution that, while the right to property is protected (Article 40.3.2), no similar protection exists for the right to a home.

Bills proposing inclusion of the right to housing in the Constitution

In September 2017, the government announced a series of referendums stemming from the Convention on the Irish Constitution. However, there was no proposal for a referendum on ESC rights such as the right to housing. In 2018, the Irish Congress of Trade Unions and the Raise the Roof coalition called on the government to 'urgently' hold a referendum to enshrine the right to housing in the Constitution. The petition organised by Raise the Roof in support of this campaign stated: 'A legal Right to Housing will benefit all citizens and provide a vital tool to help end the current housing and homelessness emergency. It would require Government to ensure that all citizens have access to decent, adequate shelter and to make this a reality through its laws, policies and budgetary decisions' (https://raisetheroof.good.do/therighttohousing/righttohousing/). The Raise the Roof motion was passed by a majority of members in the Dáil Éireann (lower house of the Irish parliament) in October 2018, which included the holding of a referendum on the right to housing.

The Thirty-fifth Amendment of the Constitution (Right to a Home) Bill 2016, introduced by Sinn Féin, sought to insert into the Constitution a right to adequate, appropriate, secure, safe and, affordable housing and sought "to place an obligation on the State to ensure the realisation of that right through its laws and policies in accordance with the principles of social justice" (Connolly, 2019). In the debate, Catherine Connolly, an Independent member of the Dáil, spoke in favour of the Bill, stating that putting the right to housing in the Constitution "is the most basic requirement if we want to call ourselves a civilised society". The Bill was defeated, with 36 members (including from Sinn Féin and the Labour, Independent and Social Democratic Parties) voting in favour and 60 (from Fine Gael and Fianna Fáil) voting against it.

The case for inserting the right to housing in legislation and the Irish Constitution

A legal or constitutional right to housing would not 'give a key to a home for all'. It would place a responsibility on government to provide a housing system that ensures everyone has adequate housing. It would be more cost-effective and better for the economy over the long term than our current housing policy. If there were a requirement to adequately house homeless people and families within a short time frame – as in Scotland, where the law states that unsuitable emergency accommodation cannot be used to house homeless people for longer than seven days – we would save the hundreds of millions of euros currently spent on emergency accommodation.

Irish taxpayers would save on the (currently necessary) costs to the health and education systems of providing supports for homeless people, and people who are homeless would have a decent home and the opportunity to fulfil their potential and contribution to society. As it is, Irish society loses out in terms of human contribution and capital, while homeless people lose their dignity. This is a loss to our societies and economies. We would also have a more balanced economy and overall better sense of wellbeing across our society if we eliminated homelessness and housing stress and poverty, and provided more social and affordable housing, relieving workers of the burden of spending huge amounts of their income on rents and mortgages.

The Mercy Law Resource Centre, which provides free legal advice to people who are homeless or at risk of becoming homeless, points out that putting in place a legal protection for the right to housing, while not a solution to housing and homelessness crises, would have a real impact on improving housing and homelessness: 'A legally enforceable right to housing – while not a panacea – would put in place a basic floor of protection in respect of basic, adequate housing for all' (Mercy Law Resource Centre, 2019: 4).

Ireland would not be an outlier in putting in place a legal right to housing, because, as explained earlier, many other European countries have already done so. Ultimately, it is "not enough to adopt laws enshrining the enforceability of the right to housing; this will not in itself guarantee people's rights" (Mercy Law Resource Centre, 2019: 15). The effectiveness of a right to housing, and ensuring people actually have affordable, secure and decent homes, is dependent on the political will to vindicate such rights through budgetary, policy and legislative choices. Thus the primary responsibility for delivering the right to housing will always remain with the elected branches of the Irish state. Essentially, it is politics, policy and sufficient resource allocation that ultimately determine whether people have their right to housing fulfilled or not.

Box 11.3: Mercy Law Resource Centre case for right to housing in the Constitution

• How would the right to housing alleviate the crisis in homelessness? All legislation and policy would have to be proofed to ensure reasonable protection of the right to housing in the same way as other rights are protected. The fact that there is no legal aid for those facing evictions in Ireland could be challenged as a breach of the right to housing.

• A right to housing would require the State, in its decisions and policies, to protect the right to housing in balance with other rights.

• As shown clearly in our last three High Court cases, there is no right to housing in Irish law nor is there a right to shelter. One has no clear legal right to rely on. The fundamental failure by the State to provide adequate emergency accommodation to a family with young children cannot be challenged directly in the courts.

• Constitutional protection would prioritise the issue, show the Government leading and show that it is a national priority.

• If there were a right to housing, there would be an obligation on local authorities to provide emergency accommodation. The word 'shall' must be used. At present, provision is optional, is made when 'reasonable' and is subject to the opinion of the council.

• We have no time limit to the use of emergency accommodation for housing homeless individuals, families and children, so there is no end to how long our families stay in bed and breakfast accommodation. They are staying there for two and a half years. How long will they have to stay in hubs? If there was a limit and it could be judicially reviewed, if the State went over the limit, it could be judicially reviewed and enforce that right to appropriate housing, not bed and breakfast accommodation.

Source: Mercy Law Resource Centre (2018)

The Home for Good civil society coalition is campaigning to insert a clause into the Constitution that spells out clearly where the common good lies in relation to the right to decent, affordable and secure housing. It argues that one of the main obstacles in the way of solving the crisis is Article 43 of the Constitution: 'The result of the primary status given in our Constitution to the right to property is that again and again, property rights trump all other considerations. Time after time, legislative measures have been brought to the Oireachtas to alleviate the housing crisis, only to be dismissed as "contrary to the constitution"' (Home for Good, 2019: 2).

A Dáil research paper, *Property Rights and Housing Legislation*, published in June 2019, shows that on 12 separate occasions over the past decade (2009–19) the constitutional protection of private property rights has been invoked in opposition to legislation proposing reforms in the housing sector. The independent report states:

> The housing crisis that has troubled the country for the past several years has resulted in a large number of Bills coming before the houses seeking to address the issue. It is a noticeable trend that the Government has frequently opposed such Bills on the basis of the private property rights protection in the Constitution, and in particular on the Attorney General's interpretation of those provisions. This paper has identified at least 12 Bills that the Government has opposed or resisted on the basis of concerns around private property rights. (Oireachtas Library and Research Service, 2019: 14)

Although it should be noted that the Supreme Court held in 2000 that obligation in Part V of the Planning and Development Act 2000 on landowners seeking planning permission to provide for 20% social housing was a legitimate constitutional regulation of property rights for the common good. This 'interference' with property rights was proportionate and based on the common good, as it was set out on legislation.

The Home for Good campaign proposes that 'the Constitution be amended to make it clear that access to adequate, secure and affordable housing is an essential part of the common good. Any amendment can preserve the right to private property, while also offering the counterbalance of a right to housing. It will unlock the barrier to essential reforming legislation and be a vital part of ending the current housing crisis' (Home For Good, 2019: 4).

The campaign is seeking a commitment from all political parties to holding a referendum and the inclusion of such a referendum in their programme for Government.

The UN Special Rapporteur on the Right to Housing, Leilani Farha, also highlights that a constitutional right to housing is important to empower those affected by homelessness and housing exclusion to feel that they have a right to housing, and that the state and society has a responsibility to them to address their housing exclusion, thus enabling them to expressly demand through individual or collective campaigning and advocacy that their right to housing be fulfilled. Fahra explains:

> 'I have worked for many years with people on low incomes and living in housing disadvantage and homelessness and I know how meaningful it is for people to have that constitutional right. It changes their relationship with the world in which they live. They feel validated and recognised as human beings and part of the human family. Human rights is about bringing us all together as a human family and recognising that we are all but humans.' (Farha, 2019)

Fahra advised the Irish government to implement the right to housing into the Constitution: "A constitutionally enshrined right to housing is not the beast and the burden that some believe it to be. If I was in the Legislature I would be proud to support the idea of contributing to people's human rights" (Farha, 2019).

Conclusion

The housing crisis is spiralling out of control and there is a need for fundamental change to our housing policy and system. The right to housing, as set out in the UN's rights-based housing strategies, should provide the framework for a radical shift in Ireland's approach to housing.

The obligation of meeting the right to adequate, affordable, decent and secure housing should be implemented in Irish housing policy and legislation, and in its Constitution. A better, fairer, rights-based housing system would create a more cohesive society and balanced economy.

Embedding a right to housing in the Constitution would provide a framework for housing policy that puts the provision of affordable and secure housing as its priority. It would strengthen government's hand constitutionally to improve tenants' protection from eviction, implement long-term leases and Compulsory Purchase Orders for vacant and derelict housing, and apply the vacant sites levy.

Holding a citizens' convention and a referendum on this issue would involve the public in a housing debate that is urgently required. It would be a proud achievement for Ireland to join the 81 other countries, such as Finland, Portugal and Sweden, that have already enshrined the right to housing in their Constitution.

The Ombudsman for Children's Office, an independent statutory body that was established under the Ombudsman for Children Act 2002, is one voice among many in favour of constitutional change. The Ombudsman for Children, Dr Niall Muldoon, stated that "the issue of enumerating the right to housing in the Constitution needs to be progressed as a matter of priority" (Muldoon, 2019). He said that he is "deeply concerned about the immediate and longer term impact that the trauma of homelessness has on children and their families – on their dignity, self-worth, wellbeing and rights. The damaging effects of homelessness on children underscore why the right to adequate housing, which is about 'the right to live somewhere in security, peace and dignity', is a fundamental human right that we must ensure all children in Ireland can enjoy."

The Constitution includes the right to primary education. Yet decent, safe, secure housing is even more fundamental to us than education. Housing is a basic human requirement for child development and health; a child without a stable home can't get an education. Why is it acceptable for a child not to have a home? Why does the Irish government not accept the responsibility to ensure no child is homeless?

Embedding the right to housing in the Constitution is a vital step towards changing the Irish housing system to one that meets people's housing needs, along with other steps outlined below and in Chapter 12 which are essential to make the human right a reality. Individual rights cases provide limited effectiveness in changing social policy and systems. It is the macro-level transformation in policy that can achieve meaningful rights in practice.

Government could also introduce immediate legislation to implement the right to housing in practice. For example, the Irish Human Rights and Equality Commission (IHREC) has recommended that Section 10 of the Housing Act 1988 be amended to place a limit on the amount time a family may spend in emergency accommodation, with an obligation on local authorities to provide suitable permanent family accommodation thereafter. IHREC also recommends regulations under section 10(11)(a) of the Housing Act 1988 in relation to the type of emergency accommodation used for families, and an assessment of human rights and equality issues in line with the public sector duty obligations of local authorities as set out in Section 42 of the Irish Human Rights and Equality Commission Act 2014. Other legislation could include extending tenants' rights, introducing protection from evictions, freezing rents, and taxing vacant and derelict buildings and land.

There is a need for the development of a new national housing policy based on a human rights approach, radically changing the way housing is provided, by massively increasing the role of the state and not-for-profit organisations in providing public, mixed-income, affordable housing, as set out in Chapter 12, and implementing tenants' rights in legislation, among other measures. Finally, at the heart of a right to housing approach is the empowerment and participation of those whose rights are being violated. A rights-based housing policy, therefore, should also provide funding to, and support for, the formation of tenants' organisations and capacity building for housing advocacy organisations and grassroots groups.

12

A Green New Deal for Housing: affordable sustainable homes and communities for all

Long-term, secure housing of decent quality is fundamental to our wellbeing and essential for every one of us to live a life with dignity. It fulfils the requirement of the basic human need for shelter and for a secure base that provides ontological security, mental and physical health; for a home in which to feel protected and to raise families and nurture individuals, especially children; and for a place that enables a good quality of life within the wider community. It is the base from which we can make friends, go to school, get a job, be a friend, partner and carer, fulfil our potential, and rest. Our home is a source of wide-ranging emotions for us, from belonging to security. Increasingly, our homes also have a central role in ensuring environmentally sustainable development and meeting the challenges of climate change. However, the fundamental role of housing as a home has been undermined by decades of neoliberal economic and housing policies to become a financialised asset whose primary value is that of an exchange commodity for investors. The real estate–finance 'industrial complex' – the banks, real estate equity funds, wealth funds, big accountancy firms, and legal and property professions – has turned homes into wealth extraction funds for the rich. As a result, housing systems across the world are failing to provide affordable, secure homes, resulting in deepening inequalities, and rising levels of housing exclusion, insecurity and poverty.

This housing shock is devastating the lives of increasing numbers of homeless individuals, families and children, and increasingly affects the working and middle classes, Generation Renters, migrants, students and elderly people. And it will continue to affect future generations. Many parents are wondering where their children will get a home when they grow up. Generation Rent is the first generation in over 50 years to experience a rupture in the social contract, without the opportunity their parents had of gaining affordable, secure homes. This is an unprecedented generational and economic inequality.

The financialisation of housing and the current market-dominated approach promises only a future of permanent unaffordability for the 'locked-out' generations. Social and economic divisions will worsen as a global 'rentier class' of investor landlords and equity funds amass wealth while making homes, cities and towns unaffordable for the average worker. We are on the verge of creating the housing dystopia set out in Chapter 1.

Private market fails to deliver affordable housing

Current government policy is overly focused on incentivising the private market through lax planning regulations, tax reliefs, 'help to buy' subsidies and 'co-living' development, creating the illusion of home ownership and fuelling house prices. It is ideologically opposed to the notion of the state, local authorities and not-for-profit sector providing affordable homes on a major scale. The ideological belief in the market has meant policy has prioritised the interests of global equity funds and investor landlords.

For example, local authorities and the Land Development Agency, a commercial state-sponsored body that coordinates land within state control for optimal use, are being directed to develop public–private partnerships (PPPs) on public land, which involves most of the land being transferred to private developers to build private housing that will be sold on the open market for maximum profit – that is, at unaffordable prices.

Such 'zombie' PPPs result in the immoral and illogical situation whereby public land is left lying idle waiting for private investors to be interested in developing it; the few sites that are being developed, such as O'Devaney Gardens in Dublin, involve huge profits being taken by the investor developers.

Unfortunately, government commitments to cost-rental housing appear to be more spin than substance. Just as the Housing Assistance Payment (HAP) scheme is spun as a way of providing social housing and Family Hubs (emergency accommodation) are spun as solutions to homelessness, a few cost-rental pilots are being spun as a cost-rental delivery programme. There is no real political will for rolling out public affordable housing on a large scale; despite being six years into the crisis, there is still no national, affordable housing delivery programme and no affordable cost-rental policy, plan, legislation, framework, funding, schemes or targets for large-scale delivery. Without this, local authorities and approved housing bodies are limited in the extent to which they can develop affordable housing.

At the heart of the housing problem is the inadequate supply of affordable housing. The private market does not, and never will, provide a sufficient supply of high-quality affordable housing. Central Statistics Office data for 2019 show a fall in residential construction in Ireland, and show that the number of new homes built in 2019 constitutes half of the actual demand. But this is not some 'natural' disaster, accident or inevitability. It results from the way in which we organise our economies and society. It results from the decisions governments at local, national and European level make about how we approach housing. It results from the operation of the private housing market and the actions of private investors, landlords, and speculative real estate funds and developers. That means it if the policies and actions of government change, the crisis can be solved.

Connecting the climate and housing crisis

The connection between housing and the environment urgently needs to be moved centre stage in both the housing and climate debates. Our understanding of the fundamental role of individual homes in our wellbeing can be conceptually extended to thinking about the role of our collective home – the planet – in our collective societal and global wellbeing. By ensuring everyone has an affordable, sustainable home, we can improve both our own wellbeing and the wellbeing of the collective home on which humanity relies for its continued existence.

Climate change and housing can be linked together conceptually and in the public imagination through the centrality of home to the human existence. The planet is our home and without a home we have nothing, as individuals, societies or a human race. A key way to stop the climate disaster is by providing sustainable, environmentally passive homes – in their design and retrofitting. But we also need to ensure people have a secure, affordable, sustainable home as part of a socially just transition. This is a central tenet of an Irish and global Green New Deal – the reconstruction of our economies to provide sustainable and socially just economic development for all, with secure, affordable, sustainable homes at its heart.

Governments and the private sector are set to build and refurbish billions of homes across the world in the coming decades. It is essential that these are sustainably designed, produced and managed homes and neighbourhoods. They should include climate mitigation measures, through green building measures, tree planting, water harvesting, underground heating systems, solar panels and wind turbines. These require a major investment that only the state (representing society) has the capacity, ability and responsibility to make. For-profit, private market housing and investors will not willingly build to the zero-carbon, environmentally sustainable standards we need; rather, they will seek out the cheapest way of delivery. Allowing the market to dominate the housing process will not ensure environmental sustainability. Market pricing and market solutions will not do what is necessary to make our housing systems climate-resilient and carbon-neutral. Leaving it up to individuals to make housing more environmentally friendly will just exacerbate inequalities; vulnerable groups and those on lower incomes who cannot afford to make the necessary retrofitting changes or build sustainable energy systems into their homes will lose out over and over again. They will be hit from increased carbon taxes, higher energy bills, an inability to afford to move or renovate after climate-related weather events such as floods, droughts and storms, and the incapacity to gain from producing renewable energy through their homes and neighbourhoods.

Building new, low-carbon housing and retrofitting existing homes to meet the highest energy rating possible reduces carbon usage and addresses fuel poverty among households by mitigating poor energy performance of homes.

As Naomi Klein explains in her book:

> Humanity has a once-in-a-century chance to fix an economic model that is failing the majority of people on multiple fronts ... a Green New Deal could instill a sense of collective, higher purpose – a set of concrete goals that we are all working toward together. Roosevelt's New Deal showed how radically both a society's infrastructure and its governing values can be altered in the span of a decade. (Klein, 2019: 26)

A new housing plan: a Green New Deal for Housing in Ireland

There are many solutions to the housing crisis. Here I outline what I believe are the most important ones for transforming our housing systems to provide affordable, sustainable homes for all. They apply to Ireland, but are suitable for other countries as well.

The first solution is developing a new vision for national housing policy and our housing system, including developing a new national housing plan based on the state ensuring a guaranteed sufficient supply of affordable, secure, high-quality and environmentally sustainable housing. This plan, A Green New Deal for Housing in Ireland: Affordable Sustainable Homes and Communities for All, would include an unprecedented programme of state-funded construction of 300,000 affordable, sustainable homes, and the extensive retrofitting of half a million existing social and private houses, ensuring that all current homes are energy-efficient and carbon-neutral by 2030. The 300,000 new, public, affordable, sustainable homes would be available for working-class and middle-income people, and for Generation Renters and Generation Stuck at Home. It would provide homes for all homeless individuals and families, women and their families in domestic violence refuges, those in direct provision (asylum seeker accommodation), and Travellers in housing need, and provide enough homes to clear the local authority waiting lists. It would include 200,000 affordable cost-rental homes, with guaranteed, affordable income-related rents and lifetime leases, providing secure, high-quality rental homes, and 100,000 affordable homes for purchase. These homes would be built in mixed-income housing developments, with, for example, two thirds being affordable cost-rental homes and a third being homes for affordable purchase.

Such developments would provide mixed-income neighbourhoods where, for example, nurses, Gardai (Irish police), teachers, retail workers, cleaners, artists, IT professionals, students, elderly people and those with disabilities can live close to their work and spend time in their communities rather than spending hours commuting with all the associated personal stress and negative environmental impact. They would provide low- and middle-income households with secure, affordable homes in strong, stable and flourishing communities. They would be built to the highest standards of architectural design and planning, creating beautiful and environmentally sustainable communities based on the carbon-neutral development model required to tackle climate change, such as developing onsite renewable energy. They would be spacious, high-quality developments, providing attractive places to live. They would include prime public spaces, libraries, retail and work units, community buildings, neighbourhood parks and play facilities.

Affordable Sustainable Homes Building Agency

A dedicated Affordable Sustainable Homes Building Agency should be created as a public enterprise body tasked to deliver this model and build the 300,000 homes in partnership with local authorities, not-for profit-housing associations and cooperatives, just as the Electricity Supply Board rolled out electricity across the country in the 20th century. There should be support for the expansion of not-for-profit housing associations and cooperative enterprises to scale up to deliver housing. Local authorities would also have key responsibility for delivery, and provided with funding to develop specific housing sections whereby housing delivery and management skills can be developed and retained on a long-term basis to deliver and manage the new housing efficiently.

This model should be developed on cooperative principles, prioritising community and place making, including local communities, tenants and owners, in the design, delivery, management and maintenance of housing. The cooperative housing approach, in particular, has significant benefits as a form of affordable housing provision that can provide strong community development. A cooperative is where people work together for a common aim, generally a social enterprise producing a socially useful outcome, and any profits are shared equally among members or reinvested back into the cooperative. A key principle of cooperatives is that the 'not-for-profit' or 'limited profit' enterprise, such as a housing development or group of houses, is owned or managed by the members of the cooperative. Cooperatives build social networks and strengthen social cohesion, which are essential elements of strong, healthy communities, by connecting residents in a sense of collective ownership over their homes and communities.

Some 3,000 homes were built in the 1970s and 1980s by housing cooperatives in various parts of Ireland. By contrast, the housing cooperative Ó Cualann Cohousing Alliance CLG (Ó Cualann) states that it currently has thousands of people on its waiting lists, but has been limited by the failure of local authorities and state bodies to make land available. Ó Cualann aims to build integrated homes in communities: 'It's not just about building houses but building communities, and that's the key here, as communities are so important' (https://www.ocualann.ie/). The state should implement legislation and finance mechanisms, including direct funding, to enable an expansion of cooperative housing and building social enterprises such as Ó Cualann. Just like the successful cooperative economy of Mondragón in Spain, Ireland could make environmental cooperatives central to its economy. There should be public educational programmes on how to develop green housing cooperatives, and facilitating and empowering communities to help set them up.

Tackling the housing crisis through a state-funded Green New Deal programme of construction would also help ensure that workers (builders, tradespeople, architects, engineers, quantity surveyors) have long-term, high-quality employment, and provide apprenticeship schemes. It would upskill and train construction workers in new green building technologies and approaches, and promote manufactured and modularised passive housing typologies that support the circular economy. Ireland could then become a global leader in environmental housing cooperatives, construction skills and technologies. Measures could include a Living Wage clause in public contracts, as well as clauses on trade union recognition and collective bargaining. This would counter the growing problem of forced self-employment among construction workers. It would also address the training deficit in Irish construction that has arisen partly as a result of the dependency of the industry on projects with short-term funding.

This approach would ensure the increased quality and standards of building (eliminating the substandard building methods that currently persist such as those found in Priory Hall, Dublin, which was condemned by fire inspectors and evacuated by court order in 2011), as well as the better planning of estates and apartment blocks as places that provide high-quality, safe and energy-efficient homes. A state-led housing body could also address the regeneration of neglected areas affected by social disadvantage and provide local community employment.

A modest increase in social housing investment in the past three years has seen the development of some very innovative and impressive examples of excellently designed, environmentally sustainable and inclusive social housing in Ireland. The 2019 Irish Council for Social Housing awards showcased some of these developments, built by local authorities working in partnership with approved housing bodies.

Reimagining public housing

Within my proposed model, there should also be opportunities for tenants to buy their home under shared ownership schemes, equity partnerships and co-ownership, 'rent and save' options. Lower rents would provide greater spending in the economy and help tenants save for deposits or take part in equity partnerships and co-ownership schemes. Moreover, such units should only be sold back to the Affordable Sustainable Homes Building Agency or local authority/ approved housing body/cooperative managing the estates. Otherwise there is a risk of repeating the mistake of the 'right to buy' schemes whereby a huge portion of the social housing stock was sold off to tenants, thus privatising and losing substantial numbers of affordable homes, and limiting the ability of the state over the long term to provide for those in housing need. This approach would also reduce nimbyism and opposition to housing developments, as locals would see the opportunities for their children of getting a home in one of these new, sustainable, mixed communities.

This new form of public housing would be built so that people aspire to live in it. This is a radical reimagination and reconceptualisation of the provision of social and affordable housing in Irish housing policy. Public housing should not just be about catching those at the very bottom in society, a 'safety net' for the most vulnerable, but instead become a service and a way of living for a broad section of the population. This would transform social housing from being treated as a stigmatised form of accommodation restricted to very low-income households to becoming a model of desirable housing available and attractive to a much broader range of low- and middle-income households.

This new 'affordable, sustainable homes' tenure would provide affordable cities and urban areas for working- and middle-class communities, artists and professionals, and give people a real option to exercise their right to live in the city and be part of flourishing communities.

These will be homes and communities that residents, housing associations, local authorities, the government and the country will be proud of and committed to protecting and expanding.

This approach is not about removing private sector involvement in housing, but would provide for a dramatic increase in the state and non-profit sector within the housing system. A good target for Ireland (and other countries aiming to solve their housing crises) then, if we are to solve the housing crisis permanently, is to bring the stock of new 'public' (non-market) housing up to the levels in countries such as Austria and Sweden that meet their citizens' housing needs much better than Ireland. That means increasing the level of public housing to between a quarter to a third of total housing stock (and to 50% in the largest cities). This still leaves private housing as the majority tenure. In Ireland, the social housing stock comprises 176,178 units – just 9% of all housing. Therefore, to bring it up to 30% of housing stock would require an additional 410,000 public affordable units. To reach this within a decade, we need to build the 300,000 affordable sustainable homes suggested earlier, and instigate a major programme of compulsory purchase of 100,000 derelict and vacant properties, 'buy-to-let' private rental accommodation in mortgage arrears and HAP accommodation.

Use public land for public and not-for-profit affordable sustainable homes

Land is the one of the most important elements in the provision of affordable housing. The Irish state owns massive land banks, and therefore has the capacity to build affordable housing on a major scale. Local authorities and the National Asset Management Agency (NAMA) alone have enough land to build 114,000 dwellings. The IDA (Ireland's inward investment promotion agency), Office of Public Works, CIÉ (public transport provider), Health Service Executive and other state agencies also own significant tracts of land, as do religious organisations. Architect and analyst Mel Reynolds (2018) found that local authorities own more than five times the declared amount in the government's action plan for housing, *Rebuilding Ireland* (Department of Housing, Planning and Local Government, 2016b). This land should be used to build 100%, affordable, 'non-market' housing developments. Some land should be transferred under leasehold arrangements or agreements to not-for-profit cooperatives, housing associations and community land trust ownership schemes. NAMA land and property sales should be halted and the remaining NAMA land used for this purpose rather than being hoarded by investors, or developed into 'co-living' pods, expensive student accommodation or investment vehicles for speculators. NAMA should be directed to fulfil its social mandate.

This model would draw on the successful Vienna housing model. Cost-rental housing (public rental housing provided by not-for-profit housing companies and public municipalities) is the norm in European countries such as Austria, Denmark and the Netherlands. In Vienna, more than half the population lives in either one of the 220,000 municipal homes or the 200,000 limited-profit housing association homes operating on a cost-rental basis. The former is more heavily subsidised and has lower rents compared with the limited-profit sector. Vienna's public housing sector is open to higher-income earners and the middle class. In Denmark, public housing accommodates 1 million people in more than 8,500 estates, owned by 550 different not-for-profit housing associations. It is financed from borrowing from the Danish Housing Investment Bank (funded by Danish pension funds). There is no income test – everybody is entitled to social housing.

Another example of a country with a progressive social housing model is Helsinki, Finland, which has made huge progress in reducing homelessness in recent years. Helsinki owns 60,000 social housing units, runs its own construction company and builds 7,000 new homes per year. The Housing Finance and Development Centre of Finland (ARA) plays a key role in funding social housing in Finland by offering grants and guarantees on long-term loans financing the provision of affordable rental housing. In addition, ARA monitors costs and quality standards, and promotes innovation and excellence.

Ireland's state housing advisory and research body, the Housing Agency, recognises the role of a cost-rental sector in the delivery of affordable housing, stating:

> A key element of achieving affordable housing in many countries is the development of a cost rental sector which, over time, provides a significant amount of housing that is affordable to a wide range of households. The main elements in ensuring cost rental achieves affordability over time are the use of low-cost land, long-term lower cost finance and funding and a not-for-profit approach. Thinking long term – 50 years plus – is key to making this work. It is a more sustainable model where assets and future rental income flows can be used to leverage further investment, building a cost rental sector. (O'Connor, 2019)

Meanwhile, the Irish government's advisory body, the National Economic and Social Council, has argued that Ireland needs to produce a large and sustained supply of new public housing available to all who choose it on a cost rental basis (NESC, 2014).

This will transform our housing system from a 'dualist' model to a 'unitary' model, where public and non-market/not-for-profit housing is allowed compete with the private rental market. Tenants will have a choice about where to access housing – in these new affordable housing developments or in the 'for-profit' private market.

Funding a new housing model

Viable developments that provide genuinely affordable homes need significant state support, including Exchequer funding, long-term, low-cost loans, land and infrastructure input at the outset. This will ensure that rents and prices are well below market rates.

The funding is available to do this. Finance could come from the Housing Finance Agency, European Investment Bank, Ireland Strategic Investment Fund (which is a €20 billion state investment fund), credit unions (which have almost €1 billion to lend) or state borrowing, which is currently available at very low interest rates. We could set up a state investment bank, providing finance for housing and green enterprise, or we could retain Allied Irish Bank as a state bank to support these social and economic functions rather than selling it off in the coming years as is currently planned by the Government and losing the opportunity to contribute to the sustainable and socially just economic development of this country. Furthermore, local authorities should be financed through a tripling of capital Exchequer funding allocations (from €1 billion to €3 billion) and be allowed to access borrowing themselves from the various bodies mentioned or on the markets, to increase capacity in terms of skilled personnel (architects, engineers and so on) to deliver the programme. Approved housing bodies and not-for-profit housing associations could also be provided with state guarantees of aspects of their finance raised from the private sector, which would enable them borrow at lower interest rates and hugely expand their provision.

There are claims that the European Union (EU) internal market and fiscal rules restrict governments in what they can do with regard to state involvement in social housing. In relation to fiscal rules, the government has flexibility on the budgetary fiscal space, which can be increased to allow more investment in areas such as housing if taxation revenue is raised to cover that increase in investment expenditure. Ireland is a low-tax economy for corporations, property investors, high earners and wealth, and there is significant capacity to raise tax in these areas. The state can also borrow to invest in public infrastructure such as social and affordable housing. In relation to the EU rules on state aid for services of general economic interest, Padraic Kenna (2019) has outlined that housing is an area of national competence, and that once the criteria of eligibility for social housing are clear and justified, investing in an expanded form of social housing such as cost rental is permissible under EU rules. Kenna has set out the categories of the population that are excluded from the housing market in Ireland, which comprise 70% of the population. While the bottom four deciles of the population are eligible for current social housing, there is very little social housing available to them because the state has not built any for over a decade. Furthermore, those in the middle deciles are not eligible for social housing in Ireland, and they cannot access the mortgage or house purchase market, or private rental market, on an affordable basis (that is, their housing costs are higher than 30% of net income). These households, in the fifth, sixth and seventh percentiles, are the 'squeezed middle'. Under EU rules, the state could finance a large-scale, affordable cost–rental and affordable purchase house-building programme for these households.

The cost-rental approach makes greater economic sense than current social housing policy as tenants on housing benefits could move into cost-rental developments, enabling HAP to be transferred from a housing subsidy for private landlords to a rent support for households in cost-rental housing provided by approved housing bodies and local authorities. In this way, the HAP subsidy could provide lifetime secure homes and a long-term investment in affordable homes.

Public and not-for-profit housing generally provides a less expensive form of housing provision than the private market. In Dublin, for example, the private sector claims it cannot build a three-bed home for less than €350,000, yet the average cost of building of a social housing unit is €200,000, and Ó Cualann has built and sold two-bedroom apartments for €165,000, two-bedroom houses for €185,000, and three-bedroom houses for €219,000 in Ballymun North Dublin. This is because the public and not-for-profit housing models have lower finance and reduced land costs, and take less profit than the private construction industry model (where developers can take 15% to 20% of costs as profit).

A new housing model underpinned by the right to housing as foundation of housing policy and law

The second solution is to make the right to housing, as set out in the United Nation's rights-based housing strategies, the framework for the new national housing policy and plan. The right to adequate, affordable, decent and secure housing should be implemented in Irish housing policy and legislation and in its Constitution. This would make a rights-based housing system the aim of housing policy in Ireland, providing a vision and policy for housing that is underpinned by a wider vision of a society and economy that provides socially just economic development for all, a socially inclusive and active democratic citizenry, and an environmentally sustainable mode of development.

This requires the Irish state to place the direct provision of public housing, not-for-profit, affordable rental and cooperative housing at the core of its function and responsibility, as with the delivery of health and education.

An equality and human rights-based approach to housing provides a framework that can guarantee access to affordable and secure housing. This approach can work to ameliorate growing inequality in the labour market and to reduce mechanisms that generate inequality within the housing and financial sphere. Housing can thus become a key factor in protecting people from rising levels of market-generated inequality and act as a tool to reduce levels of economic inequality.

A referendum to include a right to housing in the Constitution would provide an important opportunity for a national discussion about the Irish housing system, and homelessness and should housing be treated as a human right. This could include a Citizens' Convention on Housing. Putting the right to affordable, secure, adequate (and we should add environmentally sustainable) housing into our Constitution would provide a new drive and direction for transforming our housing system.

As explained in Chapter 11, there are many pieces of legislation that could be introduced immediately that would effectively implement the right to housing in practice and make the private rental sector a secure affordable housing option for tenants. These include laws to protect tenants from eviction, provide long-term security of tenure and lifetime leases, temporarily freeze rents, set rent affordability mechanisms and strengthen enforcement mechanisms of existing measures. Emergency legislation should also be introduced to make it illegal for landlords, banks and investment funds to evict tenants and home owners in mortgage distress into homelessness. If such measures were implemented and subsequently challenged and stopped in the courts on the ground that they have no basis in the Constitution, this would provide a clear rationale for constitutional change. There should also be increased powers and resources for the Irish Human Rights and Equality Commission and the Ombudsman for Children's Office to monitor, and ensure implementation of, the right to housing across the housing system. A rights-based housing policy would also provide the funding and support for the formation and operation of tenant advocacy organisations and tenants' unions, and capacity building and support for housing advocacy organisations. It would also place a much higher priority on the prevention of homelessness, particularly preventative measures and services.

A rights-based policy would also ensure that housing and land in cities and towns are planned for people as a home. This means policies that curtail speculative property investment such as:

- implementing taxes on real estate investment;
- abolishing the Real Estate Investment Trust Tax Incentive, and various forms of tax avoidance by real estate funds;
- restricting and regulating short-stay online tourist platforms;
- implementing recommendations of the the Report of the Committee on the Price of Building land (1974), known as the Kenny Report, which made proposals to control the price of land for housing, including local authorities to be given the right to acquire undeveloped lands at existing use value plus 25 per cent);
- restricting (or even removing) exemptions on the vacant site tax to force land owners to use or sell vacant land;

- introducing vacant and derelict property tax for non-principal dwelling houses and small sites;
- directing NAMA to use its remaining land, property and cash reserves for public affordable housing.

Table 12.1 sets out the benefits of a public, affordable, sustainable homes model, contrasting it to our current market-dominated housing model using key indicators of a right to housing, economic development, environmental sustainability, social cohesion, equality and wellbeing.

Conclusion: we must, and we can, solve the housing crisis

All the evidence suggests that only a radical transformative shift in housing and economic policy towards a decommodified, less financialised, not-for-profit, environmentally sustainable housing approach will achieve a housing system that can provide affordable and secure green housing to all as a human right and thus move us off the current trajectory that is causing significant housing exclusion, worsening economic and social inequality, and contributing to climate destruction.

The public, not-for-profit and cooperative affordable housing approach can address the housing crisis while simultaneously helping to address inequality, climate change and citizen exclusion. It can help overcome the growing anxiety and precarity, alienation and disconnection from our homes, community and cities.

This would provide a positive, hopeful future for hard-pressed low- and middle-income families, workers, individuals, elderly people, students and those with disabilities to have the security and affordability of an environmentally sustainable home in an increasingly precarious world.

Providing affordable, secure rental homes and cooperative, shared-purchase, energy-efficient homes will reduce poverty and deprivation and enable people to meet their bills, spend money in the local economy, reduce stress, enable people to live close to work and be more environmentally sustainable. It is illogical to rely on an inherently unreliable, dysfunctional and unequal private market housing model.

Housing systems are at a cross roads, and the decisions taken over the coming years will determine whether we compound a financialised, marketised, unaffordable housing system that creates inequality, or implement policies that achieve a housing system that reduces inequality, fulfils human rights and contributes to solving the climate crisis.

Table 12.1: Indicators of housing models: the market (dualist) model and public, affordable, sustainable, human rights (unitary) model compared

Indicator/housing model	Current market-dominant housing model ('dualist' model)	New, public, affordable, sustainable homes and right to housing model ('unitary' model)
A right to housing (adequate, affordable, security of tenure)	• Private market is unaffordable, insecure and inadequate • Insufficient supply of affordable homes results in denial of right to a home to multiple groups, especially homeless	• Ensures sufficient supply of affordable, adequate (spacious, appropriate), lifetime, secure homes • Ensures strong regulation of private market • Right to adequate housing fulfilled
Economic development	• Limits economic development, for example competitiveness • Poor allocation of resources, for example into luxury hotels, or expensive student accommodation, not affordable housing • Land and property left vacant and derelict while huge housing shortage exist • Subsidies such as HAP lost to private sector	• Contributes to economic development – social investment retained within provision of affordable housing into perpetuity • Reduces housing costs to general population – reduces poverty, enables saving, and further expenditure in economy • Reduces associated health expenses of poor housing • Provides new social enterprise – sustainable homes cooperatives
Environmental sustainability	• Very poor energy efficiency of homes – fuel poverty and high carbon emissions • Commuting – transport pollution • New private homes fail to achieve zero-carbon status and fail to incorporate renewable energy production; the market fails to incorporate carbon reduction – negative impact on climate emissions • Failure to meet climate targets	• Green New Deal for Housing ensures housing meets climate targets of cutting emissions in half by 2030 and zero emissions by 2050 • Incorporation of passive, carbon-neutral building and design into private and public housing schemes as a requirement • Major contribution to a 'just transition' by providing affordable and sustainable homes for all

(continued)

Table 12.1: Indicators of housing models: the market (dualist) model and public, affordable, sustainable, human rights (unitary) model compared (continued)

Indicator/housing model	Current market-dominant housing model ('dualist' model)	New, public, affordable, sustainable homes and right to housing model ('unitary' model)
Social cohesion (individual/community/society)	• Commuting – personal stress, reduced family time, limited community engagement • Cities hollowed out of working families and individuals • Exacerbated social divisions and political exclusion	• Liveable, family friendly, diverse cities and urban areas • Greater social inclusion and participation • Generational and social class solidarity
Equality	• Growing gap between housing 'haves' and 'have-nots' – housing affordability inequality, generational and social class inequality • Wealth transfer from renters and state to (global) landlords, real estate industry, landowners • Declining conditions of workers in construction industry	• Reduced housing costs for middle-income households • Greater equality of housing conditions • Greater generational and social class equality • Improved conditions of employment of construction industry workers and professionals
Wellbeing	Detrimental psychosocial impacts from housing stress, child development impacts, delayed adulthood, negative mental health impact of substandard housing (mould, damp), inadequate space and light, poor community infrastructure, unsafe	Enhanced wellbeing for low- and middle-income households through well-designed mixed-income homes and neighbourhoods

The housing crisis is not intractable and can be solved with a shift to alternative policies, but, given the regulatory capture of policy makers, a civil society social movement is required to bring about a major transformation in policy. To get alternative policies implemented requires a counter-power of civil society and public to force the state and government to change direction. A process of constructing cross-society solidarity is necessary. An alliance of renters, students, precarious workers and professionals, the middle class, aspirant home owners and those needing social housing should come together around the common goal of affordable sustainable homes for all underpinned by the right to housing in law and the constitution. In the words of Amartya Sen, a 'public outcry' is required to pressure the state and government to change direction. A tenants' union or organisation is needed to progress and give voice to tenants' issues.

The housing crisis in Ireland is not unique; it is part of the common policy trajectory of neoliberalism and financialisation that has turned housing into a commodity and shifted the role of the state from affordable house provider to subsidiser of the private finance development industry. We need to act at every level – as citizens, planners, architects, academics and housing practitioners – to make Scenario 2 in Chapter 1 a reality. Only by acting, by standing up, by doing it differently can we ensure affordable, secure, beautiful homes and sustainable communities – for all, not just the privileged and wealthy – will become a reality. This is a battle – a battle for the soul and future of housing and our urban areas and cities. The outcome will have far-reaching impacts.

The danger otherwise is that current levels of homelessness and housing distress and inequality will become normalised and accepted as part of the modern condition. We need a radical shift in housing policy and our housing systems to prevent the current housing shock from becoming a permanent crisis. The key question, then, is whether housing is financialised and treated primarily as a commodity, as in the current policy paradigm, or whether it is treated as a human right and social and public good.

There is a clear political choice: to focus, as governments have done up to this point, on achieving 'supply' through global wealth investors, vulture landlords and speculative property finance; or bring the state back in, in a new, reimagined, cooperative way, as a lead in a historic programme of providing affordable, sustainable homes for rent and ownership. One approach will extend unaffordable rental and house prices into the future, along with associated poverty and financial stress, for large sections of the population; the other can deliver and guarantee the human right to housing for all our citizens. It is a choice the government, and Ireland as a country, have to make. Is it to be a consolidation of the dystopia where housing is treated as a financialised commodity and wealth-accumulating asset for investors, or will our people have their need and right to a home fulfilled?

At the United Nations Climate Action Summit in September 2019, the President of Ireland, Michael D. Higgins, spoke of the need to address the three major challenges of climate change, inequality and social cohesion. Affordable sustainable housing for all can help address all of these issues. President Higgins (quoted in the *Irish Times*, 2014) has himself outlined the need for public housing:

> 'These are needs that are in fact citizenship needs ... it isn't a matter of waiting for approval from external ratings agencies or for financial matters to be made secure... It's about democracy. You can't leave the provision of housing to a residual feature of the market place.... We have to accept that we need a great, huge increase in public rental accommodation.'

This book argues that regulating landlords and capital is vital, but is not enough. The state and not-for-profit sector must become a major (in some cases the principal) direct provider of housing – not as a bureaucratic leviathan, but in the form of a cooperative, participative, empowering state that through its housing policy provides quality homes, rebuilds communities, helps solve the climate disaster, and, importantly, involves citizens as leading actors in the design, planning, delivery and management of their homes in their communities.

Deep inequalities can be seen every day in our cities, towns and across the globe. It is simply unacceptable that in a country like Ireland, one of the wealthiest in the world, there are such high levels of homelessness, housing insecurity, distress and poverty. This book is an attempt to show the Irish public (and readers in other countries too) that this social catastrophe is not inevitable, and that there are solutions. It is a question of whether or not our state and government, and society at large, want to implement them. We can create a fairer, more sustainable country for all those suffering from housing insecurity and exclusion, for everyone who wants a more equal and fair Ireland. We can end homelessness and ensure that everyone has an affordable secure home, as set out in Scenario 2, 'a future of affordable homes, flourishing communities, and a sustainable planet', in Chapter 1. It is a question of political and societal will. Let's do it.

References

Aalbers, M.B. (2015) 'The great moderation, the great excess and the global housing crisis', *International Journal of Housing Policy*, 15(1): 43–60.

Bartley, B. and Kitchin, R. (2007) *Understanding Contemporary Ireland*, London: Pluto Press.

Bissett, J. (2008) *Regeneration: Public Good or Private Profit?*, Dublin: TASC.

Bourdieu, P. (1991) *Language and Symbolic Power*, Cambridge, MA: Harvard University Press.

Brown, W. (2015) *Undoing the Demos: Neoliberalism's Stealth Revolution*. Cambridge, MA: MIT Press.

Burawoy, M. (2005) 'For public sociology', *American Sociological Review*, 70(1): 4–28.

Burns, M., Drudy, P.J., Hearne, R., McVerry, P. (2017) Rebuilding Ireland: a flawed philosophy, *Working Notes: Fact and Analysis of Social and Economic Issues,* Issue 80, pp 3-20, Jesuit Centre for Faith and Justice.

Byrne, M. (2018) 'Tenant self-organization after the Irish crisis: the Dublin Tenants Association' in Gray, N. (ed) *Rent and its Discontents: A Century of Housing Struggle*, London: Rowman and Littlefield.

Byrne, M. and Norris, M. (2017) 'Pro-cyclical social housing and the crisis of Irish housing policy: marketization, social housing and the property boom and bust', *Housing Policy Debate*, 28(1): 50–63.

CAN (Community Action Network) (2018) *Life in Mortgage Distress,* http://www.canaction.ie/wp-content/uploads/2018/11/life_in_mortgage_distress_report.pdf

Central Bank of Ireland (2019a) *Residential Mortgage Arrears & Repossessions Statistics: Q4 2018*, Statistical Release, Dublin: Central Bank of Ireland.

Central Bank of Ireland (2019b) *Ireland: Investment Funds Data*, Dublin: Central Bank of Ireland, available at https://www.centralbank.ie/statistics/data-and-analysis/other-financial-sector-statistics/investment-funds

Clifford, M (2017) 'If in doubt, "spin it out" sums up approach to crisis', *Irish Examiner*, 22 August, https://www.irishexaminer.com/viewpoints/columnists/michael-clifford/if-in-doubt-spin-it-out-sums-up-approach-to-crisis-457488.html

Committee on the Price of Building Land (1974) *The Report of the Committee on the Price of Building Land*, Dublin: Government of Ireland.

Connolly, C. (2019) Speech to the Thirty-fifth Amendment of the Constitution (Right to a Home) Bill 2016: Second Stage, Dail Eireann Debate, May 16.

Connolly, J. (1899) 'Landlordism in Towns', *The Worker's Republic*, 18 November. https://www.marxists.org/archive/connolly/1899/11/landlord.htm

Convention on the Constitution (2014) *Ninth Report of the Convention on the Constitution, Conclusions and Final Recommendations*, Dublin: Government of Ireland.

Coveney, S. (2017) 'Anti-Evictions Bill 2016: second stage', Dáil Éireann Debate, Tuesday 17 January, Government of Ireland, available at www.oireachtas.ie/en/debates/debate/dail/2017-01-17/31/?high light%5B1%5D=bill&highlight%5B2%5D=bill

Cox, L. (2014) 'Movements making knowledge: a new wave of inspiration for sociology?', *Sociology*, 48(5): 954–71.

Crouch, C. (2011) *The Strange Non-Death of Neoliberalism*, Cambridge: Polity Press.

CSO (Central Statistics Office) (2016) 'Census of Population 2016 – Profile 1: Housing in Ireland', CSO, available at www.cso.ie

CSO (2017) 'Census of Population 2016 – Profile 5: Homeless persons in Ireland', Central Statistics Office, available at www.cso.ie/en/releasesandpublications/ep/p-cp5hpi/cp5hpi/

CSO (2018a) 'Survey on Income and Living Conditions (SILC): 2016 results', Statistical Release, Central Statistics Office, available at www.cso.ie/en/releasesandpublications/er/silc/surveyonincomeandlivingconditions2016

CSO (2018b) 'Residential Property Price Index May 2018', Central Statistics Office, available at www.cso.ie/en/releasesandpublications/ep/p-rppi/residentialpropertypriceindexmay2018/non-household sector

CSO (2019a) SIA18:Income and Poverty Rates by Tenure Status, Year and Statistic, Central Statistics Office, available at https://statbank.cso.ie/px/pxeirestat/statire/SelectVarVal/Define.asp?Maintable=SIA18&PLanguage=0

CSO (2019b) 'Residential dwelling property transactions by county, dwelling status, stamp duty event, type of buyer, type of sale, month and statistic', Central Statistics Office, available at www.cso.ie/px/pxeirestat/Database/eirestat/House%20Prices/House%20Prices_statbank.asp?SP=House%20Prices&Planguage=0

CSO (2019c) New Dwelling Completions, ESB Connections by Type of Connection and Year, 1970–2016, https://statbank.cso.ie/px/pxeirestat/Database/eirestat/New%20Dwelling%20Completions/New%20Dwelling%20Completions_statbank.asp?SP=New%20Dwelling%20Completions&Planguage=0

Cushman & Wakefield (2017) 'The great wall of money', available at www.cushmanwakefield.com/en/research-and-insight/2017/great-wall-of-money-2017

Cushman & Wakefield (2019) *Winning in Growth Cities 2019/2020*, https://www.cushmanwakefield.com/en/insights/winning-in-growth-cities

Daft (2019) 'Irish Rental Report Q3 2019', available at www.daft.ie

Daly, F. (2014) 'Address to the Waterford Chamber of Commerce "Summer Lunch", Mr Frank Daly, Chairman of NAMA', Friday 4 July, available at www.nama.ie/uploads/documents/Waterford_Chamber_of_Commerce_Speech_4July2014_website.pdf

Daly, M (2019) *National Strategies to Fight Homelessness and Housing Exclusion*, Brussels: European Social Policy Network and European Commission.

Department of Education and Skills (2019) 'National student accommodation strategy', Press release, 8 May, https://www.education.ie/en/Press-Events/Press-Releases/2019-press-releases/PR19-05-08.html

Department of the Environment, Community and Local Government (2011) *Housing Policy Statement.* Dublin: Government of Ireland.

Department of the Environment, Community and Local Government (2014) *Social Housing Strategy 2020: Support, Supply and Reform*, Dublin: Government of Ireland.

Department of Finance (2019) *Real Estate Investment Trusts, Irish Real Estate Funds and Section 110 Companies as they invest in the Irish Property Market*, Dublin: Department of Finance.

Department of Housing, Planning and Local Government (2016a) *Construction 2020, A Strategy for a Renewed Construction Sector*, Dublin: Stationery Office.

Department of Housing, Planning and Local Government (2016b) *Rebuilding Ireland*, Dublin: Government of Ireland.

Department of Housing, Planning and Local Government (2016c) *Strategy for the Rental Sector*, Dublin: Government of Ireland.

Department of Housing, Planning and Local Government (2018) *Rebuilding Ireland Action Plan Status Report Q4 2018*, Dublin: Government of Ireland.

Department of Housing, Planning and Local Government (2019a) *Rebuilding Ireland Social Housing Report 2018*, Government of Ireland, www.housing.gov.ie

Department of Housing, Planning and Local Government (2019b) *Housing Statistics*, Dublin: Government of Ireland.

Department of Public Expenditure and Reform (2019) *Trends Analysis, Housing Assistance Payment (2014–2019)*, Dublin: Government of Ireland.

Dewilde, C. and De Decker, P. (2016) 'Changing inequalities in housing outcomes across Western Europe', *Housing, Theory and Society*, 33(2): 121–61.

DHPCLG (2016) *Report of the Committee on Housing and Homelessness*, Dublin. Houses of Oireachtas.

Doherty, P. (2019) 'Tax code', *Dail Eireann* debate, 17 April, https://www.oireachtas.ie/en/debates/question/2019-04-17/53/

Dolan, S. (1966) Speech to the Seanad, Housing Bill, 1965: Second Stage (Resumed), Seanad Eireann Debate, Wednesday 30 March 1966, available at https://www.oireachtas.ie/en/debates/debate/seanad/1966-03-30/3/?highlight%5B0%5D=bill&highlight%5B1%5D=1965

Donaghy, D. (2013) Real Estate Investment Trusts: Tax Policy Rationale, *Irish Tax Review* 2013(2).

DRHE (2018) *A Profile Of Families Experiencing Homelessness In The Dublin Region 2016–2018 Families*, Dublin: Dublin Region Homeless Executive.

Drudy, P. and Punch, M. (2005) *Out of Reach: Inequalities in the Irish Housing System*, Dublin: TASC.

Dublin City Council (2015) *Lands Initiative Report 8th July 2015*, Dublin: Dublin City Council.

Dublin Tenants Association (nd) https://dublintenants.com/

ECA International (2019) 'Dublin enters top five most expensive locations for expat rental accommodation in Europe', available at: https://www.eca-international.com/news/march-2019/irish-capital-enters-top-five-most-expensive-locat

Edgar, W., Doherty, J. and Meert, H. (2004) *Third Review of Statistics on Homelessness in Europe. Developing an Operational Definition of Homelessness*, Brussels: Feantsa.

Edgar, B., Harrison, M., Watson, P. and Busch-Geertsema, V. (2007) *Measurement of Homelessness at European Union Level*, Brussels: European Commission, available at: http://ec.europa.eu/employment_social/social_inclusion/docs/2007/study_homelessness_en.pdf.

Edgar, B. (2012) 'The ETHOS definition and classification of homelessness and housing exclusion', *European Journal of Homelessness*, 6(2): 219–25.

Esping-Andersen, G. (1990) *The Three Worlds of Welfare Capitalism*, Princeton, New Jersey: Princeton University Press.

ESRI (2019) 'A county-level perspective on housing affordability in Ireland', available at: https://www.esri.ie/publications/a-county-level-perspective-on-housing-affordability-in-ireland

Eurostat (2017) 'Housing cost overburden rate by household type – EU-SILC survey', EU Open Data Portal, available at https://ec.europa.eu/eurostat/web/products-datasets/-/ilc_lvho07e

Eurostat (2018) Distribution of population by tenure status, type of household and income group – EU-SILC survey, available at https://ec.europa.eu/eurostat/web/products-datasets/-/ilc_lvho02

Eurostat (2019) 'Share of young people (aged 16-29 years) living with their parents, 2018', available at https://ec.europa.eu/eurostat/web/products-datasets/-/ilc_lvps08

Faculties of Public Health Medicine and Paediatrics, Royal College of Physicians of Ireland (2019) *The Impact of Homelessness and Inadequate Housing on Children's Health*, Royal College of Physicians of Ireland, available at https://www.rcpi.ie/news/releases/faculties-call-on-government-to-urgently-address-serious-harm-to-the-health-of-homeless-children/

Fair Rent Homes Campaign (2018) 'Fair Rent Homes', available at https://ourcommunityabetterway.wordpress.com/

Farha, L. (2017) *Report of the Special Rapporteur on Adequate Housing as a Component of the Right to an Adequate Standard of Living, and on the Right to Non-Discrimination in this Context*, UN Human Rights Council, Geneva: United Nations.

Farha, L. (2019) Speech to the Oireachtas Joint Committee on Housing, Planning and Local Government, Debate, June 12.

Farha, L. (2020) Protecting the right to housing in the context of the COVID-19 outbreak, available at https://www.ohchr.org/EN/Issues/Housing/Pages/COVID19RightToHousing.aspx

FEANTSA (2005) ETHOS – European Typology of Homelessness and housing exclusion, Brussels: FEANTSA.

Finnerty J. (2002) 'Homes for the working class?: Irish public house-building cycles, 1945–2001', *Saothar: Journal of Irish Labour History*, 27: 65–71.

Florida, R. (2018) 'Is housing inequality the main driver of economic inequality?', Citylab, www.citylab.com

Focus Ireland (2018) *Pre-Budget Submission 2019: Making Budget 2019 a 'Budget for Homelessness'*, Dublin: Focus Ireland.

Focus Ireland (2017) 'One in every nine people worried about losing their home according to Focus Ireland report', 16 February, https://www.focusireland.ie/press/one-every-nine-people-worried-losing-home-according-focus-ireland-report/

Focus Ireland (2019) 'Latest figures on homelessness in Ireland', Focus Ireland, available at www.focusireland.ie/resource-hub/latest-figures-homelessness-ireland.

Fraser, N. (1990) 'Rethinking the public sphere: a contribution to the critique of actually existing democracy', *Social Text*, 25/26(1990): 56–80.

Freire, P. (1974) *Education: The Practice of Freedom*, London: Writers and Readers Co-operative.

Gaventa, J. and Cornwall, A. (2001) 'Power and knowledge', in P. Reason and H. Bradbury (eds) *Handbook of Action Research: Participative Inquiry and Practice*, London: Sage Publications, pp 70–80.

Gerstel, N., Bogard, C.J., McConnell, J.J. and Schwartz, M. (1996) 'The therapeutic incarceration of homeless families', *Social Service Review*, 70(4): 543–72.

Gramsci, A. (1971) *Selections from the Prison Notebooks*, London: Lawrence & Wishart.

Grotti, R., Russell, H., Fahey, E. and Maître, B. (2018) Discrimination and Inequality in Housing in Ireland, Dublin: Research Series Economic and Social Research Institute.

Harvey, B. (2012) Changes in employment and services in the voluntary and community sector in Ireland, 2008-2012, Dublin: Irish Congress of Trades Unions.

Harvey, D. (1985) *The Urbanization of Capital: Studies in the History and Theory of Capitalist Urbanization*, Oxford: Blackwell.

Harvey, D. (2005) *A Brief History of Neoliberalism*, Oxford: Oxford University Press.

Hearne, R. (2011) *Public Private Partnerships in Ireland: Failed Experiment or the Way Forward?*, Manchester: Manchester University Press.

Hearne, R. (2014) 'Nama is fuelling high rents by pandering to investors', *The Irish Times*, 28 November.

Hearne, R. (2015a) *The Irish Water War, Austerity and the 'Risen People'*, Maynooth: Maynooth University.

Hearne, R. (2015b) Presentation to Housing is a Human Right public meeting, North Dublin Bay Housing Crisis Community, March.

Hearne, R. (2017) *A Home or a Wealth Generator? Inequality, Financialisation and the Irish Housing Crisis*, Dublin: TASC.

Hearne, R. and Kenna, P. (2014) 'Using the human rights based approach to tackle housing deprivation in an Irish urban housing estate', *Journal of Human Rights Practice*, 6(1).

Hearne, R. and McMahon C. (2016) *Cherishing All Equally, Gender, Children and Economic Inequality in Ireland*, Dublin: TASC.

Hearne, R. and Murphy, M. (2017) *Investing in the Right to a Home: Housing, HAPs and Hubs*, Maynooth: Maynooth University.

Hearne, R. and Murphy, M. (2018) 'An absence of rights: homeless families and social housing marketisation in Ireland', *Administration*, 66(2): 9–31.

Hearne, R. and Murphy, M. (2019) 'Social investment, human rights and capabilities in practice: the case study of family homelessness in Dublin', in M. Yerkes and J. Javornik (eds) *Social Policy and the Capability Approach*, Bristol: Policy Press.

Hearne, R. and Redmond, D. (2014) 'The collapse of PPPs: prospects for social housing regeneration after the crash', in A. MacLaran and S. Kelly (eds) *Neoliberal Urban Policy and the Transformation of the City*, London: Palgrave Macmillan.

Home for Good (2019) 'For the common good; the housing crisis and a proposal to amend the Irish Constitution', available at https://www.homeforgood.ie

Houses of the Oireachtas (2016) *Report of the Committee on Housing and Homelessness*, https://data.oireachtas.ie/ie/oireachtas/committee/dail/32/committee_on_housing_and_homelessness/reports/2016/2016-06-16_final-report-june-2016_en.pdf

Housing Action Now (2013) https://housingactionireland.wordpress.com/

Housing Action Now (2018) 'Fair rent homes for Ireland', available at https://housingactionireland.wordpress.com/

Housing Agency (2018) *Summary of Social Housing Assessments 2018*, Dublin: Housing Agency.

Housing Europe (2019) 'The state of housing in the EU', http://www.housingeurope.eu/resource-1323/the-state-of-housing-in-the-eu-2019

IHREC (Irish Human Rights and Equality Commission) (2019) 'Comments on Ireland's 16th National Report on the implementation of the European Social Charter', https://www.ihrec.ie/app/uploads/2019/05/Comments-on-16th-National-Report-on-the-Implementation-of-the-European-Social-Charter-May-2019-1.pdf

IMF (International Monetary Fund) (2016) 'Ireland: Staff Concluding Statement of the 2016 Article IV Consultation and Fifth Post-Program Monitoring', 24 June, https://www.imf.org/en/News/Articles/2016/07/06/17/33/MCS062416-Ireland-Staff-Concluding-Statement-of-the-2016-Article-IV-Consultation

Institute for Fiscal Studies (2018) 'The decline of homeownership among young adults', available at https://www.ifs.org.uk/publications/10505

IRES REIT (2014) 'IRES to acquire 761 apartment suites in four properties in Greater Dublin Area', Project Orange Press Release, 29 August.

Irish Congress of Trade Unions (2018) *Charter for Housing Rights*, Dublin: ICTU.

Irish Examiner (2017) Emergency accommodation recreated in Dublin city centre, *Irish Examiner*, 24 November.

Irish Examiner (2019a) 'Tenants facing mass eviction from Cork apartments saved from homelessness', *Irish Examiner*, 29 March.

Irish Examiner (2019b) 'Success or failure? Jury is still out on NAMA', *Irish Examiner*, 4 May.

Irish Independent (2017) 'Taoiseach insists Ireland has one of the "lowest levels of homelessness"', *Irish Independent*, 11 November, https://www.independent.ie/irish-news/politics/taoiseach-insists-ireland-has-one-of-the-lowest-levels-of-homelessness-36310203.html

Irish Independent (2019a) 'Global co-living giant targets Dublin with plan for 5,000 beds', *Irish Independent*, 23 June, https://www.independent.ie/business/irish/global-co-living-giant-targets-dublin-with-plan-for-5000-beds-38243634.html

Irish Independent (2019b) 'Editorial: "Increasing housing supply only real way to fix crisis"', *Irish Independent*, 13 September, https://www.independent.ie/opinion/editorial/editorial-increasing-housing-supply-only-real-way-to-fix-crisis-38493673.html

Irish Mirror (2016) 'Over 200 families face homelessness after "vulture fund" deal for Dublin estate', *Irish Mirror*, 14 March.

Irish Human Rights and Equality Commission (2017) *The Provision of Emergency Accommodation to Families Experiencing Homelessness*, https://www.ihrec.ie/app/uploads/2017/07/The-provision-of-emergency-accommodation-to-families-experiencing-homelessness.pdf

Irish Times (2014) 'President calls for more social housing', *Irish Times*, 9 September.

Irish Times (2017a) '150 people living in three Dublin houses where fire occurred, Dáil told', *Irish Times*, 22 February https://www.irishtimes.com/news/politics/oireachtas/150-people-living-in-three-dublin-houses-where-fire-occurred-dáil-told-1.2985058

Irish Times (2017b) 'Project Eagle: loans totalling €6bn sold to US firm Cerberus for €1.43bn', *Irish Times*, 14 March.

Irish Times (2018) 'Housing crisis requires radical solutions', *Irish Times*, 26 September.

Irish Times (2019) 'Life with mortgage arrears in Ireland: I had "seizures from stress"', *Irish Times*, 2 February.

Kemeny, J. (1981) *The Myth of Home Ownership*, London, Routledge and Keegan Paul.

Kemeny, J. (1995) *From Public Housing to the Social Market: Rental Policy Strategies in Comparative Perspective*, London: Routledge.

Kenna, P. (2005) *Housing Rights and Human Rights*, Brussels: FEANTSA.

Kenna, P. (2019) 'Strategic direction for the rental sector, Irish Council for Social Housing, Social Housing 2019 Innovation', Delivery & Sustainability Conference, 10/11 October.

Klein, N. (2007) *The Shock Doctrine: The Rise of Disaster Capitalism*, New York: Allen Lane.

Klein, N. (2019) *On Fire: The (Burning) Case for a Green New Deal*, New York: Simon & Schuster.

Knight Frank (2019) *The Wealth Report*, Knight Frank, London, available at https://www.knightfrank.com/wealthreport

Local Government Board for Ireland (1914) *Departmental Committee to Inquire into the Housing Conditions of the Working Classes in the City of Dublin*, Dublin: HMSO.

Lowe, S. (2011) *The Housing Debate*, Bristol: Policy Press.

MacLaran, A. (1993) *Dublin: The Shaping of a Capital*, London: Belhaven Press.

Madden, D. and Marcuse, P. (2016) *In Defence of Housing: The Politics of Crisis*, New York, NY: Verso.

Maslow, A. H. (1943) 'A theory of human motivation', *Psychological Review*, 50: 370–96.

Mayock, P. and Bretherton, J. (2017) *Women's Homelessness in Europe*, Basingstoke: Palgrave Macmillan.

McCabe, C. (2011) *Sins of the Father: Tracing the Decisions That Shaped the Irish Economy*, Dublin: History Press.

McManus, R. (2002) *Dublin 1910–1940: Shaping the City and Suburbs*, Dublin: Four Courts Press.

McVerry, P (2015) 'Irish homelessness crisis worst since famine says campaigner', Irish Central.Com, 17 February https://www.irishcentral.com/news/irish-homeless-crisis-worst-since-the-famine-says-campaigner

McVerry, P., Carroll, E. and Burns, M. (2017) 'Homelessness and social housing policy', in *Issue 80: Rebuilding Ireland: A Flawed Philosophy*, Dublin: Jesuit Centre for Faith and Justice, pp 21–31.

Mercy Law Resource Centre (2018) Presentation to the Joint Committee on Housing, Planning and Local Government, Right to Housing Debate, 12 June.

Mercy Law Resource Centre (2019) *Second Right to Housing Report: The Right to Housing in Comparative Perspective*, Dublin: Mercy Law Resource Centre.

Milburn, N. and D'Ercole, A. (1991) 'Homeless women: moving toward a comprehensive model', *American Psychologist*, 46(11): 1161–9.

Minister for Finance (2019) 'Tax code', *Dail Eireann* debate, 17 April, https://www.oireachtas.ie/en/debates/question/2019-04-17/53/

Minton, A. (2017) *Big Capital: Who is London For?*, London: Penguin Press.

Muldoon, N. (2019) Speech to the Oireachtas Joint Committee on Children and Youth Affairs, 19 June.

NAMA (2017) 'NAMA response to a report on its performance commissioned by an ex-debtor', https://www.nama.ie/uploads/documents/Debtor_report_on_NAMA-29_March_2017.pdf

NESC (National Economic and Social Council) (2014) *Review of Irish Social and Affordable Housing Provision*, NESC Secretariat Papers, Paper No. 10: Dublin: NESC.

Noonan, M. (2016a) Speech to Oireachtas Committee on Housing and Homelessness, Debate, 17 May.

Noonan, M. (2016b) Speech to the Dail on Real Estate Investment Trusts, Dáil Éireann Debate, 19 July.

Norris, M. and Redmond, D. (eds) (2005) *Housing Contemporary Ireland*, Dublin: Institute of Public Administration.

OCO (Ombudsman for Children's Office) (2019) *No Place like Home*, Dublin: OCO.

O'Connor, J. (2019) Speech to the Joint Oireachtas Committee on Housing, Planning and Local Government Debate on Affordable Housing, 31st January 2019.

Oireachtas Library and Research Service (2019) Property Rights and Housing Legislation, Dublin: Government of Ireland.

Ostry, J.D., Loungani, P. and Furceri, D. (2016) 'Neoliberalism: oversold?', *Finance & Development*, 53(2), https://www.imf.org/external/pubs/ft/fandd/2016/06/ostry.htm

O'Sullivan, E. (2016) 'Ending homelessness in Ireland: ambition, adversity, adaptation', *European Journal of Homelessness*, 10(2): 11–39.

Padgett, D. (2007) 'There's no place like (a) home: ontological security among persons with serious mental illness in the United States', *Social Science & Medicine*, 64(9): 1925–36.

Pavee Point (2016) 'Housing/homeless plan includes Traveller specific accommodation', 19 July, available at www.paveepoint.ie/housinghomeless-plan-includes-traveller-specific-accommodation

Piketty, T. (2014) *Capital in the 21st Century*, Cambridge, MA: Harvard University Press.

PwC (PricewaterhouseCoopers) and Urban Land Institute (2017) *Emerging Trends in Real Estate® Europe 2017*, London: PwC and Urban Land Institute, available at www.pwc.com/gx/en/industries/financial-services/asset-management/emerging-trends-real-estate/europe-2017.html

Reynolds, M. (2017) 'State could save over €9bn over 30 years on social housing', *Village Magazine*, April.

Reynolds, M. (2018) *Submission to Joint Oireachtas Committee on Housing, Planning, Community & Local Government*, Urban Regeneration and Housing (Amendment) Bill 2018, www.oireachtas.ie

Rolling Stone (2010) 'The great American bubble machine', *Rolling Stone*, 5 April, https://www.rollingstone.com/politics/politics-news/the-great-american-bubble-machine-195229/

RTB (Residential Tenancies Board) (2017) *The RTB Rent Index Quarter 3 2017*, Dublin: Residential Tenancies Board.

RTB (2018) 'Rent Index 2018', available at: https://onestopshop.rtb.ie/

RTB (2019) 'Rent Index 2019', available at: https://onestopshop.rtb.ie/

RTÉ (2016) *My Homeless Family*, January, www.rte.ie

RTÉ One (2017) *The Great Irish Sell Off*, Television Documentary, 9 January.

RTE Radio (2018) 'I feel like I've been stolen of most of my life', 5 October, https://www.rte.ie/news/newslens/2018/1005/1001127-amanda-homelessness/

Safe Ireland (2016) 'Over 4000 domestic violence victims a year being ignored in housing crisis', Press Release, 6 May, available at www.safeireland.ie/over-4000-domestic-violence-victims-a-year-being-ignored-in-housing-crisis

Schwartz, H. and Seabrooke, L. (2008) 'Varieties of residential capitalism in the international political economy: old welfare states and the new politics of housing', *Comparative European Politics*, 6(3): 237–61.

Sen, A.K. (2009) *The Idea of Justice*, London: Penguin.

Sen, A. and Dreze, J. (1989) *Hunger and Public Action*, WIDER Studies in Development Economics, Oxford: Oxford University Press.

SVP (St Vincent De Paul) and Threshold (2019) The Housing Assistance Payment: making the Right impact? SVP & Threshold, www.svp.ie/news-media/news/hap-top-ups-are-putting-families-at-risk-of-homele.aspx?cat=socialjustice

Temple Street Children's University Hospital (2019) *Temple Street Annual Report 2018*, https://www.cuh.ie/wp-content/uploads/2019/11/Annual-Report-1.pdf

Tenants First (2008) 'Calling for solidarity', Press release, 19 May, Dublin: Tenants First.

Tenants First (2009) *Housing for Need not Greed, the Tenants First Action Plan for Sustaining Homes and Communities*, Dublin: Tenants First, http://www.limerickregeneration.org/HousingforNeed.pdf

The Herald (2019) 'Co-living for less rent is "exciting future" – Murphy', 21 May, *The Herald*, https://www.herald.ie/news/co-living-for-less-rent-is-exciting-future-murphy-38131965.html

The Journal (2016a) '"We're very worried" – Resident feels he's being forced out of home by 28% rent increase', *The Journal*, 13 December.

The Journal (2016b) 'There are yet more Irish laws that allow foreign property investors to operate here tax-free', *The Journal*, 10 September.

The Journal (2017) 'Government's top housing adviser: "Homelessness is a normal thing"', *The Journal*, 13 November, https://www.thejournal.ie/homelessness-normal-conor-skehan-3693850-Nov2017/

The Journal (2018) 'Dún Laoghaire residents threatened with eviction have won a key battle against vulture funds', *The Journal*, 20 January.

The Journal (2019) 'Majority of revenue on Airbnb comes from rentals which will be hit by new laws', *The Journal*, 30 June, https://www.thejournal.ie/scraped-data-suggests-that-most-airbnb-revenue-comes-from-renting-full-homes-for-more-than-90-days-4700461-Jun2019/

Threshold (2018) *Pre-Budget Submission 2019: Addressing Security, Supply & Security of Tenure*, Dublin: Threshold.

Tully, J. (1973) Speech to the Committee of Finance, Tuesday 20 November, available at https://www.oireachtas.ie/en/debates/debate/dail/1973-11-20/30/?highlight%5B0%5D=emergency&highlight%5B1%5D=measures&highlight%5B2%5D=housing&highlight%5B3%5D=residential&highlight%5B4%5D=tenancy&highlight%5B5%5D=houses&highlight%5B6%5D=housing&highlight%5B7%5D=public&highlight%5B8%5D=housing&highlight%5B9%5D=public&highlight%5B10%5D=housing

Turnbull, D. (2018) A long-term assessment of Irish house price affordability, Nevin Economic Research Institute, Dublin.

UN (United Nations) (1990) *Convention on the Rights of the Child*, New York: UN.

UN (1991) *The Right to Adequate Housing*, Geneva: Office of the UN High Commissioner for Human Rights.

UN (2017) 'Report of the Special Rapporteur on adequate housing as a component of the right to an adequate standard of living, and on the right to non-discrimination in this context', available at http://www.ohchr.org/

UN (2018) 'Report of the Special Rapporteur on adequate housing as a component of the right to an adequate standard of living, and on the right to non-discrimination in this context', http://www.unhousingrapp.org/user/pages/04.resources/Thematic-Report-1-Human-Rights-Based-National-Housing-Strategies.pdf

UN (2019) Letter from Leilani Farha Special Rapporteur on adequate housing as a component of the right to an adequate standard of living, and on the right to non-discrimination in this context to the Irish Government, 22 March, Geneva.

Uplift (2018) 'The People's Housing Plan', www.uplift.ie

USI (Union of Students in Ireland) (2019) 'USI submission to the Committee on Housing and Homelessness', 12 April, available at http://usi.ie/accommodation/usi-submission-to-the-committee-on-housing-and-homelessness

Varadkar, L. (2018) 'Leader's questions', *Dail Eireann*, 3 October, https://www.oireachtas.ie/en/debates/debate/dail/2018-10-03/16/

Weston, C. (2019) 'Cuckoo funds buy up more homes and squeeze out first timers', *Irish Independent*, 19 September, www.independent.ie/business/personal-finance/property-mortgages/cuckoo-funds-buy-up-more-homes-and-squeeze-out-firsttimers-38493718.html

World Economic Forum (2019) 'This is what Greta Thunberg just told Davos', https://www.weforum.org/agenda/2020/01/greta-thunberg-davos-message-climate-change/

Yamada, A. (1999) 'Affordability crisis in housing in Britain and Japan', *Housing Studies*, 14(1): 99–110.

Index

Page numbers in *italic* refer to a table or figure in the text.